Ursula Hegi

Tearing the Silence

Being German in America

A TOUCHSTONE BOOK
PUBLISHED BY SIMON & SCHUSTER

TOUCHSTONE
Rockefeller Center
1230 Avenue of the Americas
New York, NY 10020

First Touchstone Edition 1998
Touchstone *and colophon are
registered trademarks of Simon & Schuster Inc.*

Designed by Sam Potts
Manufactured in the United States of America

1 3 5 7 9 10 8 6 4 2

Library of Congress Cataloging-in-Publication Data
Hegi, Ursula.
Tearing the silence : on being German in America / Ursula Hegi.
p.   cm.
1. German Americans—Interviews. 2. United States—Ethnic relations.
3. Holocaust, Jewish (1939–1945)—Germany—Influence. 4. World
War, 1939–1945—Germany—Personal narratives, German. 5. World
War, 1939–1945—Children—Germany—Biography. 6. Germany—
History—1945–1990. I. Title.
E. 184.G3H28 1997
973'.0431—dc21   97-7279

ISBN 0-684-82996-7
ISBN 0-684-84611-X (Pbk)

A portion of this work entitled "Johanna's Interview" was previously
published in Prairie Schooner.

Acknowledgments

I want to thank several individuals, who read drafts of this book and offered valuable insights: Lanny DeVuono, Gordon Gagliano, Mark Gompertz, Deb Harper, Gail Hochman, Sally Pritchard, Rod Stackelberg, and Sally Winkle. Once again, Eastern Washington University supported my work with sabbatical leave and a faculty research grant. Thank you.

For my son Eric

Tearing the Silence

Contents

The Holocaust was unspeakable, and the silence—eventually—
spoke much louder than the words would have.
—Katharina in her interview

Introduction

Johanna sat across from me—serious, pale, articulate—as she spoke of seeing her first Holocaust documentary at the British consulate in Berlin when she was in her early teens. "That shook me profoundly, but what shook me even more profoundly was going home in that state of shock and wanting to talk." Her parents responded only with denial. "We didn't know. . . . We suffered so much during the war. . . . It was so awful for us. . . ."

Johanna looked at me. "We didn't know," she repeated softly. And then she said those same words again, asking them this time. "We didn't know?" Her voice had risen, revealing her doubts, her rage. She told me how her parents' denial had alienated her from them, and how seeing this film had brought her to the realization, "*If this can be done by human beings, it can be done by me.* What drove me and is still driving me is, *What can you do so this will never happen again?*"

By constantly scrutinizing herself, Johanna struggled for decades to understand the human impulses that led to the

Holocaust. She did not try to distance herself from her birth country or to compartmentalize that this could only have happened in Germany. It was rather that she seemed to understand the Holocaust instinctively on a personal and political level. "This kind of evil or negativity is really something I have to see as part of human beings, which means part of myself . . . that's the hardest work, the hardest aspect. But ultimately that is what needs to be done—what Germans particularly need to do—to look at ourselves and say: *So what in me supports this? What attitudes in me are just down that line?* And that's of course painful. I'm working in education partly because I'm still trying to make people conscious of what can happen. My emphasis has shifted—from trying to shake people up towards . . . finding my own shadow, if you want so, and making my peace with that."

From the beginning I was struck by Johanna's courage, although she described herself several times as fearful or timid. When we'd first scheduled our meeting, she'd asked if she could bring her husband along because she was afraid of driving in an unfamiliar area, but when I'd said a third person would only distract us, she'd agreed to come alone.

As Johanna probed into herself, I told her, "You have more courage than most people I know."

We have continued our dialogue beyond her interview.

Fifteen years ago I would have avoided listening to Johanna.

Fifteen years ago I walked into a mail room at the University of New Hampshire, and when I overheard two of my colleagues talk about a Holocaust documentary, I backed away, unable to speak—not because I didn't think about the Holocaust, but because I thought of it so often, and because it was too terrible to talk about. I was still within the silence, though I wouldn't have defined it that way because I didn't understand the tenacity of that silence until I began to come out of it, until I could look at it from the outside—much in the way an immigrant looks at her country of origin. Years later, after I began to write about Germany, an American friend admitted,

"I always wanted to ask you about being German, but it seemed tactless."

When you leave your country of origin, you eventually have to look at it much closer.

Born in 1946, I grew up surrounded by evidence of war—bombed-out buildings, fatherless children, men who had legs or arms missing—yet when I tried to ask questions, my parents and teachers only gave me reluctant and evasive answers about the war. Never about the Holocaust. "We suffered, too," they would say. It is an incomplete lens, but it was held up to many of our generation as the *only* lens to see through. If our parents had spoken to us about their responsibility for their actions or lack of action during the war, if they had grieved for the Jews and Gypsies and homosexuals and political prisoners who were murdered, and if then, in addition to all this, they had told us, "We suffered, too," their victimhood would have become part of the total lens.

Taken by itself, it is flawed. Incomplete. A lie.

What they tried to create for their children was *eine heile Welt*—an intact world. What was their motivation? Guilt? Denial? Justification? The desire to protect the next generation? Perhaps all of these. But their silence added to the horrors of the Holocaust.

In January 1995, fifty years after the liberation of Auschwitz, Elie Wiesel returned to the camp he survived. "God of forgiveness," he prayed as he headed the official U.S. delegation, "do not forgive those murderers of Jewish children. . . ." His prayer moved me profoundly because it challenged forgiveness in a way that was sane and realistic. Of course forgiveness is healing when it is appropriate, but only too often forgiveness is trivialized, misused. It becomes a greeting card slogan, a cliché where everyone has to forgive before moving on. And there are certain abominations that must not be forgiven. Like the Holocaust. What we must do is try to understand how it began, why it happened, and mourn every single person who was murdered. We must never let it lapse where memory doesn't reach it anymore.

A major catalyst for *Tearing the Silence* was my questioning of the silence I recalled from my childhood. While exploring that silence in my novel *Stones from the River,* I wondered if it really had been such a total silence or if, perhaps, I was the one who had forgotten. Had there been a teacher or some other adult who'd spoken to me about the Holocaust? I didn't recall any.

I decided to find out what it was like for others of my generation. There is a great body of significant personal histories connected to the Second World War—books about Holocaust survivors, Jewish immigrants, children of Holocaust victims, Germans who committed war crimes—but the personal histories of Germans who were born during or after the war and left their country of origin to settle in America have remained largely unexplored. And yet those voices belong there, along with the others, to contribute to a more complete picture of a time period we are still struggling to understand.

I began my search by contacting friends and colleagues, asking them if they knew people who were born in Germany between 1939 and 1949 and lived in America now. It didn't matter to me if they held American or German citizenship. After I published author's queries in several magazines, newspapers, and in newsletters of German clubs, I heard from more people than I could possibly interview. A query in the *Los Angeles Times* alone brought over fifty responses. Quite a few who contacted me were familiar with my books, while others did not know anything about me or my work. To each I sent a description of my project, and I began to receive letters that began like this: "A friend of a friend sent me a fax of your letter. I grew up in Germany after the war. . . ."

I phoned Karl, a minister, when he wrote me a letter after reading my work, and I met Katharina, a psychologist, while I was on a book tour, and she came up to me after my reading at her local bookstore. Both had grown up in postwar Germany and were enthusiastic about participating in my project. Karl subsequently introduced me to Eva, who also agreed to an interview.

Eventually, I heard from over two hundred individuals—three-quarters of them women—but since I wanted gender balance in my book, I interviewed nearly as many men as women. Most of the men had arrived here with their families when they were very young; two of them had been raised in German orphanages and adopted by Americans. But the women had immigrated at various ages, some as children or single adults, quite a few by marrying Americans, which explains their greater numbers.

Initially, I spoke with many of these German-born Americans on the phone to explore the possibility of a taped, in-depth interview. While I based my choice on my goal to include a wide range of life stories, attitudes, backgrounds, professions, and geography, the decision to proceed was of course not always mine because a few people I would have liked to schedule chose not to participate for privacy reasons.

In 1994 and 1995, I traveled to different parts of the United States, expecting to interview at least four individuals for each piece I would finally include in *Tearing the Silence,* but as they talked to me in such depth, I discovered there was a story in every one of them. As a result, I stopped the process much sooner than I had expected. Altogether, I conducted twenty-three interviews, twelve of them face-to-face, eleven by phone. Of these eleven, I met one personally prior to taping and three at a later time. Each interview was usually between three and five hours on tape, resulting in 65 to 125 pages of transcript. I included two-thirds of these interviews in my final manuscript.

My first few meetings were with individuals who shared with me the collective shame at coming from a country that had murdered millions, and they, too, had come to realize how essential it was to tear through that silence. Those voices were significant, but I knew that in order to have a realistic balance in *Tearing the Silence*, I also had to talk to individuals who felt justified in hating or distrusting people they considered different from themselves, and I wanted to uncover that prejudice—fed by ignorance and fear like all prejudice—without giving racists a platform for their views.

But I had no idea how excruciating it would be to listen when I flew south to meet Kurt in a Chinese restaurant after he got off from work. He told me about his years as a car salesman, how he hated "waiting on what we call dots. Indians from India. The dot on their forehead. Hate them for two reasons: they smell bad, and they do the same thing the Orientals do. Never offer you a fair profit." By the time Kurt went on to complain about Jewish customers, I felt physically ill. Long ago I made myself the promise to speak out against any kind of prejudice, even if it created a more uncomfortable situation for myself and others. But where do we draw the line? When do we say "This is not all right?" I find that the more I write about Germany, the sooner I draw that line. I've argued with a cabdriver on the way to the airport, with a colleague who prided himself on his repertoire of ethnic jokes, with students who made homophobic slurs.

But with Kurt I did not speak out.

Instead, I encouraged him to tell me exactly what he meant. I felt implicated by my silence, and yet I knew already how powerful and disturbing his words would be on the page. To confront Kurt with how I felt about his prejudice would have stopped him—not from his way of being in the world, but from revealing himself. Still, my silence remained a conflict for me even after friends assured me I was merely delaying my answer.

When Kurt talked about parallels between American gun control and the way Hitler disarmed "the citizenry prior to taking control of the country," I decided to include his misconception because it defined him and also exposed how standard prejudices of the American radical right have influenced him. In fact, Hitler inherited gun control laws from the Weimar Republic, and the only gun control law that originated under his rule was a law prohibiting Jews from owning guns, even with a permit, in 1938. Whenever factual inaccuracies revealed someone's character, I kept them in because as a writer I'm fascinated by the concept of the unreliable narrator, by the human tendency to frame the past in a way that is not historically accurate but enables us to think about it in a certain way.

I believe that as soon as we commit something to memory, it becomes distorted, and what we recall then as truth is influenced by our emotions and thoughts at the moment we retrieve that memory. In these interviews the accuracy of memory is even more debatable because many details were passed on by our parents' generation—censored and sanitized to exonerate country and family—leaving quite a few of these German-born Americans with the conviction of their parents and themselves as victims.

Jews, of course, remember the Holocaust very differently.

"A gun can't kill anybody," Kurt informed me. "I can put a loaded gun on this table, and if neither one of us picks it up, it will never hurt anybody. . . . It needs a person. It needs a human being. It needs our temper, our repressed desire to kill." He picked up his fork, held it upright in his fist, and braced his elbow on the table between us as he studied me. "I can kill you with a fork, break this glass." I felt far, far away from home, as indeed I was. Outside, it was dark, and the restaurant was nearly empty. Yet, beyond Kurt's bigotry and that raised fork in his hand, I saw the boy in the German orphanage, adopted and sent back, adopted again and sent back, several times, only to end up with an American father who "used to back me into a corner and punch me in the stomach. That was his discipline: one real healthy shot to the stomach, so hard that I couldn't breathe. Any time my parents were really mad at me, they'd say, 'You could still be in an orphanage in Germany.'"

In each story I searched for just that complexity, the flip side of what initially was most apparent. With Kurt it was his beginning in the orphanage, with Anneliese her experience of physical and emotional abandonment, with Johanna her attachment to a cult which, ultimately, made her understand what she had despised in her parents—the yearning for one leader. With Karl, who had served in the Peace Corps, that flip side was his attitude toward his mother and stepmother when he referred to them as "young chicks during the war" and told me that each got "herself pregnant." As I edited his transcript, I found myself hesitating: these comments didn't fit the compassionate man who'd let me witness his tears and pain about the Holocaust. "I've been to Dachau twice. I've been to Buchenwald. I've been to Auschwitz. And I've been to Theresienstadt. *How could this happen?* . . . I'm a German. How can this be? I've been mistaken for a Jew. How can this be? I've got Jewish relatives. . . . How can these things happen?" And yet, to cut those remarks would mean showing Karl as less complex than he is.

I approached these interviews as a novelist—not a historian—searching for the connecting themes within each story, and then lifting these themes to the surface by selecting significant material, much in the way I write a story or novel. A huge difference, though, is that the words are entirely those of the women and men who told me about their lives with such amazing openness. Another writer might have focused on different themes and story lines. I was not after statistics; I was not out to prove something or to conclude: this is what it's like for all German-born Americans; and it was not my intent to cover every possible type or trait. I was interested in examining each individual life as deeply as I could and then to uncover the story within. The more specific these stories were, the more universal they became, suggesting to me that other German-born Americans—beyond this group of interviewees—must have had similar experiences.

"Tell me about your life," I would begin, asking them to think about the significant experiences that had shaped them, about turning points. And then I listened very closely and took notes, identifying recurring themes as well as issues I wanted to explore further. Although the interviews were in English because I wanted the pattern and the vocabulary of each voice, we'd sometimes start out in German before the tape was running or lapse into German for brief moments. It became one more connection between us.

While some were insightful and reflective, others came up with disturbing and offensive material. I was not an impartial listener: I was angered, moved, drawn in, shocked; I identified, recoiled, grieved, laughed, cried, learned. The tape recorder created an odd intimacy as many revealed things about themselves that they hadn't told anyone before. Some disclosed more than they realized. Others cried as they met with memories they'd forgotten or discovered connections in their actions they hadn't recognized before. They gave voice to experiences that I, too, recalled, like being taught as a child that there was just *one* way of doing things right.

The threads of their stories emerged immediately with some, gradually with others, as they talked about their children and about being children themselves, about dreams of the night and the kinds of dreams that we all have about our lives, about what it means to them to live with the knowledge of the Holocaust. As they told me about their parents and grandparents, I got a better sense of that generation. Nothing was off-limits: they spoke of anger and love, death and work, friendship and prejudice, tolerance and homosexuality, sex and religion, loyalty and German reunification.

Some would have preferred not to talk about the war or postwar years at all and only did so when I probed. "Can we stay with that for a while?" I would ask. "What was that like? What did that feel like?" Sometimes I would reassure them about their reactions: "It's okay to feel that anger." "There's nothing wrong with crying." For the most part my questions developed from what they told me. I frequently interrupted or returned to crucial moments in their lives, asking them if they remembered specific details, going with them through the emotions it took to evoke those memories.

Sometimes I would circle back several times, as with Anneliese, a legal secretary, who mentioned only briefly that her father had been in the SS. At first she seemed uncomfortable talking about him at all, but after I came back to him several times and finally asked how she felt about him now, as a grown woman, she thought for a moment and then admitted with startling frankness: "Probably, deep down I'm proud. Not because I know what the Nazis and the SS did. I'm not proud of anything like that. The pride comes from the fact that he was an officer. He had to be an officer to be in the SS. . . . They were the elite, weren't they?" I felt repelled, saddened. And yet—as with every single one of them—I also came to a deeper understanding of her motivations and her complexity.

I had a number of questions that I've struggled with as a German-born American, and I asked everyone only those questions that had not already surfaced in their interviews: "When did you find out about the Holocaust? Did your family speak about it? Your community? Did you dare to ask questions as a child? As an adult? How afraid were you of the answers? Did you find out more when you came to America? How do you live with the knowledge of the Holocaust? How has that silence affected your life? How does it affect your life now? Do you encounter prejudice against Germans in America? Do you have any prejudices against others? Why did you leave Germany? Do you feel connected to America? How do you regard your German background now? Do you think there is a collective burden of shame? Is that different for those of us who were born after the war? What can we, as German-born Americans, do now?"

Although our individual experiences are different, we have several things in common. We were raised by the generation that lived the war, fought the war, killed, fled. And we left our country of origin to come to America. Some of us chose to emigrate as adults; for those who were children, it was a decision made by their families. Our German heritage does not define us entirely—it rather is a significant thread that weaves itself throughout our lives. I am a writer, a woman, a lover, a swimmer, a parent, a German-born American, a member of a women's group. Being a writer is a stronger presence in my life than my German heritage. Losing my mother as a thirteen-year-old has left deeper scars than coming from Germany. Yet, nothing else has ever caused me to feel this deep and abiding shame that I share with many others who were raised in postwar Germany. All this defines me. Confines me at times. Strengthens me at times.

And it is similar for those I interviewed. Not everything in their lives has to do with being German—it has to do with being human. Although their German heritage continues to have profound impact, there are also many other aspects that have shaped them. That's why their life as Germans in America is not my only focus. I've chosen to show more than that, going back to their years in Germany to understand their development prior to migration.

Why did they open up to me to such a degree? I believe it was at least in part because I shared their cultural background. Several saw me as a witness and said talking to me gave them a way to examine their lives. For some it was freeing to know that I would change names and certain identifiable details to disguise their identities. Anneliese explained her openness this way: "Because you're interested in hearing this. . . . Actually, nobody ever pays any attention to me." Kurt startled me with his hope that I'd be "a long-lost sister. . . . That would be a miracle, wouldn't it?" Perhaps he needed to imagine a personal connection in order to tell me his story, and yet he simply shrugged when I pointed out that we were born just two months apart in 1946.

Some were initially concerned about jumping back and forth in time as they told me about their lives, and I assured them I would work on the sequence during the editing process. For example, Kurt briefly mentioned his traumatic years in the orphanage several times, and I brought the strongest of those details together in one long passage and then opened his story with that passage, because knowing what formed Kurt contributes to an understanding of the destructive choices he made later on.

They knew that not every story would become part of the book, but that I would evaluate the recurring themes from all of them in my conclusion. After each interview I asked: "Are there questions you wish I had asked? Questions you dreaded?" Frequently, after I turned off the microphone, they began to talk again. With Heinrich, who described himself as not very talkative, I switched the microphone back on at least half a dozen times, and his transcript turned out to be one of the longest. After I listened to Marika's life story, both of us were reluctant to stop talking, and we decided to eat dinner together so that we could continue.

I told them the interviews might evoke further memories and encouraged them to write to me if they wanted to add anything. Some I contacted with follow-up questions. A few times I was concerned how their openness would affect them afterwards, particularly Joachim, a gay ex-Jesuit who lives a solitary, closeted life and hasn't been in a relationship in seventeen years. Our phone interview took us further than a face-to-face conversation could have, because it protected his privacy even more. "You're away in Washington over there," he said. "I've probably told you more over the phone than I've ever told anybody about my personal life." I was moved by Joachim's dignity, his honesty, but while I had the story of his life to work with, he was left with having revealed so much of himself to someone who then disappeared from his life. I wondered if he could go back to that personal silence in his life. Would he want to? He'd never been in therapy and had no one close enough to him to even discuss the impact of the interview. To make sure he was all right, I called him a few weeks later. Soon after, Joachim sent me a letter, telling me he was proud to have "participated in the interview process with you. The 'revelations' to you have helped me to put a lot of things into a different perspective. Whatever happens with the material I willingly gave you, I feel I am a better person for having talked to you."

Each transcript went through over a hundred hours of editing. I preserved the spontaneity and uniqueness of each voice in a first-person narrative, careful not to cut any material that would have changed the meaning and intent. While using only each individual's words, I made grammatical corrections and minor clarifications, such as substituting "my father" for "he." I composed some life stories in chronological order; in others I moved back and forth between present and past. My focus in editing down a wealth of information was to understand the character and story of each individual in all its complexity—positive and negative aspects—and I selected and arranged the words to illuminate what I saw. And that's where my presence exists in each piece—in the background.

Since I wanted to guide each voice into the world and let it stand on its own, I chose not to intrude with analysis. I decided against any grouping to make distinctions, because that would have labeled people, made them the other, confined them to something less complex than who they are. In determining the sequence of the voices, I juxtaposed them to create tension between them.

While writing my introduction and conclusion, I often felt conflicted in determining the level of my critical involvement. I did not want to judge, did not want to slam down, and yet I had strong reactions that I wanted to lift out. I finally resolved to deal with this by placing my own life story at the beginning because it establishes the direction from where the listening and the questions are coming. Since my essay evolved and changed over a span of several years, it naturally differs in form and introspection from interviews that were held over a span of hours. It provides a window through which to see these life stories, re-creating the journey I took while interviewing, and letting my readers develop their own insights before I offer mine in the conclusion.

Part One

Ursula: Tearing the Silence

Ursula

Born: 1946
Age at time of immigration: 18

Tearing the Silence

September 1984: My son Eric is fourteen when I move with my children across the country to the state of Washington. He brings a new friend home with him from school, who asks me about being German. "Does that mean you are a Nazi?"

I can't breathe.

As a young woman, I tried to shed my German heritage, to make myself nationless. I wished I'd come from another country, another culture. There were times when I would have given a lot not to be blond and blue-eyed, not to fit that German stereotype. I wanted black, curly hair, wanted my accent to disappear so that people would not ask immediately, "Where are you from?"

April 1984: I'm driving in my car with a lover, who notices a Velcro holder for my cigarette case on the inside lid of the glove compartment. "How efficient," he says. I want to spill coffee on my sweater, create a mess in my car—anything not

29

to be called efficient. To me efficiency means the German efficiency, the concentration-camp efficiency. That terrible saying—about German trains always being on time.

I was born in a small river town a year after the war ended.
When I immigrated to America, I was eighteen and thought I
could reject my country of origin. My father's alcoholism had
spiraled in the five years since my mother's early death, and I
would have gone just about anywhere—"even to Siberia," I remember saying—to get away. Moving to another continent
fed my belief that I could start a new life. America seemed perfect for that—a wonderfully classless society without prejudice. After growing up within the rigid German class system
and the strong distinction between adults and children—
"Grown-ups are always right"—I loved the informality of my
adopted country.
     Slowly, I realized that barriers between classes and ethnic
groups existed after all, though they were more subtle.

I found that Americans my age knew much more about
the war years than I. Gradually, I learned more about the
Holocaust: I listened; I read; I ran from what I found out; I hid
in the familiar silence for years, surfaced again and again,
feeling increasingly distant from Germany until I could no
longer run from it and had to know as much as I could find
out, until it burst through in my writing.

1988: When I talk with my children about the silence of
the postwar years, Eric reminds me that I told him about the
Holocaust when he was seven. He tells me about the impact it
had on him, how important it was for him to learn from me
about the war before he found out in school.

1950: The lens through which I am allowed to see as a
child is narrow. I live within a family, a church, a school, a

country that preaches obedience. My questions—even at age four—are met with reminders that it is a sin to doubt.

I wander into a room where my parents and their friends are talking about some trains. They sound upset. When they see me, they stop. I ask about those trains. No one answers.

I don't want to go beneath that silence again.

Writing has often been my way of understanding, of revealing things to myself that I didn't know before. In the late eighties, when I worked on my novel *Floating in My Mother's Palm,* I wanted to capture the significant truths in the lives of individual characters. Unlike my two earlier books, which were set in America, this new book was set in Germany. When my editor kept focusing on the impact of the postwar years, I protested that I wasn't a political writer, that I wasn't intending to write about the war.

"But it's evident throughout the novel," she said.

It wasn't until *Floating in My Mother's Palm* was published that I fully recognized what had emerged along with the stories of the characters—a larger political truth about the profound and eerie silence that existed when I was growing up. And the presence of the war was there throughout the novel, though it was set in the fifties.

As I went deeper into my research and writing, I realized that for many Germans of my generation this silence was normal—and normal is a terrible word under the circumstances—yet, we grew up with that silence. We didn't know the right questions to ask, and whenever we felt the pressure of undefined questions rising within us, we also felt the danger of asking. Questions about the war were far more taboo than questions about sex.

Those of us brave enough to ask about the war were told not to dwell on the past but to focus on the good things in our lives.

• • •

September 1995: I'm giving a reading in Connecticut. After I autograph books, a woman stays behind. She tells me she's Jewish, the wife of a rabbi, and that she was born the same year I was born. In her family, too, there was a great silence regarding the Holocaust, and she wonders if she has protected her seven-year-old son too much with that silence.

As we talk, her son comes up to us and asks me for an autograph. I pick up my pen, and he tells me to write my name on his forearm.

I hesitate. "We have to make sure that's all right with your mother."

She smiles. Nods.

But as I move my pen toward her son's forearm, I see hundreds of arms, children's arms tattooed with numbers. I go hot, then cold, start to shiver. "I can't." My eyes race past the boy to his mother, whose face reflects the same panic I feel, and in that instant we're both rendered inert by the sum of our inherited histories.

Her son waits. His forearm lies on the table in front of me, and all I want is to protect him. "You know what?" I say. "I do much better with autographs on paper. Let's find some, okay?"

His mother quickly gets us some blank paper, and I write my name for him. Then I ask, "Will you give me your autograph, too?"

He looks pleased and carefully prints his name for me.

"How about a hug to go with the autograph?" I ask, and I close my eyes as we embrace. When I open them, I see his father watching us from across the room, solemn, silent.

"But what happened during the war?" I remember asking my parents and teachers, and they'd tell me: "We were hungry. We were cold. We were afraid of the bombs. . . ." They always had coats ready to throw over their nightclothes and suitcases packed with their most important belongings and papers. When the sirens sounded—often several times a day and during the night—they were prepared to grab their coats and suitcases. Mothers would snatch small children from their beds and run into their cellars. Usually, the bombings didn't last very long, but sometimes they were in the cellar for long hours with their deadly fears while mothers tried to calm their screaming children; while people cried, prayed, complained.

December 1960: We do know that Adolf Hitler was evil. In Catholic boarding school we speculate that Hitler is still alive, hiding in some cloister, dressed as a nun. What could be a better disguise? We scan the nuns' faces.

Behind these cloister walls, our teenage passions are channeled into religious ecstasy until most of us fantasize about becoming nuns. Brides of Christ. We sigh with chaste lust as we witness yet another young, white-gowned postulant drift down the aisle toward her eternal union with the eternal bridegroom. What could be more fulfilling than this? We, too, want to become brides of Christ. We know what is expected of us— chastity, obedience, and poverty—and we spend many hours in earnest discussions. Two of these vows, I figure, will be easy—chastity and poverty. At fourteen I haven't been in love yet, and I've never been poor.

But obedience, I'm certain, will be almost impossible for me.

Nights, after the nuns turn out the lights, I read with a flashlight under my blanket: Wolfgang Borchert and Karl May; Franz Kafka and tales of saints; Edgar Wallace mysteries and Goethe; Dostoyevsky and the catechism; Heinrich Böll and Anne Frank.

Earlier that same year, a few months before I had watched my mother die from complications after surgery, she had become upset with me when she found me reading a book my Catholic youth group leader had given me, *Das Tagebuch der Anne Frank*. When I wanted to know why my mother didn't want me to read it, she said: "Because Anne always talks back to her mother." At age thirteen I believed my mother's reason because obedience was important to her, especially a child's unquestioning obedience to her parents, and Anne Frank was definitely talking back to her mother—not only in words, but also in the thoughts she confided to her diary. Obviously, my mother had read the book. What I wouldn't understand until much later was that her discomfort went far deeper because Anne's talking back to her mother was symbolic of her talking back to authority, to society, and because by writing her diary Anne Frank had broken the silence.

Three decades after my mother's death, when I stood inside the Anne Frank House in Amsterdam, I thought of my mother's reaction again and wished—as I had many times before—that I'd probed her answer that long-ago day.

A few years ago my godmother, Tante Käte, gave me a letter my mother sent to her. Its ink has faded. It was written in 1944 during the bombings of the Rhineland—two years before my mother would give birth to me, sixteen years before she would die.

My mother is worried about the low-flying bombers, but mostly about my grandmother, who has become so nervous and frail that she might not outlast the war. For two days and two nights they have been hiding in a bomb shelter. "*Wir sind alle halbverrückt*—We are all half crazy. . . . *Mutter ist diese Woche auf dem Weg zum Bunker so fürchterlich hingefallen*—This week Mother fell terribly on the way to the shelter. . . . *Bei dem Angriff auf Neuss sind hier Sechsundachtzig Bomben gefallen*—During the attack on Neuss, eighty-six bombs fell here. *Was soll nun werden?*—What is going to happen? *Ich glaube wir gehen hier alle drauf*—I believe we're all going to die here. . . ."

My mother is afraid for my father, who is a soldier, and she wishes she could talk with him about everything. "*Als Frau steht man diesem allen doch so hilflos gegenüber*—As a woman one is helpless in the face of all this. . . . *An frühere Zeiten darf man garnicht mehr denken*—One cannot let oneself think of earlier times. . . ."

Spring 1990: I meet an exchange student from Germany—half my age—at a reading in Moses Lake, Washington. We discover quickly that we grew up with the same shame of being German, with the same uneasiness at any display of nationalism. "Even as schoolchildren we could never be proud of our nationality," she says, and I know exactly what she means.

After talking with her, I'm finally able to identify why I'm so uncomfortable around uniforms. It troubles me that I find it difficult to see beyond a military uniform. Until now I have considered myself free of prejudice. But uniforms make me uneasy—even school marching bands. To me, love for your country and identification with your country feels suspect. Although I know that nationalism does not have to mushroom into what happened in Germany, I feel the potential of danger when the American national anthem is played and people rise with their hands above their hearts. I flinch when I see the unquestioning pride that many American children take in their country.

February 1995: I visit the University of Washington to hold a seminar on memory and history. When asked if I was politically active during the Vietnam years, I reply no, that I even used to be married to a man who'd fought in Vietnam and was rather conservative, that it was not an issue between us in the early years when we raised our children, but became one later when I grew more politically aware.

A woman asks if my children feel as encumbered by Germany's history as I do.

"How can they?" I reply. "I'm the child of a soldier. They're not."

There is silence in the room.

Finally, a man asks, "Isn't your sons' father a soldier?"

I cover my face for a moment. When I drop my hands, I say, "I didn't realize till now that to me soldier means German soldier."

The German exchange professor next to me admits she hadn't even noticed my slipup because for her, too, soldier of course means German soldier.

Some immigrants keep seeing their world through the lens of their birth country. I yanked out that lens when I came to America, wanting a life that was new and clear and separate. But now I've picked up that old lens once more, and I'm trying to find out what it means to be linked to two cultures. I waited many years—too many years, perhaps—to write about Germany, but once I began, my writing took on an extra layer, a deeper way of seeing.

In the early years after arriving in America, I wasn't interested in meeting Germans. Americans would assume that I'd want to be introduced to others who'd come from Germany, but I'd usually make excuses and avoid them. Now I seek them out in order to understand. I also speak more German than I did in the first two decades of living here.

Whenever I meet Europeans of my parents' generation, I turn into the well-behaved girl of my childhood. It surprises me, amuses me how my manners skip across decades of independence to the child-politeness that was drilled into me. After all these years in America, where I've valued the relaxed boundaries between the ages, I'm still not immune to that old formality.

1969: Some of the Germans I've come across here—like the bank teller in Connecticut whose name, too, is Ursula— still talk about the "old country" as though they lived there.

They order their shoes or coats or chocolate from Germany because they believe the quality is much better than here in America. They save their money to return "home" every summer. Such a different sense of belonging . . ."Don't you miss home?" they ask me. They don't like it when I shake my head.

I don't feel German.

Didn't feel German when I lived in Germany.

I don't feel American either.

But every year at Christmas I become German. I make *Sauerbraten* and *Kartoffelklösse, Rotkohl* and *Apfelmus.* I serve *Lebkuchen* and *Stollen.* I set up the manger with the little plaster Jesus and the plaster sheep and the plaster Virgin, and we listen to old records with *Weihnachtslieder*—Christmas carols—sung by a choir of boys who by now must be quite middle-aged.

My childhood memories of Christmas Eve are flawless, splendid. Whatever conflicts and disappointments there were—my father drunk, my mother rigid with embarrassment and silent anger—have fallen away over the decades to leave me with memories of the perfect Christmas. And it's that idealized Christmas I tried to re-create for my children when they were growing up. What they liked best about their German Christmas was that they could open their presents the night before their friends received theirs.

Prior to Christmas, I'd scout out the most beautifully decorated tree in some yard half an hour or so away, and Christmas Eve we would trudge through snow or slush to come upon that tree, lit. . . . My children were not very enthusiastic about the Christmas walk because it meant a delay in getting their presents, but for me it was a journey back into those childhood years when we and several other families spent three weeks every December in the Black Forest. Christmas Eve we were bundled up and pulled by our parents on sleds through the cold, clear night. As we followed a path into the dense forest, some of the adults carried lanterns, and we all sang Christmas carols. Suddenly, amidst giant pines, we'd discover a small spruce, its snow-covered branches ablaze with red candles. Each year it felt magical to find a tree alive with lights in the middle of the dark forest, and though we got older and too heavy to be pulled on sleds, we never lost that deep sense of wonder.

In my first apartment in New Jersey, I clipped candleholders to the branches of my Christmas tree and lit dozens of the thin wax candles I'd found in a German deli on Eighty-sixth Street in New York. But I no longer light real candles on my Christmas tree. It makes Americans too uneasy. They accuse me of creating a firetrap and lecture me on wooden houses in America versus stone houses in Germany.

September 1985: One of my friends, who grew up in America with German parents, tells me her family used to speak German until she started school in 1943 and her teacher called her a Nazi. After that her family spoke only English at home.

What I brought with me from Germany was a strong distaste for politics. A distrust of politics that made me shun political involvement until I was in my early forties. From time to time, I would remind myself that I should know more about what was going on in the world, that I should get involved. Uncomfortable with my lack of political knowledge, I would read newspapers, listen to the news. But after a while I'd grow disillusioned. It would become a duty. And I'd stop. Until the next time.

In 1993, I would learn from a German-American friend, the historian Rod Stackelberg, that many Germans of my generation shared this distrust of politics because it was passed on to them by their parents and grandparents, "who don't trust their political instinct. What's right and what's wrong. They've lost their political compass and are afraid to choose because their culture took what turned out to be a destructive course."

April 1989: The Aryan Nations compound near Hayden Lake in northern Idaho is less than forty miles from where we live in Washington. There have been increased incidents of racial violence in the region. Alarmed that the neo-Nazis are planning a parade, I've thought of joining a human rights demonstration in Hayden Lake to counteract the Aryan Nations' gathering. But along with others, I'm concerned that any kind of public attention will only validate the neo-Nazis. Already, the local media has given them an enormous amount of coverage.

The morning of the demonstration I'm on my way to a meditation group, but halfway there I stop at a public phone and call my partner, Gordon. "I have to go to Hayden Lake," I tell him. "That's how the people must have lost their power in Germany—by staying out of politics, by staying silent. It didn't start with the Holocaust there—it ended with the Holocaust. It started with people not objecting when a neighbor was harassed, when a neighbor was beaten, when a neighbor was taken away."

"I'll come with you," Gordon says, and together we drive to Hayden Lake, where the human rights demonstration is already in progress. Nearly a thousand people are there. At first I feel awkward—I've never been in a march and I don't know the songs—but deep in my gut I understand how essential it is for every one of us to be part of this, to pitch our voices, our beliefs, against those of the Aryan Nations.

May 1965: My first job in America. I work with a Jewish man, Sy Hecht. When he asks me if I feel guilty about what happened in Germany during the war, I feel stunned. Accused. Defensive. I answer him—and I cringe at that young and blind answer now—that I was not alive during that time. That I have different values. That I detest everything the Nazis did, everything they stood for. I ask him how I could possibly feel guilty. I even remind him—and once again I'm mortified by my response—that, theoretically, he could have made more of a difference than I because he was alive during the war years. I tell him I didn't have anything to do with what happened in Germany. Yet beneath my words—though I don't want to feel it—is a deep and unsettling disquiet that I cannot name for myself.

Nearly two decades later, German Chancellor Helmut Kohl, confronted with the same question in Israel, will seek refuge in *"die Gnade der späten Geburt"*—"the grace of late birth"—suggesting that the question of guilt was not all that relevant to Germans who were not of age during the war and therefore not involved.

If I could talk to Sy Hecht today, I would begin with an apology for my ignorant and offensive words. I would tell him it has taken me many years to be able to write and speak about Germany because I feel encumbered by its terrible heritage. I would tell Sy Hecht what I've struggled against and come to accept over the years—that I grew up in a country that murdered millions of children, women, and men, and that I cannot sever myself from that country, though I have certainly tried to do that.

And that's where the conflict lies for me: since I cannot separate from Germany, I have to understand it, have to come to terms with it, though—many times—I still wish I'd been born in another country. I would tell Sy Hecht that we must never forget what happened in Germany—not because I believe that this will stop history from repeating itself, but to remain aware that whenever history does repeat itself, it rises up in a different form, and that it then becomes the responsibility of every individual in the rest of the world to stop the conscious genocide.

• • •

June 1991: I have been invited to speak at the Writers' Symposium in Sitka, Alaska, on personal vision and the responsible voice. The focus is on the writer's connection to the community. My voice shakes as—for the first time in public—I talk about my connection to Germany, which has influenced how I perceive community and, quite often, resist community. Ever since I received the invitation to Sitka eight months earlier, thoughts and feelings have been churning, forcing me to find words for them. They are not something I've talked about, except with a few close friends. It's as if I've carried on that tradition of silence, that habit of silence that I've raged against.

But now, in Sitka, I'm no longer silent. I tell my listeners that I keep redefining the boundaries in my struggle between preserving my personal vision as a writer and being part of a community. A lot of that depends on how much we identify with our community of origin. I envy the Chickasaw writer Linda Hogan and the Inupiaq educator James Nageak who are on the panel with me, who both come from cultures they regard with admiration and loyalty, whose personal visions reflect those of their communities.

But I spent the first eighteen years of my life within a culture that has a history of oppression and violence—I can neither trust that community nor identify with it. I feel no loyalty to preserve the secrets of that community—only the loyalty to myself to tell the truth as I perceive it, regardless of how flawed my vision might be. And to preserve the integrity of my vision, I have to risk not belonging to any community.

After my presentation a Jewish writer, Hugh Brody, takes me aside and tells me I'm taking on too much of a burden, that what happened in Germany has far more to do with human nature than with one particular country.

Awed by his generosity, I ask him, "Would you feel that way if you were German?"

He hesitates. "I don't think so," he says.

• • •

I returned to Germany in 1986 after a fifteen-year absence. I would have stayed away longer, but I had applied for a research grant to work on *Floating in My Mother's Palm,* and I had made a pact with myself that I would go back for three weeks if I received the grant. When I opened the letter with the good news, I felt upset. Afraid. Now I would have to go.

It felt confusing to rediscover places I used to love, especially the Rhine River, where I'd walked as a girl when I wanted to be alone, where I'd written my first poems as a six-year-old, where my parents used to take me sledding, where I'd swum out to the barges as my brave mother had when she was a girl. But as I rediscovered the landscape and wrote about it, I began to reconcile some of my conflicting feelings toward my country of origin. It was all right to love people and places in Germany, while detesting so much of the history. I began to remember people who'd meant a lot to me in my childhood— school friends and teachers, relatives and friends of my parents, and especially my beloved *Oma*—grandmother who'd helped raise me until her death when I was three—and I knew I would not wait that long again before returning to Germany.

I knelt by my mother's grave and lit candles. Cried for her. For us. The hardest part of my trip was trying to confront my father. But he was almost senile, and I finally acknowledged and mourned the real loss of him, which had happened many years earlier when I was still a child.

1993: Perhaps those of us who leave Germany are more constantly aware of the legacy of being German than people who live in Germany. By becoming citizens of a foreign country, we are instantly marked as being different. For many we become representatives of "the German." Every possible stereotype—efficiency, racism, obedience, punctuality, rigidity, loyalty, denial, cleanliness, arrogance, persistence, responsibility—is measured on us, applied against us, searched for in us.

•   •   •

January 1974: I'm skiing at Gunstock Mountain in New Hampshire. On the chairlift a man asks me where I'm from. When I tell him I come from a town near Düsseldorf, he nods. "Ah yes," he says as though he'd been there many times, "I know about Düsseldorf . . . from *Hogan's Heroes*."

After I completed *Floating in My Mother's Palm*, I began work on two novels, one set in the Pacific Northwest, the other in New Hampshire. But the month *Floating in My Mother's Palm* was published, Bob Edwards interviewed me for National Public Radio, and one of his comments—which did not become part of the aired interview—was "I hope we'll hear more about these characters."

I told him I was finished writing about the people of Burgdorf, that fictitious German town on the Rhine River; yet, when I walked out of the studio and into the spring air, one of my favorite characters, the dwarf woman Trudi Montag, began knocking about inside my head, demanding to have her own book. With complete scenes and images she lured me away from my projects and pulled me into the early years of her life, into 1915, the year of her birth, and through the thirties and forties when—as someone who looked different—she would have been very much at risk.

I knew then that *Floating in My Mother's Palm* had only been the first step in my journey of writing about Germany. I was frightened. Ready.

Around that same time, the German-American writer Ilse-Margret Vogel contacted me to tell me she'd read *Floating in My Mother's Palm*. Ilse, who'd left Germany in 1950, was the same age my mother would have been had she lived; yet, Ilse talked openly about the war years and her involvement in the resistance against Hitler—documented in her latest book, a memoir, *Bad Times, Good Friends*. I was able to ask her many of the questions I couldn't ask as a child, and over the course of long phone conversations and letters, we developed a friendship. When Ilse sent me her memoir—still in manuscript form at that time—I wished I knew of people in my own family who also had resisted, who also had hidden Jewish fugitives.

Spring 1991: I'm afraid of writing Trudi's book, afraid of what I'm going to find out. If I could leave all of this alone, if I knew of a way to leave it alone, I would. But I cannot avoid looking into that time period. I've opened some kind of window—regardless of how small. It's impossible to keep the war out. It's pushing itself into my life.

It was as though during the year after I'd completed *Floating in My Mother's Palm* the character Trudi Montag had been developing on her own—independent of my conscious imagination—presenting me her story as a gift. For a while the material for *Stones from the River* came too fast—quite a change from my daily writing habits—and I would take notes while driving or while sitting in restaurants. Finally, I bought a cassette recorder so I could listen to Trudi and transcribe her words onto tape while I walked or drove around.

My conversations with Ilse gave me the courage to ask one of the few surviving adults from my childhood—my godmother Tante Käte, born in 1903—what she remembered of the war. I was surprised and moved by her willingness to record her memories on tape and help me with the research. But by then she was deeply worried about the neo-Nazis and ready to talk about the parallels she saw.

When I received Tante Käte's tape, it took me a while before I could bring myself to listen. I expected atrocities, secrets about my family. At first her voice was hesitant, but then it grew more confident as if she'd forgotten the tape recorder and was talking to me directly.

The first time I listened to Tante Käte's voice, I thought I wasn't finding out enough; yet, when I listened once more—without that hunger and dread—I heard so much more and understood that what she was giving me was her personal experience against a background too threatening to look at for very long. I felt the presence of a *Schleier*—a veil—of memory as she tried to focus on the positive, a lifelong habit that filtered out many things, as she revealed memories that obviously were disturbing and painful for her. Though it was the only angle of vision she could allow herself, I felt grateful to her.

January 1992: I'm reading more and more about the war. Much of the time I'm filled with despair. I want to stop the reading but can't. I try to read something else; I can't. It keeps coming back to this. A journey that has chosen me.

Though Tante Käte encouraged my questions, she was troubled by some of them. "You've lost the pride in your country, Ursula," she wrote to me. "We are a nation that can let itself be seen in the entire world. We are known to be industrious, loyal, intelligent, clean and orderly . . . many good attributes. How this whole unhappiness came into the world through one individual—that is very regrettable, but it has not spoiled the entire nation. There are a lot of artists and poets and composers who are very famous throughout the world . . . great scientists. . . . You don't have to hide for being German. I will send you some books about people who were in the resistance so that you can read about *them*."

"What did my father do in the war?" I asked her. "My mother?"
Tante Käte sent me books about the German resistance and a second tape, confirming what I'd been told as a child—that my father had been a soldier on the Russian front. My mother, she said, had always been against Hitler and stayed in

our hometown, taking care of my sick grandmother. And Tante Käte—a teacher during the war—used to demonstrate her resistance by not raising her hand in the *Heil Hitler* salute whenever possible, and by praying with her students.

"How about the Jews in your neighborhood?" I wrote back to her, knowing I was pushing her. "How about *their* suffering?"

On her third tape Tante Käte talked about the Liebermann family across the street. "They were honorable, dear people. Herr Liebermann was taken away in his pajamas on Kristallnacht, in November 1938. The entire night his wife stood by the window, waiting. At dawn she saw something crawling in the street. First she thought it was a dog, and then she ran downstairs, realized it was her husband, dragged him upstairs. . . . It took a lot of her strength."

Perhaps I could have written back to Tante Käte: *"And what did you do then? Did you help the Liebermanns?"* But she was nearly ninety, and she'd already answered many of my difficult questions.

Her description of the woman waiting by the window stayed with me until it grew into a chapter in which Trudi's father waits with Frau Abramowitz, the neighbor across the street, after her husband has been taken away. Trudi watches as Frau Abramowitz stands framed by the splinters that stick from the window frame as if she'd always been there. When the texture of night wears thin, Trudi spots something crawling across the intersection, an injured dog, perhaps, or some ancient beast dragging itself toward the dawn of mankind, the doom of mankind. Just then Frau Abramowitz loosens herself from the window and flies from the house toward whatever it is that's crawling toward them. And Trudi—Trudi and her father help her carry her husband home and tend to his injuries.

February 1992: Much of the research material is in German, and I'm living more within the language than I have in twenty-seven years. I move deeper and deeper into diary entries of people in concentration camps, read interviews with Holocaust survivors. I dream about them, think about them when I'm away from my desk. During a car trip to Oregon with Gordon, I wake up while he is driving. Outside, it is night. I'm cold, stiff, drowsy, and my first thought is of Jews being deported in cattle cars. I'm ashamed of even acknowledging my minor aches. Yet, already, those thoughts are becoming the catalyst for a scene when Trudi and her father, Leo, are driving to Dresden in June 1944 to search for the Abramowitzs' daughter, Ruth.

I remember a woman at one of my readings, years ago, crying as I read my short story "Tina's Room," and thanking me after the reading: "You write about things most of us don't dare to look at."

Some of Trudi's book, *Stones from the River,* was growing out of my struggle with being German. At times it seemed that things which happened in my personal life were connected to German history, evoked it. Like the seminar I taught in black literature. I found it impossible to talk about slavery without bringing up the Holocaust and how dangerous it is when individuals or nations consider themselves superior to others and then act on that belief, justifying it. It not only happened in Germany during the Third Reich, and in America during the many decades of slavery, but it continues to happen in political and personal conflicts throughout the world. To keep that sense of superiority going, people use others as fuel: slaves, Jews, spouses, children. The cost of sustaining that superiority—which is an illusion—is enormous: the cost to the victim; the cost to the oppressor, which is a hardening, corruption, and deeper descent into illusion.

The impact of that illusion was becoming one of the major themes in *Stones from the River,* explored through the perspective of Ilse Abramowitz, who used to travel all over the world.

But by 1942 her world had shrunk to one room in a Jewish house that she shares with her husband, Michel.

March 1992: I'm in Germany to do research for *Stones from the River*. In Berlin uniformed men with muzzled dogs patrol the train and subway stations. On a crowded sidewalk by the ruins of a cathedral, a skinhead with a young puppy passes me. Although the puppy is not on a leash, it completely obeys, staying next to the left heel of its owner as he strides through heavy traffic. I'm chilled by the incredible amount of training that must have shaped a dog this young into such obedience, such terrible precision.

How could it have happened? How did it begin? Those were some of the questions that had drawn me into *Stones from the River*. They were answered—at least in part—by what I'd written in my journal during the Gulf War.

January 18, 1991: A peaceful demonstration in Spokane to end the Gulf War. We sing songs of peace, listen to speeches in front of the Federal Building, and then walk to the Marine recruiting station, where five members of our group are arrested. I feel angry, disillusioned, afraid. Within minutes we are surrounded by police and military men, very much outnumbered, and beyond that line of uniforms hundreds of people collect, watching us—the other—with hate and contempt though they don't know us. The arrests are crisp, efficient. One of the peace activists, Nancy, gets her wrist hurt, while another, Allen, has a policeman push a thumb into the soft spot behind his ear.

I'm troubled by the change in language I have observed over the past months. It reminds me of Germany. That blind allegiance to the leader. Up to now I have valued the freedom we have in America to express our opinions even if they differ from those of the government. But ever since we sent our troops to the Middle East, the language has become narrower. There is no space for disagreement with the government. We become suspect. A scraggly bunch of people. A minority. Ineffective. At risk.

The media talks about the war as though it were a cartoon or video game where someone gets shot or maimed but there's no blood. TV news refers to it as the showdown. Soldiers are interviewed on camera and compare their wait in the desert to training for the Super Bowl and finally getting to play. Bombing missions are compared to touchdowns. Ironically, while most Americans are expressing approval of the Gulf War, Germans—hundreds of thousands of Germans—are marching in protest against the Gulf War, evoking worldwide criticism of Germany's failure to support the struggle against Iraq, which threatens Israel's security.

Furious at the lack of information, at the distorted facts that recruiters gave the young, I took training sessions to become a draft counselor. My son Eric was twenty at the time, and recruiters were sending him and many young men his age propaganda in handwritten envelopes, tricking him into opening something he'd usually throw away unread. The letters promised him adventure, travel, benefits, education, and the money he'd receive *after* he got out of the service.

Even a pack of cigarettes bears the warning that it might be dangerous to your health, but none of the recruiting propaganda we read mentioned danger.

Eric developed his file as a conscientious objector and voiced his reservations about what the government was doing. His language was strong. His opinions were strong. One evening I watched the German film *The White Rose,* about the German students who were executed for expressing their opinions, and it struck me that fifty years ago in Germany my son could have been killed for expressing his beliefs.

• • •

1956: I'm helping my mother peel potatoes in our kitchen. She suddenly hugs me, tells me I'm fortunate that I was born a girl. "Girls are lucky," she says. "They don't have to go to war."

March 1992: On my way to Buchenwald in the former East Germany, I take the train along the system of tracks where thousands and thousands of prisoners were transported. I get off the train in Weimar, a beautiful old city, famous for the great artists who lived here, among them the writers Goethe and Schiller. Their graves have become elaborate shrines where people come to honor them.

I'm terrified to continue my journey to the anonymous mass graves of Buchenwald—only a few miles outside Weimar—where 65,000 Jews and political prisoners were killed. But that's why I've come this far. As a German-born American, I have to go there. When I enter Buchenwald, my first thought is: *But it's so small.* I have prepared myself for something vast and terrible, but this clearing—surrounded by barbed wire fences and forests—is far too small for 65,000 people to have lived here.

And then the horror becomes more real than it has been in books and documentary films. Of course they didn't *live* here all at once. The systematic, day-to-day killing went on for years. Most of the barracks where prisoners froze, starved, or lost their sanity have been taken down. But the disinfection quarters with the showerheads are still there. The stable where prisoners were killed with a shot in the neck. The crematorium. The mass grave is outside the fence along a path in the forest. Someone has left a bouquet of flowers next to birch twigs that have been shaped into a cross—not a Star of David. I don't hear a single bird in the trees.

1994: I receive many letters from people who have read *Stones from the River*. Some move me deeply. One letter that brings me to tears is from an old Jewish man in Florida. He tells me he escaped from Germany during the war. Every member of his family has read my book, and he wants me to know that I'll always have a home with him and his family.

"You don't seem German," someone will say to me from time to time.

It is intended as a compliment.

As an eighteen-year-old, I would have welcomed those words. Now they make me angry, sad. I could ask, in return: *What do you think Germans are like?* I could talk about prejudice in its many forms as I will if someone makes a racist comment. But I usually don't. Because I feel the speaker's uneasiness beneath that compliment, and the attempt to bridge that uneasiness by separating me as an individual from the history of my birth country. I can understand that impulse only too well because I've followed it for many years.

But the fact is that I come from Germany. My initial stage of that journey was far more than geographical—it was a wrenching away that I assumed would be forever. Each subsequent stage of that journey has changed me, and now I've begun to reach across with my writing, to tear through the silence, to try and understand with all the compassion I can summon.

Part Two

The Interviews

Johanna

Born: 1949
Age at time of immigration: 35

The Longing for One Leader

My mother gave me tranquilizers when I was twelve. She couldn't handle my aliveness—my getting angry or being sad—so she encouraged me to take Valium. She took lots of drugs, too. She wasn't happy where we lived, never took the initiative to say: "Let's move somewhere else." She really had victimized herself, was very depressed. I remember coming home from school when I was sixteen, being unhappy and talking about it—oh, I had a bad day—and my mother trying to convince me that we should commit suicide together. There she was with her bottle of Valium, and she started to swallow them, very desperate, wanting to drag me with her. I have blanks there in my memory. I see her holding the bottle in front of me. I also remember grabbing the bottle, slapping it out of her hand.

It was the only time. She never tried, only threatened, to kill herself. She started to do that when I was five. I remember her lying in bed and saying: "I want to die," and my father saying to me: "You've got to be nice to your mother." He was also not happy. He was very weak. I wanted him to protect me from my mother. I was convinced he knew what she was doing because she was also abusive with him. Verbally. With me physically. He did not stand up for himself or for me.

I raised a father and a mother. I did.

I had not much childhood: I was responsible for my mother's survival, and my father wanted from me the affection that he didn't get from my mother. He wanted me to show him all the time that I loved him, that I needed him. I would call my relationship with him emotionally incestuous. He was not sexually abusive. There was this suggestion that I was the most suitable partner emotionally for him, that I understood him better than his wife did. And I think I played on that, too—it was a classic triangle. I felt I knew my father better and related to him better and loved him better, but I also remember feeling like a hypocrite. The legitimate anger of a child who doesn't want to take care of a father, who is already bruised from the abuse of a mother. All I wanted was a father to support me and help me and take me out of there.

The memory is one of utter exhaustion. With my mother I never felt safe. I'm still carrying a lot of fear. It's hard for me to feel safe with anybody. It was either abuse or abandonment from her—I never knew which, and I never knew which one to fear more. She would all of a sudden pack a bag and say, "Bye." Here I was, six years old, my mother was gone, my father would come home and say, "Where is your mother?" So it was my fault.

Then there was the verbal abuse, the continuous grinding me down: "You're like your father. . . ." "You're a failure, a zero. . . ." "You won't be anything without me. . . ." In hindsight, I know she is a crazy woman. As a child, I didn't, so I gobbled it all up. Meaning fear: *What's next?* A lot of shame: *If she does that, I must really deserve it, so I must be a bad person. Really bad.* I couldn't defend myself, didn't have the power to say: *Go to hell.*

Now I visit my parents once a year. I have come close to

saying: *I never want to see those people again, especially my mother,* but I just know that is not the solution. It's difficult. It takes me usually at least a month to recover. Now there is a new bungee cord—my father being sick with Alzheimer's—and being the only child, I can't say my brother is going to take care of it or my sister. I'm sure it's still the leftover: *I have to take care of my parents.* I obviously have guilt feelings: *How could I do this to them, going so far away, moving that far?* But it was important. It's been very good. Yet, I get homesick.

I can remember being very little and wanting to get away. I had an aunt in New York. I saw her twice as a child. She came to visit and brought an energy that I had not ever encountered—very positive. She affirmed me, and I had never experienced that. She would send me toys and clothes, and I liked her very much.

I was very shy, timid. I found my refuge in books. That was my world. I've never had many friends. I've never been a popular in-girl, but I've always had one or two friends I could completely trust and relate to, with whom I felt safe, and who really accepted me. I feel very fortunate. It started in kindergarten when I had a very good friend, and in the *Gymnasium*—secondary school—I had some very good friends.

I got to go to the *Gymnasium* when I was ten. That wasn't quite our social class because my parents were not educated, and I wouldn't have gone had my teacher not insisted. Most girls there had parents who were lawyers or doctors or pharmacists or teachers . . . far more educated and richer. I felt I had no right to be there. I was trying to act like I was comfortable with them, hanging out with the in-group, trying to dress like they dressed, trying to speak like they spoke, trying to—again—to belong, to be accepted.

I was a very good student. The abuse was still going on, and I lived with it somehow—in exile, I would call it. When I was twelve or thirteen, I used to go to a foreign film club at the

British consulate in Berlin. There'd usually be a documentary before the actual movie. One time—I wasn't warned about it—I saw a film of Auschwitz or Dachau, and that shook me profoundly, but what shook me even more profoundly was going home in that state of shock and wanting to talk. The response was that of denial: "We didn't know. . . . We suffered so much during the war. . . . It was so awful for us. . . ."

We didn't know.

We didn't know?

Okay, let's even assume they didn't know! I could grant them that. And I do feel a lot of compassion for these women and children sitting in burning buildings. It's not like I say: *Well, you deserved it,* which for a while was my attitude. But it's always like: *Well, wait a minute, why was all this happening?* And that question is not asked. What I did pick up was a condoning of Hitler, of the war, of camps, of the hatred of Jews, of blaming Jews, of scapegoating. Now I would call it all the shadow aspect projected onto Jews. And that was scary for me. From then on I felt a deep split between me and my parents. *Oh my God, they could have actually done this. Or maybe they even did. Who knows?* My mother had lived in the countryside, so I assumed she really didn't know much. But it was this deep sense of: *My very own parents. . . . They are not outraged. We're on different sides here.*

It was the first time I had seen something about the Holocaust. I had heard remarks: "Well, there were those damn Jews, and we're not allowed to say that anymore." As a child I always wondered why my parents weren't allowed to say something. It amazed me, shocked me. The only times I would ever see my father get hateful—not angry but hateful—he'd say, "Those goddamn French" or "Those . . ." He would swear, which I'd never heard him do. Everything that wasn't German was goddamn. And I remember that hurt me, a deep spiritual anguish that my father could have hatred against people in that way.

My parents never mentioned camps. And nobody else in

my family or our acquaintances. There was nothing. Not in
school. But somehow I picked up that I wasn't being told the
whole story, that there was something that wasn't being said.
When I saw those films, I knew, and I would say that has absolutely directed my life. The most profound insight that
came up for me then was: *If human beings can do this, then I can
do this.* At that age. But that's how deep it went. *So if this can be
done by human beings, it can be done by me.* What drove me, and is
still driving me, is: *What can you do so this will never ever happen
again?* It drove me to deep questions. There were no superficial solutions.

I couldn't identify with my parents, and I couldn't identify
with being German. I wanted to burn my passport. I was afraid
and ashamed to go to foreign countries. *What do I say? I'm not
going to tell anybody I'm German. They're going to hate me for that.* I
was always told I was too serious. "Why don't you enjoy your
life?" With that background—impossible.

I'm living now in a country where there are Jewish people
and even survivors. . . . In Germany there were no Jews. I
never met one. When I came here and talked for the first time
to a Jew, I was lucky it was a sensitive woman, and we cried together. We could do that.

Memories coming up . . . In the *Gymnasium* I had friends.
Twins. They weren't the best students, more the fun-loving
kind, but my mother said I shouldn't be hanging out with
them: they weren't a good influence. I kept probing: "Is it because they like to joke and chat in class?" Then I heard her
say: "Well, they're half Jews." I hadn't known, but then I became aware of it. I hung onto them—they were my friends,
and I really liked them. I could not understand that my
mother would bring this up.

So I realize I did know Jewish people. At the university I
knew another woman. I didn't have the courage to ask her
whether she was Jewish, but I had heard it from someone. I re-

member feeling a bit awkward around her, and I have that issue now. Some of my good friends are Jewish, and there is always this part of me that feels: *Well, they can never really like me. Because I'm German.* You can talk about it, but that's about all. I mean, it is there, as a reality. This person next to me could be a survivor. But I guess I wouldn't dare ask. So I carry of course the shame. Feeling ashamed for my parents, for that generation. And there is nothing you can do about that. That shame is just there.

I have heard my mother talk negatively about fascism and Hitler, and it's taken me a long time to figure out that she supported it in her own way. With her it's more subtle—you have to listen more carefully than with my father. Probably in order to not provoke conflicts with me, she'd say: "Yes, this was really horrible . . ." and "These old Nazis . . . I don't like being around them." But then she would go and do what many women did, being part of it in their own supportive way. I mean, that's part of enabling this whole thing. Caring about real responsibility, you'd say: *No, no, I don't want to do this. Those are not the kind of people I want to be with.* It was a pretty thin veneer. There'd be these walks almost every Sunday—it was a ritual—my father and this man, an old Nazi, in front walking together, and then twenty or thirty meters back my mother and this man's wife. I remember being bored. I wasn't interested in what my mother was talking about with this woman. They were killing time, interacting because they had to. Many couples do that. Sometimes I'd be with the men, and all they would ever talk about was *the war.* And this battle and that battle and: *What if we had only . . .* They were still winning the war. *If we had only . . .*

My father had been with the air force in Russia. Fifteen years ago he got a pretty good job through one of his war buddies, who had an influential position in one of the big insurance companies. I learned then that once a year these guys meet at military bases, military airports, to travel and talk about those old days. They once traveled to Sicily to a military airport, once to England. So they are still playing war, still very engaged.

It was last year that I finally realized people didn't go to Russia to play golf. My father was in Russia—meaning he was there to kill. Interesting that it never came to my mind. As a teenager, I asked both my parents: "Where were you? What did you know? Why did you follow?" What I wouldn't ask was: *Did you see killing? Did you kill? Did you see atrocities? How did you feel about it?* I did not dare become that concrete. My father said he kept the books. I bought that. I thought he just kept the books, and then it dawned on me, that's exactly it— *"I just kept the books."* My father was one of those very obedient men, following orders, very much looking for an authority figure. Now he has Alzheimer's. I can ask him, but he probably won't answer. Convenient.

It took me a long time to understand that the people of this generation are angry at Hitler—not because of what he did, but because he lost the war. They make it sound as if it's because of the atrocities and the Holocaust and the whole ideology, but that's not the reason. They're angry with Hitler— *their Hitler*—because he didn't give them what he promised.

At seventeen I started reading—I called it my three staples, which have been part of my life—Buddhism, especially Zen Buddhism, Marxism, and psychoanalysis. Always these questions: *How could this be? Who are we that we can do this? And why would we do this?* I've always needed the approach from several sides; one seemed never enough to explain this unexplainable thing.

Puberty was also a time of extreme confronting—confronting people in my family and friends of my parents. Sometimes, I think, they didn't want me there because I would lead the discussion to the Holocaust. They have this word *Nest-beschmutzer*—the person who dirties her own nest. I got called that. *Nestbeschmutzer.*

When someone gave the typical argument of "Well, he built the *Autobahnen* . . . ," I'd just fly into a rage: "How can you say this?" Which was painful, almost a self-destructive thing, because I drove myself into a deeper and deeper alienation. But I had to do it. I think what I was looking for was someone who'd say: *I know how you feel. I'm as struck by this* . . . That kind of mirroring, confirmation that what I was feeling was a sane feeling.

I didn't talk with friends about it. It wasn't talked about. In school I didn't get answers either. History ended somewhere in the Weimar Republic—if it ever got that far. We went through world history probably three times in nine years in the *Gymnasium,* and miraculously—whenever we got to 1933, it was vacation, or there was nothing left. So it was always like hitting a brick wall. From my family and friends I got the feedback that I was the weird one, that I was somewhat hysterical, that I was overdoing this, that I was—again—too serious. So I felt like a stranger.

When I moved away from my parents, I was twenty-one. It was painful . . . hard. I was very dependent and felt I couldn't do anything without my parents. I carry a lot of fear. I was scared to go to the university; I was scared to find an apartment; I was scared to make decisions for myself and say: *Yes, this is what I want. This is what I want to do.*

While I was going to school to become a translator, I was involved in drugs. I think it was my way of drawing my boundary. Doing what was forbidden. Finally daring to be disobedient. That lasted about two years. But then from one day to the next I decided: *This isn't it.* I could do it. I was very lucky. I remember getting up and saying: *This isn't going to work for me. This is not the solution.* And I brewed myself a cup of very strong coffee and said: *No, this is not going to continue.* And that was that. I never returned to drugs.

Now, when I go back to Germany, I feel nothing has changed. There are still comments like this: "Oh, this is over now. . . ." "This has been fifty years. . . ." "Look at what they're doing in *fill-in-the-blank*. . . ." Even people of my generation—and that's what scares me—don't want to think about it too much. That is a shock. I talked to a woman in her thirties who said to me: "I don't want to hear it anymore. They have bombarded us in school with this stuff." When I went to school, there was nothing, but there's this claim now that it's been overdone in school. Well, I can only say then that they haven't done it right. It's still a form of denial.

I read somewhere that, being born in 1949, I'm not actually responsible for what happened, but I am responsible *now* every time the subject comes up. Every time people talk about it, I'm responsible in my own reaction, my response. I don't know whether I would call people equally guilty when they say: "I don't want to hear it anymore. . . . " or "The *Autobahnen* are nice. . . ." I don't like the word guilt anyway. But I would say these people are still denying something there.

It is a big dividing line for me with people. Sometimes I try to talk—it depends on the person. It brings up my fear of that thinking and that mentality, and of course it brings up the fear of that being part of myself. This is what I've been working towards—that I cannot solve this problem by saying: *I don't want to see Germany again.* This kind of evil or negativity is really something I have to see as part of human beings, which means part of myself . . . that's the hardest work, the hardest aspect. But ultimately that is what needs to be done—what Germans particularly need to do—to look at ourselves and say: *So what in me supports this? What attitudes in me are just down that line?* And that's of course painful.

I'm working in education partly because I'm still trying to make people conscious of what *can* happen. My emphasis has shifted—from trying to shake people up towards digging in my own mud. Finding my own shadow, if you want so, and making my peace with that. And that takes courage because you're really looking at a monster. I have found that this monster is pain that has hardened. This rage and anger and hurt—you either turn against yourself or you are turned against someone else.

It has forced me to dig deeply and not ever put up with anything easy. So in a way it's been a gift to have been born at that time in that country, to have the opportunity to work this beast, to work evil, darkness, negativity, in a specific form. I mean, Germans have this very organized evil. It's not hatred with a passion—like you kill someone because you passionately hate that person. It's a very much thought-through process. You have all the arguments there, all the reasons, and that is the aspect—I think—you can't compare to anything. People say: "Well, there's the Holocaust, and there's Vietnam, and look what's going on in Rwanda. . . ." I don't buy into that one because I was born in Germany and have that cultural heritage, whether I like it or not. There is a specific quality there, that of thought-out, planned, organized, rationalized evil that makes it different from all those.

I'm not saying Americans shouldn't do their own work on their cruelties, but what many Germans do is take away from their responsibility by saying others did it, too. And that doesn't work. To tattoo a number on a person's arm, to then gas that person a few days later is . . . that is unique. It kind of blows your mind.

Those are the spots that are very hard for me to comprehend and see in myself. I know my tendency to overorganize or rationalize things. I know the mentality of the so-called *Schreibtischtäter,* a person who didn't exactly work in a camp but who signed the papers to send another person to camp. During the trials these people would always say: "Well, I just did my duty. . . ." "I just followed orders. . . ." This authoritarian spirit is another element that's scary and that I know very well.

How could this have happened? Always the question. But there was still something deeper that wanted answering, so I got involved in Zen Buddhism. I did it in good German fashion, always very serious, a good student, till I realized I was getting just too German about it, that there was no fun in my life. At that point in Berlin, where I grew up and lived, the leader of one particular spiritual group came into the picture. He was from India, and he simplified many of the different approaches. He brought all aspects together, all religions. What attracted me was that he was against any dogma of any church, of any ideology. There were dogmas of course in this group, but it took me time to understand that.

It was a large group in Berlin, and they seemed to really have fun—which is not what Germans think is the goal of life. Pursuit of happiness is not in our constitution. The group had nice discotheques, and I liked dancing there, liked the idea of enjoying my life. It was an intense group, confrontational, very much out there, different, which is what I needed to do. To the whole society. At that time it probably was the most controversial thing you could do, walk across the street or into a store or bus wearing the red clothes and a mala—a chain of 108 beads and a locket that had the picture of our leader in it. You'd get a lot of energy, a lot of juice. It was almost like running along naked. I felt kind of safe being a bit outrageous, but not doing it for my own sake. It was just what you did . . . a real convenient thing: *You can act out, but you're not responsible because you're following.*

Most of his disciples were Germans, which is interesting. I came to the United States because the main ashram, or center, was here. I visited during a festival, and I liked it. About 18,000 people were there. Part of the worship was the ideology that work is worship, so people built a dam and created a huge lake. We're not talking a little group getting together once a week. They created a city. It was huge. And when there wasn't a festival, there were still 2,000 permanent residents.

While I was there for ten days, I met my husband, Bob. What attracted me immensely was his generosity, taking it easy . . . a total opposite of that whole German uptight thing of how things need to be done, and if they're not done like this then they shouldn't be done at all. My Germanness really hits his attitude there and leads to a lot of conflict. But it was healing to be around that, just to see: *My God, there is a chance you could live life differently.* We were really attracted to each other. Very opposite. The longing was there to become part of the ashram and have that be my life, and I had a strong impulse to be done with Germany. Everything happened that same year: I was here in July; in September, Bob visited me in Germany for two weeks; a few weeks later we decided on the phone we wanted to be together; in October, I came to the United States; and by December we married at the ashram. Marriage was the only way to be here and not be on a tourist visa. But what was also in me was the search for home and family, for belonging and feeling protected.

I projected a lot of that on Bob. Then began the long walk of working on a marriage, which was hard because we didn't know each other, and here I came with my whole baggage—psychological and cultural. We've done a lot of work with each other, and I'm feeling a lot safer now. It wasn't always fun. Since we are so different, I've become aware of my Germanness. I'm trying to hide it, and it's impossible with Bob.

I used to spend three, four weeks a year at the ashram. To belong again, to have a place where I was accepted and loved, not alienated. The structure was fun-loving, but also very hierarchical. There was a big emphasis on work. People who lived in the ashram—which I never did—basically didn't have an income. The ashram took care of you: you had food; you had a bed; everything was taken care of. But you had no money. You cleaned or you worked in a store or the disco or the restaurant. I had a deep longing to abandon myself to that extent, to say: *Okay, this is it. I'm just going to give my whole life to this ashram now and this path, and forget about the rest.*

But I didn't.

I just didn't.

And I don't know why I didn't.

There was some obstacle inside of me that said: *No.* It reminds me of getting out when I was doing drugs and just saying: *Okay, this is it.* Like this intuitive valve someplace. And it says: *No, wait.*

Eventually the whole thing collapsed. I hear it's still going on big in India. It was a controversial group. Some people called it a cult, a sect. I'm careful with that. I mean, I would call Catholicism a cult, too.

The leader of our group was very controversial; he attacked especially the fundamentalist Christians. He made fun of them, and people didn't like that. So there was pressure building up—to a point that I didn't like it anymore. The group became paranoid. Militant. People were toting guns, and the government got involved. Our leader was accused of having come to this country for the wrong reasons. Well, it ended up he had to leave the country.

I may never know the truth, but supposedly someone tried to poison a salad bar in the area so the group would have the majority during an election for the school board. For me this was going over the limit. It stopped at the same time for Bob and me. We had heard rumors, and there'd been negative books, and the press had been negative, but we'd known that it was part of the whole thing. Then Bob found a book at the bookstore that was written by a former bodyguard. It was a good book. I mean, there are people who were part of a religious group, and they go out and sling mud to prove that they're now altered and better, that it was all a mistake. I don't see it like that. And this man didn't write it like that either. He wrote about what he had learned and what phase of his life this had been, and he described why he couldn't be there anymore. I liked it because he basically carried on the spirit of what this group had professed to be. He was, in other words, saying: *I'm staying true to why we were all here, and that's why I'm telling what happened.* It really touched me. It felt sincere. Bob started reading it, and then he started reading aloud. At first I didn't want to hear it, but we stayed up all night and read the three hundred pages to each other. At five in the morning we were done, and it was clear.

I remember crying for days. I felt a real sense of void. I had also learned enough to deal with that void, to accept this as an experience that had enriched me and helped me in my process. I had a phase of being angry, of feeling betrayed. It was hard letting go of another identity that wasn't anymore. But I didn't have regrets because I felt that what I had learned far outweighed the negative side.

What I learned there was my need for an authority figure telling me what to do.

I had been at a point where I was willing to do anything. Had our leader said, *You need to go to India and work at the ashram there,* I would have done it. That was quite a lesson. I saw similarities to my mother not taking responsibility, just wanting someone else to do it for me. Not owning my life, not taking responsibility, acting out all the things that you are not supposed to do, and then you can blame it on this leader. I felt an understanding for Germans. *One thing to follow.* That was hard, painful. I realized I had the same personality structure I had learned about at the university, this *Schreibtischtäter,* this person who's just signing papers but not actually doing anything, and then afterward says, "I just did my duty." I didn't like it. It was all very scary, but I didn't try to deny it. I said: *Okay, here it is.* That was another piece of the answer to my question: *How can this happen?*

It may sound strange . . . for me it is positive to know about that weakness in me and to not condemn myself for it, but to say: *I wasn't alone, we were all doing it.* To say: *So this is who we are, and this is what we do.* It gave me the awareness that we have a long way to go.

I cried a lot. I questioned what I was doing here. I questioned my marriage, because it had been part of that. It was a difficult time, a very difficult transition. *Who am I if I'm not part of that spiritual group? And what am I going to do with my life?* I started doing therapy with a woman, getting into my personal history, really looking. I think I was forty. It had taken me that much time and that much space away from Germany to be finally able to say: *This is what happened. Yes, it was all those horrible things.* And to process it and feel it.

I'm again doing my spiritual work. Working with a group of people . . . meditation and so on. The main attraction here is that it's democratic. Everything—teaching and planning—happens in teams. You don't have one teacher who will be the guru again. With our leader it was the devotion that counted. This here is not about a teacher—this is about a teaching. Which is a huge difference. I do my own meditations at home—about two hours a day—processing the past along certain questions, clearing up, understanding my past. It's not judging it. It's looking at it: *So this is what it was like.* And at the same time cultivating what you might call a witness, a part within that is not subjective, which really then helps to look at your past more honestly.

I consider this my space and time to heal.

I love being out here in nature. I could do this forever, being in a forest and camping by a stream and running around. You don't need clothes. You are alone. You don't find that in Germany. It is crowded. So I'm enjoying the space. And I am appreciating that people are a lot more easy on each other here. It's comfortable and a great relief. There is more space between people, a friendliness, even if it's superficial, a civility that you will not find in Germany. It's like: *Just because you are another human being, I will treat you friendly.*

Sometimes, though, I miss that old enmeshment, people everywhere, and everyone has an opinion, a judgment. I'm not sure about living in Germany again. This is always an open question. I miss particularly one friend. I'm very close to her. And I miss being in European cities. I like being around museums. So it's not a total yes to staying in America.

I teach German at a college. For me it's important to not just teach a language but to tell the students about what it means. Lots of the students who take German are conservative, have a German background, and are pretty much in denial. So it's tricky to let them know this part of learning about Germany, the culture, without alienating them. In one contemporary issues class we read German magazines and newspapers that had a lot of articles about neo-Nazis. The movie *Schindler's List* had just come out, and it was scary for me because it is personal. I don't want to judge my students when I see them reacting in the sense of: *I don't want to hear it.* But it was interesting how involved they got. One brought a tape about a camp, and they watched it. Several students cried. About half of the semester we were on that subject. This is important to me. How can this be done in such a way that they can assimilate it and process it, that it will deepen them?

For the first time in my life I feel an equal—and not because of any role I take on. I love working with young people, but it's a real trap, a danger of identifying with the role of teacher and taking that for being me. But I learned that's not me either. That role is just a role, and when you're in that role, you get a certain type of interaction, you have a certain power, and you can identify with that. I think that's dangerous. Of course, coming from that history, it would be just the thing to compensate for my past. But I'm aware of not doing that. I know I don't want that power. Students can make you feel important and powerful. And to not take that on, but to kind of give it back . . .

What I want is to be an equal among equals. I don't want to be a victim. I don't want to be a victimizer. I don't want to follow anymore.

I also don't want to be the leader.

Ulrich

Born: 1946
Age at time of immigration: 8

It Is at Least My Responsibility to Be Aware

In conversations with American friends, I frequently say: "You know, what happened over there, the abuse of the minority in Europe, could also happen here." Many years ago people would say: "Are you crazy? It could never happen here." But we've gotten closer to that. And so I'm very much a pacifist. I feel we always need to talk about a conflict, no matter what it takes, and in discussion we will find some solution that is going to be adequate for both sides.

Even though the individual may not be at fault—I mean, those of us who were born after the war didn't participate in the horrible events and therefore cannot be found guilty by any jury—it's not just the individual. It's the collective. It's the culture that bred individuals who created these problems, and since I'm part of that same culture and my children are to some extent part of that culture, it is at least my responsibility to be aware and to pass that awareness on because we need to make sure that's not going to happen again. We can't run away. We can't say: *"I'm not interested in that,"* or, *"That's horri-*

ble—I don't want to read that," or, *"I don't believe that."* We need to understand it, need to confront, and need to make sure that we're not going to fall into the same trap our forefathers fell into.

My father was in the war as a musician, a choral conductor. He was not in the front ranks but entertained the troops with music. He was not a very good soldier, I'm sure. He's Prussian but not very athletic. He tells me he never fired a shot once during the war, and I believe him because he's a musician— not a fighter. He apparently was lost in this forest behind the Russian front line with three or four other soldiers. Since he was the highest-ranking soldier, he had the responsibility to get these soldiers out of danger. He let somebody else take command, and apparently they got back to the German side.

When my father was a Russian prisoner of war, he created a chorus out of German soldiers in this prison camp. Now Russian choral music is not that different from German choral music. Apparently, these Russians liked the music my father was performing, and he was offered a good position in Russia; but he declined because he was interested in my mom—they weren't married yet—and he wanted to come back to Germany after the war. A Russian woman doctor or nurse got him and some members of his chorus out of prison. It had something to do with his music. She created some fictitious report that these men were ill, and that they couldn't take care of them.

My father wanted to have an orchestra, but after the war there weren't any orchestras in Germany. The only opportunity in music was to have a chorus, and so he changed careers and became a choral conductor. Germans like to sing, and in all these little towns the men got together as well as the women and organized choruses. That was the entertainment after the war. Interestingly enough, the Germans in the United States also formed choruses, and my father got an offer from a chorus in New York. My parents left Germany primarily because of the economic situation. A secondary reason for leaving was probably a fear of communism because the Cold War had started. My father feared communism for many years.

I was eight when we moved to America. We spoke German at home, and I grew up in a German cultural environment. Every night my father would go to a different chorus and rehearse. His choruses consisted of native Germans—from recent immigrants to those who'd come here after World War I. Because I was the only child of the conductor, everybody knew me, treated me well, and said: *"Ach, wie schön der deutsch sprechen kann"*—"Oh, how beautifully he speaks German."

I witnessed their conversations as they spoke of the past and the present, compared the U.S. to Germany. Never did my parents or the Germans speak sympathetically of Jews. They'd say something like: "Of course it was wrong, and it was terrible, and we didn't do it. But the authorities, the Nazis and the SS people, they were awful. They were pigs. But the number of Jews gassed was exaggerated. There weren't that many Jews in the world. It couldn't have been that many." I remember such comments as: "There was a chaotic time in the twenties, and there were so many political parties, and we had inflation, and then this fellow came along, who had a good plan, and he built the *Autobahnen.* . . ."

Everybody seemed to always talk about the *Autobahnen,* that example of great achievement of the early Nazi years, and that economic and social problems were being resolved because this new political party brought some stability and law and order. The Germans who, after the war, ended up in the United States thought that was a noble thing to do, that the initial years of the war were okay. They said: "Germany was mistreated after World War I and didn't get a fair shake. Therefore, these people needed some *Lebensraum*—living space—and had to take the initiative to regain some of the

lost territory." Most of the Germans I met here in the United
States had opinions like that, and when we were talking about
the later war years when everything started falling apart, they
said: "Well, Hitler then became crazy and lost his mind and
didn't know when to stop, but he had done much good in the
beginning. . . ."

I don't believe I ever witnessed anyone discussing guilt.

I remember one fellow once said: "What we need in this
country is a Hitler, who would solve the social problems rather
quickly. . . ." I think he was referring to the racial problems we
have here. This fellow would say: "Well, we ought to get these
blacks jobs and get them off the stoop. That's what Hitler
would have done, and that's what we need to do here." He
also would say something like: "They just have too much freedom here, and freedom is good, but you need a little law and
order, too."

That would be a very modern position, actually, because
our Republican friends have pretty much the same position.

I remember seeing the ruins in Germany. I'm not sure I
understood what that meant or where those ruins came from,
but I heard many stories about fleeing in the war, my mom in
bomb shelters in Berlin, scared and screaming and experiencing the horror. I wonder how these people actually have survived until this time and to what extent their lives have been
affected by the horrible memories of their youth.

My relatives passed a lot of stories on to me. Everybody
likes to tell this story about my uncle, butchering a cow in a
pasture to get food for the family, putting his life at risk. He
brought back pieces of the meat wrapped in newspaper or
sacks and distributed it to friends and family. The British gov-
erned Lower Saxony at that time, and apparently this crime of
stealing or butchering somebody's cow was punishable by
death. We were about a dozen people living in two rooms. Our
whole family had fled from Ostpreussen, away from the ap-

proaching Russian armies towards the Americans in the west, and congregated in this small town called Scheessel, where I was born in 1946. Since we were *Flüchtlinge*—refugees—there was very little to eat. Apparently, everybody begged and in some cases stole milk and eggs for me, who had just arrived in the world.

Since these small towns in Lower Saxony were never bombed, the society was pretty much intact. The farms were there; they had their chickens and cattle and sheep. The farmers had plenty of food but weren't necessarily friendly to *Flüchtlinge*. If you were an outsider in that society—even if you were German—the farmers didn't particularly want to help you. My mom didn't have much luck when she begged for eggs. She went into the chicken coop and tried to steal some eggs. Farmers would put fake chalk eggs, *Kalkeier*, in the nests to remind the chickens to lay eggs. My mother was apparently very nervous, and she came home with some real eggs, but also with one or two of these fake eggs. My family was not very lucky when it came to theft. I have an aunt who took a sack to the train station, stole coal off the train, jumped from the coal wagon onto the ground, and broke her leg.

I had a little brother who was a blue baby. I believe there was a hole in the heart. Somehow the heart didn't pump properly, and the skin color turned bluish, which would indicate a lack of oxygen. My brother died before he was three. I was fourteen months older than he. I remember two things about him—probably my earliest memories. I gallantly protected him against the local bully. Soon after that my brother was laid out on this huge bed. Individual roses were placed around his body and covered his body. I felt he couldn't just be still, lying there without movement. If only I could touch him, he would react and this charade of grieving would end. But of course I wasn't allowed to touch him. Thinking about that in retrospect, I should have been allowed to touch him. I've never forgotten that feeling, as well as seeing him on that bed.

For years I wanted a friend, a companion. I grew up as an

only child, and I always thought very fondly of my brother and wished my parents would have another child. They chose not to. My best companions later on, as I grew up here, were always in Germany . . . always far away.

Coming to this country as an eight-year-old, I didn't feel comfortable. America is a very conformist society. Maybe today we've loosened up a little bit because there have been new waves of immigrants from Asia and Hispanics from south of the border, but at that time America was even more conformist than it is today, and if you didn't wear the same clothes that people wore here, didn't do the same things, or didn't eat the same things, you were an outsider.

The local kids made fun of me because they'd probably never seen *Lederhosen.* They taunted me to the extent that I retreated into our railroad flat and did not venture out to play again—so my memory claims—for two months. I was probably a very insecure kid anyway. We lived in Ridgewood, New York, in an apartment under the elevated, that portion of the subway which is above ground. These structures are very old and rusty. They were probably built around the turn of the century and rattle when the subway comes. It was funny. It took some while to get used to sleeping there.

All through my teenage years I felt like an outsider. We moved to Forest Hills, a better residential neighborhood of Queens. A high percentage of the population was Jewish. It was very European. There were European bakeries and the first German butcher shop. They had very good sausages, *Leberwurst* and *Mettwurst,* and they would import bread from Canada, which we always bought.

On Jewish holidays we did not have classes because there weren't enough non-Jewish kids to make for a class. I had one Jewish friend, but everybody else avoided me. I spent unhappy junior high and high school years. One year I tried out for the softball team—I was a fairly good athlete—but I didn't make the team even though I could probably play better than most. I thought it was because I wasn't Jewish. I blamed myself for not making the softball team, for being German.

Most of the teachers were Jewish, the student body was about 75 percent Jewish, and I was known as "the German," sometimes as "the Nazi." Kids will always call other kids names, and the name I was called when things became hectic was Nazi. I felt that this was a terrible injustice because I was not a Nazi. I was German. I had an identity, and I had a name that others didn't recognize. I don't want to use the word "discrimination" because I believe it should be used for more serious mistreatment, people who are really being discriminated against in this country and also in Europe. But I was shunned. I was a very sensitive teenager, and being treated as an outsider and a foreigner in a Jewish area did affect me.

I grew up in my own world, living on the side of most of the action. I did not go to dances or do things other teenagers normally do. Now there may have been also other reasons for developing that way. My personal experiences at home, I'm sure, played a large role. Perhaps it was also my personality that didn't let me adjust adequately to the environment here. I felt very unhappy and wanted to go back to Germany because all my relatives were there, aunts and uncles, my grandmother and my grandfather, whom I loved very much. There was really no extended family here.

I had more and better friends in Germany. As a junior in high school, I spent a year in Germany and went to school. My parents stayed here. I experienced *Fasching*—carnival—that year. *Fasching* was great fun because there weren't any rules anymore. I was about fifteen, and the fun was in trying to get girls behind the door so you could kiss them, which normally you couldn't do. We wore masks, and the adults all got dressed up, went to restaurants, and totally let loose. There was a lot of drinking, a lot of coquettishness, people sitting on different people's laps and making believe they were somebody else.

I went back to Germany almost every year until I was about nineteen or twenty years old. I've always dated German young women, even here in this country, and I ended up marrying a German-speaking woman.

Choral conductors are always in charge in their job. My father was like that also at home. He ran the show, and he was very Prussian in the United States—not much humor, but very intense, very stern, very dictatorial. My mother basically had to adhere to his wishes. He decided when we should buy something new. He decided everything. My mother tried to fight that, but she never really succeeded in changing anything. Adults were always right in my family, and it was not wise to contradict them, especially my father. He was very stubborn and didn't want to discuss anything. In my own way, I rebelled against that even though I knew I would suffer for it. I wasn't hit that much, but I was yelled at, and there was also the withdrawal of affection.

The choruses would have a Christmas concert and a spring concert or other festivities, and my father would go and perform. I would go along. The first or second year here, I was supposed to recite a German Christmas poem. For a month my mom worked with me to memorize it. It was awful. When the day came, they put me on this pedestal in front of what seemed like thousands of people but was probably a group of fifty. My father was proud of his only son. I was very nervous. It was dark, smoky. The Christmas tree stood right next to me, and I sang "Jingle Bells." My father was furious for days. Here's this nice German kid who's going to say this nice German poem, and then the kid escapes into this awful cheap American song "Jingle Bells." I must have learned that if I wanted to irritate my father, this was how to do it.

Contradicting him was my way of controlling him. I realized that when I saw my kids grow up; they were controlling me by being stubborn or by not doing what I wanted them to do. What I wanted to accomplish in life was bringing up my children differently. It was the most important thing to me, and I'm not sure I succeeded to the extent I wanted to succeed. Maybe others might not be as hard on me. Maybe if some more time passes, I won't be as hard on myself. But right now I feel I failed a little bit. When my younger son, Martin, was a teenager, I had a lot of difficulties with him. In retrospect, it was probably similar to the problems my father had with me. That was a very painful experience—not being able to transcend that.

We are all a little bit stubborn: Martin was stubborn, and I'm stubborn, and my dad is stubborn. And when Martin was a teenager, he stopped communicating almost totally. We'd moved to the Twin Cities just before this happened. In retrospect, it was not a wise thing to move a teenage boy, and if I could do it over again, I wouldn't do that. It was a very scary situation because my communication style is to try and talk common sense—at least what I think is common sense. With Martin it never worked. Frequently, I would explode and say, "Why can't you talk to me? Why don't you answer?" I think Martin was in a lot of pain and basically shut down. Sometimes I saw him cry. He had an inability—and he still has difficulty—to communicate with his parents, and what I've tried to do over the last seven years is to give him more space and leave him be. Our relationship has really improved. We do a lot of things together now, although he still communicates on his terms. He has his way of saying, "Well, Dad, I'm just not ready now." But when he does communicate, it's so precious, and he smiles, and then I feel rewarded.

My other son, Ulrich, was just married in Las Vegas. He called us three hours after he was married and said, "Okay, Mom and Dad, you've always wanted a daughter-in-law." He told me he didn't see anything wrong with getting married in Las Vegas because it simplified things. "Well, Dad, that's how you raised me—to seek my own path and to do nontraditional things." It took me a little time to get over that because I raised him with the understanding that family is important, and that special occasions need to be celebrated with the family. But outside of that, anything goes, and you have to choose your own path.

I just visited Ulrich and discovered that eight days is too long. Young couples want some privacy, and after a while Dad is in the way. A couple of days is nice, but then it becomes old. I couldn't help but think about my parents, who come to this country every year and want to stay as long as possible. My mom just told me they have made plans to come for a month. Somehow I didn't have the courage to say, "Jesus, that's a long time . . . a month." Interestingly enough, I escape into my work. My father said, "Ulrich, you work so hard. It's nice to see you take care of things, but you need to rest more." So we play games—I escape into my world, and in turn my father thinks that I always work this hard.

Coming back from Düsseldorf last week in an airplane, I sat next to a young African-American male who'd just come from central West Africa. He had visited his father, who was ill, and he said he felt he owed his father something since his father had taken care of him so well. He smiled when he said he loved his father dearly and would do anything for him. This was such a wonderful experience, to hear somebody talking positively about a father, because my own relationship isn't that positive.

My father still is very much a Prussian. He is about seventy-six, retired, and lives with my mother in Langenberg, Germany. Even though she has a license, she isn't allowed to drive his car. And they lived in New York for twenty-five or thirty years. My mother worked in the city as a secretary or book-keeper, and today she's living on this hill with a nice view, but with absolutely nothing to do. She does a little *Handarbeit*—needlework—and reads magazines. My father is one-sided and opinionated. They don't discuss anything. Probably the one thing they still have in common is music. My dad, as a young man, was very flashy, very handsome, and played the piano. Apparently, many women flocked to him. My mom was a very attractive young woman, and they had something in common back then.

Now she walks down the hill to go shopping, and my dad has to pick her up to carry the groceries back up the hill. It's kind of funny and sad. I've tried to intercede over the last thirty years, but now I let them be—simply because this is their life and the relationship they have fallen into. They obviously both feel comfortable with it. Who am I to say that either my mom or my dad ought to change? So I've accepted it, but whenever I go to Germany—basically every year—I never stay with them. I don't feel comfortable sleeping there, because they still treat me as if I were a little kid. I stay with my aunt and drive over for a day to see my parents. And that's it. Interacting with them is very difficult because we always get ourselves into some sort of a box. My father is *jähzornig*—hot-tempered—and can explode without warning, even though two hours later he might regret it.

He was like this as far back as I remember.

I felt very uncomfortable as a teenager and left home as soon as possible. I had graduated high school and was a confused young man. Actually, my father helped me get a job at this German travel agency on Eighty-sixth Street, in Yorkville, the German area of New York. Next door was Café Geiger, and there was a movie theater still showing German films. On that one block were a lot of German shops, a couple of other restaurants, and another café. Of course, at that time Yorkville was already falling apart a little bit, but they say back in the forties and fifties everybody spoke German there. All the people who worked in this travel agency were German—some second-generation—and most of the customers were German. I spoke German there and ended up dating somebody who had just come off the boat from Germany.

Living alone in New York wasn't working out. My earnings weren't sufficient, and my mom had to give me an extra ten dollars every week or so. I was at the travel agency from 1964 to 1965, and then I took all my savings, bought a ticket, and basically escaped back to Germany. I thought I would enter a *Lehre*—an apprenticeship—but after four months I decided to go to college and came back to the States.

I met Marga in a German literature course at the State University of New York at Albany, and we ended up marrying. She'd been born in Germany, too, and had come here when she was twelve. Her parents fled the Ukraine and met in Ulm after the war. At first they lived in barracks, and the good Ulm *Bürger* looked down on the family because they spoke Ukrainian and were considered to be *Ausländer*—foreigners. When Marga came to this country, she was relieved to get out of Germany.

I ended up taking more German courses, and I continued with *Germanistik,* the study of German language and literature, probably because I wanted to learn more about the culture I came from. I ultimately learned much about twentieth-century German history, focused on the modern German novel, and wrote my dissertation on *Hundejahre* by Günter Grass.

Marga and I are still each other's best friends. There are ups and downs, as everybody experiences, but we basically are happy together. We have the same interests and solve problems in a similar way. *Wir gleichen einander aus*—we balance each other. We are compatible. I probably got married very young because I wanted a companion. We had two children right away, thirteen months apart. I was a graduate student living off a teaching assistantship, and Marga was doing babysitting. My parents-in-law would bring food and every once in a while slip us a twenty. Interestingly enough, my mom always contributed money without my father knowing.

I felt very happy because I had my own family. Here was my opportunity to show my dad, to do things differently, to raise my own kids my own way. They were not baptized because I felt baptizing children is cruel. I felt when they were old enough and if they were interested, they would pursue religion or spirituality. I'm very pleased about that decision because both have found their own spiritual paths and have high moral values without belonging to any particular religion. My father is Protestant, my mom Catholic, and they always argued about it. I was supposed to be baptized and raised a Catholic, but my father forced me to be baptized and raised as a Protestant. Whenever he'd see my mother pray with the fingertips extended, hands flush against each other the way Catholics pray in Germany, he'd become very angry.

Early in my teens I decided to rebel against the religious activities I was doing. I chose my own path. Today, I consider myself to be an atheist, and my wife is seeking her own spiritual path. Thomas Merton is very important to her, whereas I'm not interested in a spiritual quest at this time. Although we do discuss it, we have learned to accept each other's differences.

I was very involved with my children when they were young. I was at home struggling with writing my dissertation, which took me forever. I saw the kids off to school in the morning, got them back from school, and took care of the home. I baked French breads and *Brötchen,* went mushroom hunting. We always did a lot of outdoor things, and my children spent a lot of time in the woods and on the lake or near the ocean. Marga supported the family. She had a full-time job at the University of Connecticut library, and I was doing odd things, teaching here and there in the summers. I was a research assistant at the University of Connecticut. In the evenings I went to the library and tried to do some work. We basically got by.

Germany and German culture are obviously very important to me, because we gave our children German names, even though Marga is Ukrainian. We spoke German at home for the first four or five years of my oldest son's life. At some point we switched to English because Ulrich would say, "What do you call this?" and, "I didn't know what that was." Today we speak English almost exclusively.

All of the German culture I inherited as a child, I passed on. We had a Christmas tree that we always decorated in our unique way with *Lametta, Kugeln,* and *Kekse*—tinsel, balls, and biscuits. We baked *Stollen* and *Lebkuchen.* We went over to Germany and brought back a lot of books and fairy tales and children's music. We raised our children singing German songs like *Hänschen klein,* and we did all the Grimm *Märchen*—fairy tales—all the *Struwwelpeter* stories. They're pretty terrible—I mean, if you don't behave in those stories and fit in, you're going to become mutilated.

I finally got my Ph.D. in 1981, but then I became frustrated with the prospect of a job and then perhaps not getting tenure and moving every year or two. The only jobs open were one-year appointments with salaries between $14,000 and $15,000. I couldn't afford to raise a family on that. My kids were already getting older—Ulrich was eleven, Martin ten.

We had a neighbor, a salesman who was very entertaining and always had great stories about his travels. He influenced me a lot. He said: "Ulrich, you have a gift of gab. Why don't you become a salesperson?" After a lengthy analysis of the situation, I decided I would try to initiate a sales career. A large company that makes consumer products hired me as a salesman. I started with a salary of $20,700 and a company car, and I thought that was wonderful. I moved to Buffalo, New York, was successful, moved to Seattle, Washington, and then they brought me into company headquarters here in St. Paul, Minnesota, to make me a marketer. After three years, there was a local opening for a sales position, and I grabbed it. So that's what I do right now. I love it. I have an ability to do this type of work. Company headquarters is fifteen minutes down the road, and I work out of my home office. I'm totally independent, able to schedule my own workload. I've always gotten along well with my supervisors, and they have left me alone so that I can basically run my own business.

At work is this man I really like—in fact, I report to him. We are unlike in many ways: Al likes Rush Limbaugh, and I don't; Al doesn't read, and I do. But we can talk about politics and gay issues and stuff like that. The first time I came into Al's office and we talked about our backgrounds, he said, "I didn't know you were a Nazi." It really took me aback. It did sting. He's never mentioned anything like that again, and I have not addressed that remark. I don't plan to either. I did inquire at the time though with the human resources manager, who investigates complaints against the company. He said, "Maybe I'm going to see you soon in my office." But I didn't file a complaint. It's settled. In retrospect, Al was not trying to say anything negative or mean with that comment—he thought it was a funny quip perhaps. Apparently, this mentality is still with us.

Growing up in this country, I was exposed to war films that showed the Allies as being wonderful and the Nazis as being ungodly. They always said: *"Achtung"* and *"Sieg Heil."* These old films were pretty stupid and simple. They were not very helpful because they weren't very historic, but somehow I increasingly became interested in Germany and what happened to the Jews. Every once in a while I would initiate a discussion or comment about 6 million, and my father would say: "Well, there just weren't that many." When I was studying *Germanistik,* I strengthened my pacifist position. My position is that of course the war was wrong. The problem is that Hitler ever came to power.

I grew up during the Vietnam years, and I was very antimilitary, probably because of the experiences I grew up with. At one time I was classified as 1A and went to Toronto to explore what was going on there because I was not going to let myself be drafted. Since I had kids and my family was young, I basically got out of that situation where they wanted to make a soldier of me. I don't think I'd be a very good soldier because I don't take orders well and don't believe in that type of discipline. And that's how I raised my children—I did not want them to become soldiers, and they did not. We sent them to a good private school, and I told them I would take care of the bill—that cost a lot of money, and I still have debts—whereas a friend of theirs went to ROTC and is now in the military. He chose that as his path, which is fine, but I was not going to recommend that to my boys.

I've been against all the wars we've since been involved in. In fact, I was shocked at the war against Iraq. I never thought we would initiate something like that. I felt we had to keep talking somehow, that we could not just go in there and bomb the heck out of these cities because maybe bombing soldiers is one thing, but we did not just bomb soldiers. I was the only one in my circle of friends who was against that war.

Right now it's the fiftieth anniversary of the American forces liberating Germany, and in Germany they're showing a lot of films that Americans made when they liberated individual cities. My uncle, who is now retired there—even though he lived in the United States for thirty years—was very interested in these films, taping them, whereas my aunts said: "God, why don't you stop this? We just can't watch this destruction anymore."

It's a very painful experience for my aunt from Berlin to see pictures of her beloved city destroyed. She doesn't want to talk about it, doesn't want to relive those horrible experiences. We talked about the issue of Dresden again—that still is very controversial. You read these British fellows with their quotes: "We just had to do it." And the Germans who experienced it say it was horrible and unnecessary.

Whenever people talk about the war, it's difficult.

My uncle commented that some American soldiers took potshots at anybody who moved when they entered the city. Apparently some soldiers—and this probably makes sense because it's the nature of war—may have had fun firing at civilians. This is the first time I've ever heard a negative comment about American behavior. What I've always heard is that the Germans all wanted to run towards the Americans and away from the Russian soldiers and their supposed barbarism. They would shoot to kill, to maim; they mistreated the people; they raped the women. What I read when I was older and did some research was that the Russian troops were kind of wild and chaotic, and of course they let out their resentment on these Germans—or Nazis, as they may have been called—because of the pain they'd suffered back in their homelands.

I have mixed feelings about not having stayed in academics. Sometimes I feel I sold out to money. I have never been fond of business interests, and I have never gotten along with business people because frequently they are conservative. But I do have to make a living. I started so late earning an income, and we had a lot of catching up to do. We live in a society that offers all its citizens a lot. It just takes money. And that involves choices. Right? So I made my choices. I feel fairly good about them, but sometimes I wonder whether they were the right choices, and I feel a pang of guilt. My guidance to my children was to not sell out, to study in college what they were really interested in and then later in life find a way to earn a living.

What I really live for is reading. I've read about half a dozen of Nabokov's novels within the last year. He is a wonderful writer. There are so many good books, so many interesting subjects I want to explore. I enjoy reading what physicists are discovering and what these discoveries mean. I've thought about getting back into teaching, but I don't think I can reenter the world of *Germanistik* after fifteen years of not reading Goethe and Schiller. What I'd be interested in would be twentieth-century literature, but I don't think anybody would give me the salary I need to stay alive, to feed myself, and I still have responsibility for my children.

My number-one interest is my family. We try to spend a lot of time together. When the kids are around, I always make myself available. Now that they are older and don't need me that often anymore, Marga and I go to the theater a lot. I like to see experimental things. Sometimes they're terrible, and I don't know what they're talking about, but I still enjoy seeing what the young theater people are doing.

I do most of the cooking in the family—that's my hobby. I learned to cook from my grandmother and aunt, also a little from my mother. I cook German basically, meat and potatoes and vegetables with gravies. One of my favorite spices is *Maggi*. I don't like going to German restaurants because I can cook better, and because they're so fake. They play up the stereotypes with awful decor, cheap cuckoo clocks and pictures, the steins of beer, and the owner running around in *Lederhosen*. That's the image of Germany that Americans have from Bavaria, of course. I went to some of these small towns. They were so touristy that I would never go there again. One town was re-created to look medieval. Busloads of tourists from Japan, the U.S., and other European countries were all taking pictures of these natural-looking Germans.

Most people say I don't have an accent in English, but because my name is unmistakably German, everybody knows I'm German. When I was in Germany on business, I was known as the American who spoke German. You're always a little bit the outsider. Somebody once told me I have a different personality when I speak English, that when I speak German I'm more serious.

At first I felt German values were better, more meaningful, but now I feel very comfortable here. I would not ever think of living in Germany—I'm much more Americanized than that—but because of my extensive experience with German culture, I am not totally Americanized. My children, I suspect, are going to become more American than German, and then the next generation will become totally American.

I guess that's the experience all immigrants had coming to this country.

Anneliese

Born: 1942
Age at time of immigration: 10

I Don't Want to Know

M y father was in the SS during the war. It's not something I'm ashamed of. Probably, deep down I'm proud. Not because I know what the Nazis and the SS did. I'm not proud of anything like that. The pride comes from the fact that he was an officer. He had to be an officer to be in the SS. There is a certain criterion you have to meet. I mean, they didn't take any old farm boy. They were the elite, weren't they? And that's the part where I think: *Hey, that's all right.*

But I don't tell just anybody that.

How can you? You don't go around bragging that your father was in the SS. Now my mother says he never did anything bad. I don't know. I mean, if you were in the SS, you had to have done something. If I ever thought that he hurt anybody, I would just . . .

I'm real sensitive about that. I can't watch those movies about concentration camps. The only thing I've ever seen was accidental. Maybe *60 Minutes*—completely unexpectedly— comes out with pictures of the graves and the skeletons. If it flashes on, I quickly close my eyes. And I don't read about it. I don't know if it's because I'm German, or if it's because I'm me. I think it's just because of the way I am.

Of course, nobody ever lets you forget it. It's been fifty years, and it's always mentioned. I mean, it was a horrible, horrible thing, but it's time to let it go, to a certain extent. What I object to are those horrible newsreels and pictures. Anything like that, it just constantly works on my mind, and I can't get it out. So I avoid it. And if anybody ever wants to talk about it, I say: "I don't want to hear about it."

I don't have to.

I don't want to know.

You couldn't pay me to go into the Holocaust Museum in Washington. There are millions of people who buy tickets and line up because they want to see that. Why in the world would I want to go into a pretend cattle car? And I understand they have shoes of the victims. To subject myself to that . . . I'd probably faint.

I don't think anything like that could ever happen again. Although, you know, other countries are exterminating their unwanted. Look at Rwanda and Yugoslavia, where they're just wiping each other out. Why didn't the United States step in and do something when it started? That's how things started in Germany when the Nazis first started wiping out the Jews. People knew what was happening. But nobody stepped in either.

I live my life very much on a surface. Maybe that's why I don't remember whole sections of my life. Years. It always amazes me when people say: "Oh, when I was three, I did this or that." My life is a complete blank except for certain things that I remember. I don't know if it's because it was so horrible, or if it just didn't sink in. Things just don't make that much of an impact. It's strange.

What I feel about my birth father is hard to say, because I've never really given much thought to it. I don't know much about him, except the bits and pieces I've heard from my mom, none of which are good. I've taken her word for how he is. And her word is that he didn't care about my brother or me. Or her. We never got a birthday card or Christmas card. He knew our address in America because my mother got a little bit of child support—not voluntarily, but through channels in Germany that made him send money, which stopped promptly on my eighteenth birthday.

I don't know what went on between my father and my mother. You know, maybe something turned him bitter. Or maybe he's just a cold person, who could push away his wife and two little children. Maybe that was easiest for him. I have no idea. But I have pictures of him. He has blond hair. What's a German without blond hair? Nice-looking. Left-handed, which I inherited. He was an accountant. And he was a prisoner of war for several years. Of the French, if I remember correctly.

I don't talk much about this to anybody.

Actually, nobody ever pays any attention to me. . . .

My father took off and went into hiding when he realized how the war was going for the Germans. When my mother found out where he might be, she hooked up with some people who volunteered to take her across the border. I don't know which border, maybe into Poland. That must have been around the spring of 1945. My mother said it was dangerous because you never knew if you were hooked up with good people who really wanted to take you across the border, or people who would take you to the Nazis. As traitors.

Anyway, she did find my father, and he was living with this woman. He wanted to marry her and said he didn't want to be married to my mother anymore. What could she do? She hooked up with another group, who took her back across the border. Here my mother was stuck with me and my brother and my grandmother, and all the neighbors knew that her husband was an SS officer. When the Russians invaded our part of Berlin, my mother went around and begged neighbors to not tell them that her husband was in the SS. Because then the Russians would just take us all off to a camp or shoot us. Evidently, none of the neighbors reported us.

We lived hand-to-mouth. I have class pictures of my older brother. He is four years older than I am. Sunken cheeks. Cheekbones that stick out. Teeth that look way too big for his mouth. He is obviously undernourished. In my picture I look all right. I'm not chubby, but my cheeks aren't sunken in. Evidently, they made sure that whatever they had, I got first because I was the baby girl.

One of my mother's girlfriends had emigrated to the United States, and they'd kept in touch. When she was getting ready to divorce her husband, she kind of recommended him to my mother. He became my stepfather. He also is German. He left Germany in the late 1930s when he first started seeing how the Nazis were going. He was in town one day and saw the Nazis beating up an old man. So he left for America. As soon as possible he became an American citizen.

My future stepfather and my mother started corresponding. I guess he proposed to her in a letter. All this time we were still in East Berlin. You couldn't move from there to the United States. You had to go to West Berlin and then to America. They started the paperwork for us to move to West Berlin. My mother didn't tell me why. Finally, we did manage to go to West Berlin, and that's where I first met my stepfather. My mother said: "Well, this is going to be your new father, and we're getting married next week. Then we're going to America."

I was ten years old. Can you imagine? That was the most traumatic thing in the whole world. Nowadays, with any change like that, they would get you counseling, but back then it was like: "Hey, kid, this is what's going to happen, and you don't have anything to say about it." That's definitely the

German train of thought. They're probably getting away from it now, but that's the way it was back then. And you're the one who has to learn to adjust.

I asked my mother once: "Why didn't you tell me that all this was coming about?" And she said she was afraid I might tell my friends, and then they would tell their parents, who would report us, and we wouldn't get out of East Berlin. I said: "I wouldn't have told anybody. I was a responsible person."

My relationship with my mother is real iffy. I used to say she was my best friend. But as I get older, I get more resentful about the things she didn't do. She should have made it a little easier by giving me emotional support. My little granddaughter is eight now, and in a couple of years she'll be ten, the same age I was when all of this happened to me. And I think how differently I would handle a transition like that.

But then I feel bad. Because here I am . . . fifty-two years old. That should be all water over the dam. It never is, is it? Until you get it resolved somehow.

When my mother and my stepfather took off for the United States, my brother and I couldn't go with them for six months. My brother got farmed out to stay with friends of his, and I got farmed out to this Catholic convent. A boarding school. Not only was I separated from my mother, but I was separated from my grandmother and my brother.

My grandmother—she was the love of my life, and I was hers. I wish I could remember more about her. I called her *Malein*. She stayed behind for a while in West Berlin, and then she came to live with my mother for several years. When she went back to Germany, she went into one of these . . . for the older people. *Ja.*

I've never wanted to go back to Germany. Maybe it's because I was ten when I left, and Berlin was completely bombed out. I remember playing in the rubble of buildings. Climbing over bricks and mortar and seeing metal joists sticking out.

When I came to the States, I made up my mind that this was going to be my home from now on, that it was foolish to give in to being homesick or wanting to go back because I knew I couldn't. I probably trained myself to push Germany aside.

My mother has horror stories about things that happened there during the war. We were practically starving, and she used to go around and beg the neighbors—not for potatoes, but the peels—so she could make a bit of soup. That was the biggest, most horrendous part of her life, trying to keep body and soul together. To get enough food on the table and keep two little kids protected. Look how long the war went on. Not just the war itself, but the events leading up to the war, and then of course the events afterwards. For us, who were children, it's a fraction of the impact.

I don't remember knowing about the Holocaust. I think I just heard about that over the years. I understood more when I came over here. I have a few snatches of memory of the war. One is being carried on my mother's shoulders to the bomb shelter at night. She said I was a real happy child, always singing. The neighbors could hear me singing and said: "Oh, here comes Ellen with Anneliese." I remember going to the school yard and watching the Russians practice their fencing. After the war, the old bomb shelter was converted for storing potatoes, and Russian officers stood in front of it, guarding it. I have a picture in my mind of brown uniforms. I remember a carnival. A few little booths and a carousel. My mother and I on the Ferris wheel. When we got up to the top, they stopped the Ferris wheel because on the ground some Russian soldiers were shooting. I guess they were drunk.

My husband said that my mother told him things that happened to her during and after the war, things she never told me. I said to him: "Don't tell me. I don't want to know." Maybe sometime I will. I'm sure she was raped. By the Russian soldiers. They saw a woman, and I'm sure that's what they did. She said the ones they sent in the front line into eastern Germany were the most ignorant ones, the plowboys, the farmers, from way out in the Ukraine. Those soldiers used to pour honey on people and then send a swarm of bees. My mother said they came and drank the rubbing alcohol. She buried all the good glasses—Roman wineglasses and the crystal—in her backyard.

Evidently, my real father married this woman he was living with. A long time ago my mother told me he had a daughter. I would like to go to Germany and find her. My husband, Paul, really encourages me. In fact, it was his idea. He said: "Aren't you curious? Don't you want to know?" At first I thought: *No, I don't want to have anything to do with that part.* He kept pushing it: "Just think, you've got a sister." And he finally got me around to thinking that way. So now I'd like to find out what's what. But when I asked my mother if she knew anything about this girl, she said: "Oh, she is not your real sister. I don't think his second wife could have children. They adopted a girl."

I don't believe that. I think she just doesn't want me to delve too deeply.

The only time I remember seeing my father was in November 1952 when my brother and I flew from Germany to New York and had a layover in Frankfurt. My father met us there. And do you know what? This is terrible—I'm going to sound so bitter—but he didn't pay that much attention. He took us to dinner, but he didn't make a big fuss over me at all. I had gotten my hair cut real short. When I landed in New York, where my mother and stepfather met us, she asked me: "How was your meeting with your father?" I said: "Well, he didn't . . . it was like I was just some person." She said: "Why, no wonder, look at you. Look at your hair." It's awful how you remember some things that really cut you to the quick. That affected me so much. I thought: *Well, I guess I wasn't cute or pretty enough for him.*

It was pretty traumatic. My mother was out like this— about two months shy of giving birth to my half brother. We drove from New York to New Jersey, where we lived. I remember asking her if we were safe now in America, if there would be any more bombs. My stepfather was very Prussian, and if you didn't keep up with his intellect or whatever, why, you were like nothing. My mother just sat back and let him rule. It was always: "Well, don't do this because you'll embarrass me in front of your stepfather."

I started school right away in fifth grade. I didn't understand one word of English and didn't know what the hell they were talking about. But I just kept on. I was lucky because everybody was nice and kind to me. Nobody threw rocks or called me names. I picked up the language from paying attention. A young GI tutored my brother and me two or three nights a week. But mostly I taught myself. I love to read, and I read comic books to start out and progressed from there. I tried real hard and wasn't kept back in school.

When my class put on a Christmas play and I was in it, my mother didn't come. I couldn't have friends over because it was too much of a bother. And with my stepfather she didn't give me any emotional support. It was always up to me to be understanding. Why couldn't he try to understand me? He was the adult. I was a child.

I joined a sorority in high school, and that was fun. My parents were very strict about dating, and I had an eleven o'clock curfew when I was a senior. So very, very German. Needless to say, I got married almost immediately out of high school. I married my son's father, and I stayed married to him about three years and then lived on my own for six months. I was married to my second husband for about three years. It sounds terrible: *I married him for three years and then him for three years.* . . . But there wasn't that much to my first two marriages. I don't remember. My mother and stepfather did not approve of my first husband because he was a truck driver. So that was like lowest-of-the-low in their eyes. We had a religious ceremony, and at first my stepfather wasn't going to come, but my mom talked him into it at the last minute. My first husband ran around, so I thought: *Well, I don't need that.*

I didn't like the way my second husband treated my son. He wanted to spank him. He was too domineering, too strict. He was a spouse abuser, *ja.* After the second time, I thought: *No, no, no, I don't do that. I don't believe in that.* So I moved out and got my own apartment with my son.

It's funny. I've never really been without a man in my life. I've always kind of met somebody right away. My girlfriend fixed me up with Paul, my third husband, on a blind date. He was in the military, and we liked each other right away. But he was still married . . . separated, and we lived together for eleven years before we got married.

As a legal secretary, I've worked with lots of Jews. They all loved the fact that I'm German because they knew I was a hard worker. They've all bent over backwards to be nice to me. In fact, the first attorney I ever worked for would take off Jewish holidays, and he would let me have them off. So I had Jewish holidays and Christian holidays off.

But two or three years ago the law firm I worked for took in a new partner, who is Jewish, and he flat out told me that he hated all Germans, that he lost too many of his family during the war, and that he never buys any German products. Well, I thought he was an ass for telling me that, because obviously he didn't realize the potential for all kinds of lawsuits. If they ever wanted to let me go, I could say: *Well, they're letting me go due to my being German.* It was very foolish of him to say that. Also pretty ignorant. Because he didn't know me. We had just been introduced. So how dare he?

I think I said to him: "I buy all German products if I possibly can." I don't. I'd love to be able to afford a Mercedes, or a BMW. I made light of it. What was I going to do? That was the only time I've encountered prejudice for being German.

My prejudice is that I have a real thing about Indians. India Indians. I don't know why. It's silly. I've certainly never had a run-in or anything. Whenever there are some downtown, I walk far enough away from them. Maybe I'm prejudiced against them because my grandmother told me one time she was walking through downtown Berlin, and an Indian came up to her and said: "Well, you're not long for this world." And within two years she died. Maybe subconsciously that's why. I don't want them to come up to me and say: *Hey, hey chick . . .*

I consider myself a German, without a doubt. I have a German passport. Yet, America is my home, and I feel at home here. But I don't feel like an American. Maybe because I've never taken out citizenship. I guess I'm sort of a split person. I do feel connected to America, and I definitely don't feel connected to Germany. But I am German. Maybe I would feel more American if I became truly an American citizen.

I don't know how that fits together with not having been back to Germany.

In terms of my identity I'm a German Virgo. The Virgo part is that I'm very structured, which also is very German, isn't it? Very clean. *Everything has to be in its place. Don't get me off my schedule.* Very focused. *This is the way it's done because it's my way, and my way is the best way.* It works for me, but it makes life difficult because it always throws surprises at you. The biggest surprise was my mother marrying my stepfather and coming over here. Maybe that's one of the reasons why I'm so structured. I don't like change, and I don't like being surprised. Still, I didn't have any hesitation about leaving my husbands. That was certainly a change. But that was my choice. *Ja,* that's right.

My third husband, Paul, is completely the opposite of me. He can't see how I can stand living in such a structured way. And I can't see how he can stand living in such an unstructured way. He says: "You've got to relax. The dirty dish in the sink will be there tomorrow." But I don't want it there tomorrow. So we've learned to adjust. It's mostly me—I've had to adjust to his way. He certainly would never be the way I am. It's just not in him.

I'm proud to be German. I don't think it's anything to be ashamed of. But I'm not proud of what happened to the Jews and the Gypsies and anybody else who didn't fit into the norm according to the Nazis. However, you know, nobody ever says how many Jews and other people Mussolini exterminated. I'm kind of torn between being proud to be a German—I think it's a great heritage—and being ashamed of what happened.

Every now and then I have the same nightmare. I still have it to this day. I'm a child playing in the rubble. I know I'm going to come across a corpse in the rubble. Feelings that you have in dreams are so strong and vivid. . . . I don't know if I ever see the corpse. But it's enough knowing that—while I'm playing in that rubble—I'm going to come across the corpse.

Karl

Born: 1946
Age at time of immigration: 2

I'm a Chameleon

I listen to people all the time. I watch how people grow up. I watch how people screw up their lives. Most people want you to be interested in them—and that's my job as a minister. I see how people make it and how people don't make it. And you say: *Well, why does one person make it and another person not make it?*

I have no conscious memories of Germany.

If I had stayed there as a German, I would have been a different person.

I came to America when I was two-and-a-half years old. My father was a linguist and had joined the U.S. Army to get away from his first wife. He was married to a very old woman. The family myth is that he was looking for his mother because he and his sister had been orphaned.

My father was in his forties when he was in the American military government in Germany. He met my mother, who was born in 1923. She has a story that would be worth ten novels if she would tell it. She was married to an Iraqi, who was in the Iraqi Air Force and part of the diplomatic community of Berlin. I've seen pictures of the fellow, a very handsome man. At the end of the war when Berlin was evacuated, the SS didn't let my mother go with him. They saw her as a traitor to Germany because of her consorting with this Arab.

She and another woman marched across Czechoslovakia to get away from the Russians. Because she spoke English, they got through the lines. She quickly got hooked up with my father. You weren't supposed to fraternize with Germans, but my father did, and I was the result of this. A lot of German people wanted out of Germany, and one way to do it—if you were a woman—was to do what my mother did. My father got an old Nazi to deliver me C-section. In the process of doing that, the doctor messed my mother up on purpose. He did some things to her that imperiled her life because she was a German messing around with Americans. My father married my mother to get me to this country. She was not the nicest of women to be married to because she's pretty tough and self-centered.

In Paris my father picked up a French woman. She and my mother were young chicks during the war. Since my father wanted to marry the French woman, he came back to America with her and my mother. He finally divorced my mother and married the French woman. That turned out to be the happy marriage of his life.

You can almost categorize broad groups of people by decades. People who grew up in the thirties, whether it was in this country or Europe, were badly scarred and bruised. Europe had Nazism to deal with; we had the Depression to deal with and then the war. You can't be blinded, you can't be bombed, you can't have your parents killed, you can't be hounded everywhere without that affecting you.

And I think it affected my mother.

• • •

My mother and I don't have a loving relationship. I'm a dutiful son. We get along. We don't fight. I see her a couple of times a year. We've had several talks about the war. There is enough public information that you can get the facts, but then you try to fit in your own story. How did people I know fit into this? My mother was fifteen in 1936, and nineteen in 1940. When I was nineteen, I wasn't battered with the propaganda and all that. It's a mystery.

Families tell stories. Sometimes they tell stories and don't realize what they're really telling, right? When my mother was fourteen, she was in this car accident—fractured skull—and her father slapped her in the face. And that's abusive. But then I know other stories about going to the North Sea in the summer or going to the Harz Mountains. One of our family stories was that my mother went to the Olympics in 1936. She met Jesse Owens, who played with her pigtails and talked to her about her blond hair.

My mother's tall, attractive . . . typical Aryan. During the war she was in the Hitler *Jugend* in the *BDM, Bund Deutscher Mädchen*—the League of German Girls. Her parents both died in air raids. She was on the outskirts of Dresden when it was fire-bombed. When a phosphorus bomb went off near her, she was blinded for a week.

I've asked my mother: "What about the Jews?" She said: "All I can remember is that people were suddenly gone. We had Jewish neighbors, and they were gone." That is the extent that she's aware of that. She doesn't remember things now that she told me about Germany and the war. In the fifties, she went to a psychiatrist, and he told her: "There are things that are better just left up on a shelf. You've put them in a jar. Those are demons that are better just left there." And that's what she's living. It's not age—she's not forgetful otherwise. She's forgotten because she's chosen to forget.

• • •

"What happened in the war, Daddy?"

That's something that has consumed me, preoccupied me. On a large academic level: reading books, traveling to Europe; and on a personal level: trying to sort out who my mother is and who my father is.

And who am I? Am I a German? Am I an American? Am I an American-German? Am I a German-American? I'm a chameleon. I can be different things. And that's part of the problem with all of this. When I talk to the Germans in this church where I am a minister, I highlight the German side of me. I can talk in German. One of the German women in my church has said: "Sometimes I feel guilty about the war." I don't feel any sense of collective guilt. I've come to terms with that part of it. Bad Germans did things. Bad Americans have done just the same. I know enough bad people to know who's capable of what.

When we came over, my mother laughed because I said to another baby on the plane: "Shut up, baby! You make me nervous." I told that to my wife, who is into counseling, and she pointed out what an awful story that is. "Why would a two-and-a-half-year-old say that? Because he's heard it."

There's a fair amount of violence in German child-rearing practices, and my anger might come from some of that. My mother has some of that obviously in her. I've never felt like I was abused or misused, but I'm also conscious of the fact that my mother was a German. I base that on my own experience. And I have some very specific views on how Germans look at stuff because I've seen enough of them in action. I've read Dietrich Bonhoeffer's biography twice, and his family believed in home schooling because in Germany your spirit was crushed twice, first in school, and later in the military.

When Germany was being reunified, there was an essay in

the paper by a Jewish psychiatrist who had this study done by students who went to public playgrounds in Copenhagen, Frankfurt, and Italy. They tried to get the same socioeconomic area for each playground, and then they just watched. The incidence of physical and verbal abuse in the German playground was much higher. In Copenhagen there was a little bit; in Italy there was practically none; and in Frankfurt there was a lot. The psychiatrist said he would be a lot happier if he could know what was going on in the German character in terms of why there was all this abuse.

My mother was taken in by my father's sister in Laconia, New Hampshire. My aunt was a very loving woman, and she took care of me. As an adult, I realize what a wonderful gift she's given me. She was married to a Jewish fellow, whose father came from Latvia around the turn of the century. A whole bunch of Eastern European Jews came to this country about that time because of pogroms there. They went to New England and became junk dealers. And that's just what my uncle and his father were, junk dealers.

Some people thought I was my uncle's blood nephew. I went everywhere with him, to the barbershop or to the firehouse, where we talked to his buddies, the firemen. Lots of people knew us. He was a father figure to me, and I was the little boy he would have liked. I grew up with him and his father from Latvia, and all their relatives in Boston and Dorchester, and so I had that kind of ethnic flavor in my background.

My mother, who was coming out of postwar Germany where life was still pretty nasty, would put big plates of food in front of me. If I didn't eat them, I would get a spanking. She got a job cleaning the movie theater in town. Then she moved down to New York City. I have no memory of how often I saw her. My father was still in Europe. He stayed there until 1950.

My aunt and uncle became my emotional stability. Over

the years, they were the ones who saved my life—emotionally—because they gave me love. Laconia, New Hampshire, is my emotional home.

When I was in first grade, my mother flew me to New York City. My aunt thought it was horrible to take me from a beautiful environment in Laconia to urban New York. I don't remember being upset. I don't remember being excited. When you're a kid, you roll with the punches. We lived right next to Riverside Park. Grant's Tomb was down the street, and Riverside Church was around the corner. I have very nice childhood memories of riding the subways. I remember the smells of the subway, the smells of New York. I remember the American Museum of Natural History with the big, stuffed whale. There's an aura that goes with all of that, which is part of me.

I went to an Episcopalian parochial school. They skipped me through the second grade. We lived in a one-room apartment like that of *The Honeymooners*. The only difference was that Ralph Kramden at least had two rooms. My mother had a boyfriend, a powerful politician from Iraq. His apartment was very lush. Uncle Raschid, I called him. My mother was going to marry him. My uncle, who met Raschid, spoke very highly of him, praised him as a gentleman.

My mother got herself pregnant again and had my half-brother. When he was born, she shipped him to cousins in Maine. They raised him—sort of the way my aunt raised me. The reason my brother is halfway sane, I think, is because of the stability they had. My mother went to work as a secretary. I would come home, call her on the phone. Then I was by myself for several hours. They didn't have day care and stuff like that.

My father married the French woman. My aunt and uncle were humble people; they saw her as typical "French" and didn't have much use for her. But my father loved her dearly. He was in New Jersey, a couple hours from us. One time he called from around the corner and said: "I'm here. I'm going to come see you." I remember being very fearful and trying to call my mother. Within a few minutes he showed up. He had his French wife with him, and he delivered some German magazines. I can still see those magazines, real crummy paper that didn't compare to a *Life* magazine in terms of quality.

At that point in my life I knew I had a father. I had gone to visit him a couple times. He bought me a cowboy suit. And once, driving, he slammed on the brakes, and I went right into the windshield and cracked it. They put a fifty-cent piece on the bump on my head to make me feel better.

But between the first and fourth grades, I was made to feel guilty I had a father: "Your father is awful. . . . He doesn't want anything good for you." At that point it became not good to mention him. What I discovered down the line was that he tried to be my advocate and father until that time. He really put himself out to get me into this country, and he tried to get partial custody of me. When my mother wanted to move to Baghdad, he didn't let her. He said: "You can go if you want. You're not taking Karl with you." She didn't.

The French woman decided to get herself pregnant when my father was about fifty. She did that to bond with him and get me out of the picture. She had a little girl. It was about that time my father gave up and stopped having much communication with me.

I think—and I've watched this with my parishioners, too—we are all egotistical enough that we cannot imagine someone would conceive us and not want us. The sexual act of having a child. That's why adopted children go berserk trying to find their real parents. *How could someone make me and then not want me?* That's a real burning thing all people struggle with.

Raschid died. He went to Baghdad and died very suddenly. If he had been here, they would have saved his life. He was an older man. My mother still has his picture at her bedside.

I was ten years old. It was me and my mother. My brother was still in Maine, being cared for by relatives. My mother decided "We're going west," and she packed up everything. We came down the coast, through the South. Her goal was California. She got a good secretarial job in New Mexico. They introduced computers into this company, and she had the aptitude. She was thirty-five at the time, had two kids, was without a man, and finally got her life together. Things settled down. She bought a house, got my brother out there, and the three of us started living a normal life.

She was not a warm, loving person. She was not a totally cold and distant person either. It was sort of . . . she was *there.* Her Germanness came through. She was not demonstrative. She could be harsh. She could rise to the occasion if it suited her at the moment. Since she was strict and no-nonsense, we didn't do bad things. We got good grades and were good citizens. Because that's how it is when you're a German. I think she did the best she could, but she is also a selfish person, and she comes first. It wasn't until we got to New Mexico that she started doing things for us. No—that's not true. I can remember that she started getting settled even in New Jersey. She made little flowers and things to sell at the office for a quarter a piece so she had some money. I'd get like a train set. So I think my anger towards my mother comes out of the German side of her. The cold, colder, more distant thing.

In one of my sermons I said: "If I had to do it over again, I'd rather be an Italian."

That bugged one of the Germans in the church. But in my mind, Italians are warmer. I read a book in college that contrasted the dark German nights with the sunny Mediterranean days. And the pull of Rome and Greece on the German mind and German literature—that really spoke to me. On an emotional level it comes down to wanting to be Italian, being free, being able to express, to wave your hands and hug.

If you know anything about child-rearing, the sins of your infancy and childhood become evident in your adolescence when private problems go public. My adolescence was a rocky time. I did not act out. I turned inward. As a sixteen-year-old senior who weighed 210 pounds and was six feet four inches tall, I looked twenty years old. So I was getting away with it physically, but not socially.

I wanted to be a writer, but I wasn't driven to do it. You get visions of yourself as the artist. Camus has this character in *The Plague* who is stuck on the first line of his novel. That's how I felt and have sometimes felt as an adult: *stuck with that line*. It's like there are these pathways in my brain that are blocked. If a couple of those pathways would open, I could express things—I've done that in sermons, but not regularly. And I've done it when traveling. My mind starts thinking in terms of words and images and trying to create things.

Kafka was one of the writers who molded me. And Camus is important. Do you know where he wrote *The Plague?* In Le Chambon-sur-Lignon, a little village of French Huguenots. There's a wonderful documentary, *Weapons of the Spirit,* about how this village of 5,000 Christians sheltered 5,000 Jews in the midst of German occupation. When I learned a couple of years ago that Camus wrote *The Plague* in that village at that time, I was overwhelmed. Here's a book that has influenced my view of things, and it's a parable about Nazis and the occupation.

Going to New Hampshire for the summers was always a good time. Rattling back and forth across the country on a bus. I worked in my uncle's junkyard. We would scrap cars, take them down to Boston. Dirty work, but it was fun. He paid me twenty bucks a week and gave me all the gas I wanted and a car to drive. One summer day he was drunk. We were sitting on the porch, and he made the comment that Germans are not good. I can't remember his words, but it was a negative comment coming out of the Jewish-German experience. I chalked it up to his drunkenness, to his ignorance. It was one of those things you let go by you.

I dreamed about bumming around Europe. In 1964 my mother gave me the money for the trip. I flew to London, hitchhiked and took trains, went through France, had my eighteenth birthday in Naples. When I hitchhiked through Germany, a German picked me up. I was dressed in *Lederhosen* and had a rucksack. When he realized I was an American, he wouldn't talk with me. The next day I was thumbing for a ride when a convoy of American soldiers went by and one gave me the finger.

Who was I?

In Osnabrück I visited my mother's relatives, who knew me when I was a baby, although I didn't remember any of them. One of them said: "You and I used to play in that *Sandkasten*—sandbox—there." A word popped into my head that I didn't know, my German coming out of me. My relatives were very gracious. Two of them were farmers. One day we went to a village fair, and I was talking to a man, very sharp-featured, about the war. He said: "There was a toss-up who was going to capture us—the Russians or the Americans. The happiest day of my life was when I heard someone say in English, 'You're now a prisoner of the American expeditionary force.'"

So these things were rattling around. I was a kid trying to figure them out. *So now I'm a German. I can look like a German. People think I'm a German.*

I took a picture of a freight car sitting out in the field by itself. That car—for me—was the Holocaust freight car. I had an image of people crammed into it. I was very conscious of the Holocaust. After all, my uncle is Jewish. And as a kid in the Southwest, I used to baby-sit for a Jew who lived across the street. He had a book in his library with pictures of the Holocaust. So I knew what the Holocaust was. I mean, you never had to convince me that it happened.

How did it start?

It's a question I have worked on for so long. . . . As I have gone through Germany and Poland, I have wondered how this country would feel if we suddenly removed most of our black population. There would be so many lingering ghosts. There would be all of the names and places and influences that simply couldn't be removed from our land and culture.

I went into the Peace Corps because it fit what I believed in. I was part of that generation, and I got a draft deferment out of that. I went to Tunisia. We lived in the medina, and I learned Roman history. I met my wife in the Peace Corps at a riotous New Year's Eve party. She was like me—I mean, she read the same things. She was smart. My father sent us a Corning Ware dish as a wedding gift. Pretty crummy. It was his wife who did it, you know? I didn't write to them for years, and he was aware of that.

We went to Rome twice. We went to Spain in the summertime and on the way home took another tour through Germany and Austria. I met more of the family. One distant relative had a *Gaststätte*—restaurant—in Wuppertal. Very gracious people. He had been in the SS, and he described how in the field, right behind the *Gaststätte,* people had been killed as the tanks came through. One of my relatives, a farmer, had been captured by the Russians and didn't get out of Russia till 1952. We were sitting at the table with his two daughters. We had these big plates of food, and he just sucked it up. He told us: "We had a saying, 'The way home lies over the bodies of our comrades.' We ate poison ivy. It would take the hunger out of our mouths." The war had devastated him. He said: "You know, there was no crime when Hitler was in power. Hitler cleaned up the streets."

• • •

On that trip my wife and I went to Dachau. That was moving. I learned that it wasn't just Jews that died in places like that, that it was socialists and university professors and homosexuals and pastors. Twelve million people died in those places. I'm irritated by the Jewish lobby's insistence that 6 million Jews died. They're doing a disservice to the other 6 million people who died. And I think that's wrong. I've been to Dachau twice. I've been to Buchenwald. I've been to Auschwitz. And I've been to Theresienstadt. *How could this happen?*

You say: "How can this be?"

You say: "I'm a German. How can this be? I've been mistaken for a Jew. How can this be? I've got Jewish relatives. How can this be? How can these things happen?"

In 1989 I went on a trip with a man who has developed a whole ministry to Eastern Europe. That trip was one of the most freeing experiences of my life. We were in Berlin three weeks after the Wall came down. Our job was to meet Communists, East German Christians, and Polish Christians. I was asked to address one congregation in German. That was really neat to be able to speak and be heard and understood.

Part of that trip took us to Auschwitz. That's the hellhole of the world as far as I'm concerned. I gave the meditation that day, and one of the things I said was: "This ground is soaked with blood." It was December, cold and dreary, and there was no snow on the ground. Like out of a movie. We went to the barracks where they'd torture and beat you. The gas chamber was right next to the SS cafeteria. We went into the oven part. We stood there and sang: "Were You There When They Crucified My Lord?" I came out of there limp.

The thing that haunts me about Buchenwald is the little room where they would measure you, and while you stood there, they put the gun through a little hole and shot you in the head.

• • •

My view of the Holocaust comes out of that German awareness, that Jewish background of my own. We have this fascination with evil, with why people could do this. Camus and that whole incident of Le Chambon-sur-Lignon are personally important to me because there you had good people who didn't do it, who said: "We're going to be good." And the Germans who were there knew what was happening. They participated in the goodness. I have a book called *The Altruistic Personality*. The authors asked people why they did good even though they risked their lives. Religious people and non-religious people did it, educated and uneducated. The bottom line was that the persons who did good were persons who said they'd been raised to do good. That simple. Eichmann made the statement, "No one ever told me what I was doing was wrong." And somebody raised the question, "What if Eichmann's secretary had said to him: 'What you're doing is wrong'?" Because whenever the Nazis were challenged, they stopped. Bulgaria saved tons of Jews because the church said: "No, we're not going to do it."

My initial reason for going to seminary was to not get drafted in 1969. I had never been overly religious, but I had been preoccupied by spiritual questions and God questions. When I was a kid, one of my ministers had said: "Have you ever thought about being a minister?" And I said: "No." To me that was for sissies.

But there's all this deeper stuff like Dostoyevsky and Kafka and Camus. Existentialism. And I was on a spiritual journey. The seminary gave me the luxury of doing that academically. I did well in seminary because I'm a German. You do well. You make the trains run on time. I struggle with the fact that I was raised in a way that when you do something, you do it right, and if it's not right, you do it over until it is right. I see that as the pull in me: *Get to a task and do it, and do it well, and do it thoroughly—and then let things go to pot sometimes.* That's not a very German thing to do.

In our church you do three years of academic work and then a year where you work at a church. I was sent to California. That's where our first child was born. And that was my first experience of being with adult Christian people. I found out that you could be an adult Christian and not be crazy or stupid or a sissy. There are some very impressive men in that church who really showed me how to be a man and a Christian, and that—with authenticity—I could be a minister. I went to a little town in the mountains and labored there for five years between the Apaches and the Navahos and the Mormons. There I kind of got everything together. I was thirty-two and doing my thing. I had two children.

Now I have lots of veterans in my church. They don't want to talk about their killing times. I finally realized that, for them, this is because they have repented, become Christian, and really do not want to recall who they once were or what they once did or were capable of doing. Veterans I know who didn't repent, by and large, have become alcoholics. One way or another, the past must be left behind.

I always wanted to go back to Germany and live there long enough to become fluent in German. I still may do that. I can work through the church and do that. My daughter has fulfilled my dream. She's living in Germany. She married a soldier, and he's over there as an enlisted man. She's been to Poland, Italy, Greece, France, and England—but she hasn't gone to northern Germany to visit the relatives. What does that mean? She's an American, and she's basically indifferent to them.

In 1991 we went over, all of us. And what blew me away was that here I was, visiting my daughter on this American army post, eating pizzas and using American dollars, but I could walk right off of it and be in Germany. Go back and forth. The army post in Würzburg was an old Nazi garrison on a hill overlooking the town. It was beautiful. Absolutely lovely. There was a big field that used to be the airfield. Hitler had flown in there. I heard these stories, and everything got even more complicated in terms of identities.

One of my seminary professors once said that the best you could hope for in this life is that someday your parents will forgive you. I mean—

No. The best you could hope for is that someday your child will forgive you. As I've raised four of my own children, I think there's something to that. We do the best we can, and we make mistakes, and we inflict damage; and our children do their thing and come to terms with it. They learn and say: "Well, Dad did the best he could, given things." And I'm doing the best I can. I feel I've done that with my mother. I could make a list of things she could have done better, but I think she did all right.

I've counseled people when they're estranged from their children. I've said to them: "Just wait. You'll hear from them." And you know, I've had three people come back to me and say: "You're right."

I finally wrote my father a letter when I was in my late thirties: "I was raised to feel guilty that I had a father, but I remember all these things from when you were in a relationship with me. I've been intimately entwined with your family. Your sister raised me and loved me. I'd like to come see you." I got a long letter back. He'd kept records, letters he wrote in the forties and fifties, telling his side of the story, telling the truth, and he sent me copies of all those things. That's how I know he loved me up to a certain point. He said: "No need to come see me. It wouldn't be good."

It was awful, but I said: "Okay." His French wife was still

alive. She was twenty years younger than he, but she dropped dead one day when she was sixty-five. After I heard about it, I waited a year or two, and then I told my father a lie: "The church gives me money every Christmas. I'm going to be in New York. I'm going to come see you."

In my mind he was a big man. The thing that shocked me most was to see him as a small person. I spent a couple of nights at his house. Basically, all that part of me got put back together. We talked—very superficially, just swapping stories. He told me some funny stories from the war and the occupation and tricks they had played on people. I told him one of my memories of taking a bath with him when I was five. He'd had a potbelly then, and I'd seen his belly button going in like a hole into his stomach. I'd said: "What is that?" And he'd said: "Oh, that's where I got shot in the war."

You try to integrate things, integrate your life. And I've got all of these things everywhere, you know, from Germany to New England to the Southwest. The mysteries . . . Rex Stout wrote all the Nero Wolfe mysteries, based on the same formula: a situation is very complicated, and they can't figure out what has happened until something that happened twenty-five years ago comes to light, and when that secret is unearthed, all of it makes sense. I thought a lot of that in relationship to that silence from the war, and there are all kinds of secrets people are harboring. What they did or what their feelings were or what happened. Maybe by bringing to light what happened fifty and sixty years ago, we can make some sense out of what's happening today.

I think in one sense that's why I fret over the Holocaust. There are clues to why we are the way we are today. By *we* I mean all of us in this culture, American and European. I've done a lot of study on cultural history. You can look at that globally or you can look at yourself and say: *I'm part of this.*

Things are evolving, and we haven't seen the end of where we're headed.

So, where does that leave me?

Sort of like Franz Kafka, wandering the streets of Prague, writing these weird books—in German.

Eva

Born: 1941
Age at time of immigration: 24

Just Because I'm German Doesn't Mean I Am a Nazi

In March 1945 the Russians were already close by, but my mother had to wait for the birth of my youngest sister. The beginning of May we had to leave the Sudetenland. We started walking. With a whole bunch of people. The baby was in one of those buggies, which was good because my mother could store a lot of stuff in that. My older sister, Grete, was five. And I was just four. Both of us had little knapsacks on our backs with a change of clothes. I still remember the hiding and screams in the night. Women . . . attacked. *Ja.* You could hear. Also those low-flying airplanes, bombing. Even nowadays I don't like low-flying airplanes.

At night we would sleep on farms. Sometimes in a barn. Or they would let us have a little room. Most of them were kind, I would say, because they saw this young woman with three little children. Sometimes they gave her potatoes. My mother exchanged some silver and got a whole pot of lard, which really saved us. It was her best possession at that time. At least that's what she says now.

It took us six weeks to walk most of the way to Berlin. Sometimes somebody would take us along the road in a little wagon. And once in a while we caught a train. I remember one freight train with a flatcar full of potatoes. There was nothing around, and all we had to hold on to was that baby buggy. My mother told me: "Put potatoes in the baby buggy." They lasted us almost all the way to Berlin.

My mother and father had promised each other: *After the war, we'll meet here in Berlin again.* When my mother got to the area where they used to live before the war, everything was in ruins. We luckily found some good people. One family kept us for a night. Two nights we slept in the schoolhouse. Another person had pity on my mother and said: "Next door is an apartment. Nobody knows about that yet. If you go to the *Wohnungsamt*—housing office—they'll probably let you have it."

Fantastic. She did get that. It was a very small apartment, just a kitchen and one room. It was between floors, where the *Hausmeister*—superintendent—used to live. If you went from the first to the second floor and didn't know there was an apartment, you would miss it. That was lucky, because when the Russians came, they missed that door: it looked like a storage room. They just stormed up to the other apartment. You could hear the screaming.

All of us were sitting under this kitchen table. My mother's sister and her little boy were with us. You grew up with "Sshh, quiet, don't cry." My mother would nurse the baby—she didn't have much milk—just to keep it quiet so the soldiers wouldn't know where we were. I really didn't know what those Russians would do, but the women . . . how afraid they were. It was something bad—you knew that. I remember sitting under that table. They put this big, long tablecloth over us. The Russians didn't get in there. So my mother and my aunt were really lucky.

I guess the first year of living in this apartment was the worst because everything was in ruins. My mother and aunt used to look through the ruins. See what they could find. We'd get potato peels, and they would boil those through again. On the Kreuzberg, the biggest little mountain in Berlin, we'd pick *Brennesseln*—nettles—and my mother would cook them like spinach. We didn't starve. I don't remember ever going to bed hungry. People who have been hungry probably won't forget that. But we managed. And my mother was lucky: one day she found a whole bunch of briquets. *Ja.* At that time that was like gold. She took a few and covered the rest up. That night she and my aunt took a little wagon and got those briquets. We didn't freeze that winter.

After a while, I guess, we got rationing stamps. Since Mother had three children, she could afford to have my aunt and the little boy there, too. They weren't supposed to be in that apartment. Once they started giving out rations, we had to stand in line. Because my mother and aunt could do something else, they sent my sister, Grete, or me. And we stood there and waited patiently until it was our turn. Sometimes you got there, and nothing was left.

On my fifth birthday, the eighth of April 1946—I'll never forget—we were standing outside, waiting for my uncle and aunt, and here was this other soldier, my dad. I didn't remember him, you know. He had a little chewing gum and chocolate. He'd been a prisoner of war in France. They were going to transport a section of his unit to Russia. When they put them on those trains, my father and a friend jumped off and made their way to Berlin. He found us because my mother had left a message on the wall where the old apartment used to be.

And then things were easier because he was there. Of course, my aunt had to leave because there was not enough room. My father was a trained saddler and upholsterer. Nobody needed saddles anymore in Berlin, and he did mostly upholstery and window treatments. We were just working-class. He would always say: "I'm just an *einfacher Arbeiter*—simple laborer." He was the most talented man, and he could do anything: electrical, wood, whatever. He made us sandals out of wood and leather straps. Like Birkenstocks. If he just had patented them, he might have been rich.

For a while he worked with my uncle, who had a carpentry shop, making doors and windows. At that time, slowly, they started building. So my uncle had enough work. My father could get the wood cuttings, which was lucky. We weren't freezing. Once or twice a year—and this is embarrassing for me to think about because nobody else had wood—my cousin would come with the *Lieferwagen*—delivery truck. We had this whole load of wood put in the cellar. It made me feel kind of bad then already. We did give some here and there, but mostly we had all that wood.

My father was very strict. Okay. And he was not very loving with kids. I don't think parents—men at that time—were anyway. I knew other German fathers, and they weren't either. But I think he was a good father. What can I say? We loved him because he was family. You're supposed to love your parents. And I always looked up to him. Because he knew everything. I guess I'm Daddy's daughter. If you needed something, he always would get it. My mother would always look to my father, too. During the war years and while she was *auf der Flucht*—on the run—she had to do it herself, but anything after, it was always *Vati*—Daddy. *Vati* made the decisions. I don't think that's quite the right way to do things. If *Vati* said it was okay, it was okay. And if you wanted to go somewhere, you had to ask *Vati*. She really put him on a pedestal.

And she grew a little weaker in this. But I guess she was a good mother. Things didn't go all that well after the war. My father wasn't that nice to her. And she just took everything. Well, nobody's too proud about it. If you know your father made your mother very unhappy . . . Most men who came back from the war wanted to live. And try to forget. Even as a child I always thought: *Why is my mother taking all this? Why isn't she speaking up? Why isn't she leaving him?* Right. Right. . . . It's hard. And I can see her point of view: *Three little kids. What could I do?* But I thought: *Well, you wouldn't have starved to death.* She had sisters who would have taken us in. But I guess she really loved my father. She forgave him everything. I don't think I could. I'm more like my dad, I guess. In everything.

There was not much time for vacations. We would go to East Germany because one of my father's brothers lived there. And we would pick whatever fruit was in season from his garden. Mother would preserve it. Both my parents were very hardworking people. No luxuries. Of course not. But even later on when times were better, luxuries were low-key. If we had candy at home, my father would buy it once a week, and we would each get just one piece at a time. I still cannot eat a whole bar of chocolate. Even with my kids I always rationed out.

Whenever the friend my father escaped with and other friends came to the house, they talked about the war. And the women always talked about the hardships they went through. As a small child you just sit there and listen to all those terrible things they went through. I guess it was the only thing, really. A lot of people had that in common. But after a time you forget the stories. About two, three years after the war, they tapered off. Because there was no use in bringing up all this old stuff. There was nothing we could do about it anymore. Still, when an old *Kriegskamerad*—war comrade—would come, they'd talk about the times they'd had together.

My father was at the front in Russia. Then in France, too. I guess that's where he was captured, because I have one letter he wrote as a prisoner of war. It was mailed from France. He was drafted in 1940. I found out because I had his *Soldbuch*—pay booklet. His picture was in it, and the times he went on leave. I found out he got wounded once.

After I left Germany, we did not talk about it much. Sure,

later when I came home, I did ask about Hitler, and all my father would say was: "Well, *der war verrückt. Wahnsinnig. So viele Menschen umzubringen!*"—"He was crazy. Insane. To kill so many people!" But that was about it, mostly just about the war and what they experienced. It was the same with the women. Otherwise, there was not much talk about it. Almost everybody at that time said: "Why, Hitler just got *grössenwahnsinnig*—megalomaniac. The way it started was okay. He did so much for the Germans in the beginning. And he did build the *Autobahnen*. But then it went to his head." This old story that you always hear . . . part of it is true.

I would say there were people who knew, but there were so many who didn't, and so many who wouldn't believe something like that could happen. I'm sure my parents really didn't know that many Jews were being killed. Before living in Berlin, they both lived in a tiny farming community where anything like that wasn't coming through that much. I don't think they knew about concentration camps and about what happened to those millions of Jews. My father was just a *Gefreiter*—private. And then a corporal. He just was drafted. He was nothing in the army. Just one of those people who had to go along, I guess. My parents knew people were being picked up from their houses and taken places, but I don't believe they thought they were being gassed or whatever.

Because if you are normal-thinking, I mean, you cannot comprehend that things like that go on. And if you really are not much into politics, maybe you would say: *No, that cannot be.*

But it was.

And that makes you feel guilty somehow.

In a big city like Berlin there were a lot of crimes after the war. Kids disappeared. Girls were raped. *Ja.* We were always kind of watchful. You had to be careful. I hated to go down into the dark cellar. I was so afraid somebody was going to grab me. I guess I grew up kind of scared, easily intimidated. Loud noises would scare me.

We lived in the American sector of the city. At that time there was no wall. The street ran through. On the other side was the East. They had the East *Mark,* and we had the West *Mark.* My mother, thrifty as she was, sent Grete and me—the little one was too small—to East Berlin to buy potatoes and bread because it was much cheaper. I was always afraid I was going to get caught. We had to stand in line. And we had to carry everything home. It was not like across the street, I tell you. At least forty-five minutes. Most people used to do it. Especially if you lived right across. But they didn't send their kids. I guess my mother didn't think there was anything wrong with sending us. She thought they wouldn't do anything to little kids. I hated that. I really did. When I'd look at the bread and see it was getting smaller and smaller, that meant I'd soon have to go to East Berlin again. It was scary.

My parents always told us: "If they ask you, tell them you live in East Germany." One time we did get caught. My sister and I had to take the train to my uncle's garden outside of Berlin. It was quite a way. You couldn't walk to it. On the way back to the station it started raining like crazy. We had little jackets and put them over our heads. We each carried a knapsack and a *Körbchen*—little basket—filled with fruit. At the station were East German border guards and two Russians with guns. They asked where we were going. So we put in our little lie—what my mother had told us. I guess they could tell we were lying. They gave us a talk. "You shouldn't be lying. Don't let us ever catch you here again."

I guess my parents decided not to send us anymore. I talked about that to my children. I don't think I would have made them do that. I would have been too protective, afraid for them. When I told my mother that, she said: "Well, I had other things to do while you were doing this."

The Russians shut off the entire city because they thought this way they would get the Western forces out. But the Americans, with the help of Canada and France and Britain, brought food and coal—everything that was needed—in by plane. Those airplanes got the name *Rosinenbomber*—raisin bombers— because apparently they had raisins in there, too. Every three minutes, if I'm correct, one of those airplanes landed with stuff to keep the city alive. They did this for almost a whole year. The Berlin Airlift. That was one huge undertaking. To keep a whole city—two and a half million—alive. Fed and clothed. Right.

Silence in school.

During the elementary years, nobody talked about the war. But when we got to high school, we did. It was not very extensive, but it was facts. We would talk for months about different countries. I knew a lot about America, about Greece. But Germany . . . it was always very brief. Very seldom was there anything mentioned about how many Jews died in that war.

I took English and French. I went to Spain one year and loved it. We had one French teacher. Madame Souchons. I guess she'd married a German man. Their house was bombed, and her husband died. She was lying under the rubble for a week before they found her. She was burned. You could see. Her face . . . She had legs like sticks. And her hair was white. Once in a while she would talk about it. But nobody there would really say anything bad about the Hitler years. I guess she couldn't anyway, in her position. She sticks out in my mind, what she went through, and that she still decided to stay in Germany and teach German children French. I thought that was remarkable.

Around my graduation we read *Das Tagebuch der Anne Frank—The Diary of Anne Frank*. That was when it really started, I think, talking about it. I read other books from the library about the Holocaust. So we were aware of it then. When we graduated, the mayor gave us all this little book by Lucie

Adelsberger: *Auschwitz: Ein Tatsachenbericht*—a documentary report. I still have it. The book said we would never forget what happened, and that the youth of Berlin should not take an unpolitical stance. Because of the mayor, there was a little bit more awareness in schools. Maybe he was Jewish, but I don't know for sure.

One of our theaters had the play *Das Tagebuch der Anne Frank*. It made a deep impression on me. I felt terrible reading the book and watching it in the theater. Up to now even, I do feel somehow guilty. Maybe guilt by association. Because I am German. Most people you meet don't say anything. They know you were too young. You had nothing to do with what happened at that time. Still, it makes me feel uncomfortable sometimes. Some Germans here tell me I'm silly, but I do feel guilty. And I guess that's why I was glad when I got away from Germany. That's why I really enjoy being in the United States.

It's not that I want to shed everything that's German in me. I cook German meals. Both my children speak German. I kept that because it had nothing to do with the war and Hitler. Lots of women who came over here did not teach their children any German at all. But I wanted them to talk to their grandparents when we go to Germany. Deep down, I'm probably still German. But I never did flaunt my Germanness or said: "Oh, I came from Germany." Well, with people who knew you, you would. But I would not go out of my way because I always thought: *They're all blaming you.* Most people probably wouldn't, but certainly there are some who would. I thought: *Maybe these are the people who will get at me because I am German, because they had a big sorrow or somebody died.* You cannot blame them if they have a Jewish background.

After tenth grade I got an apprenticeship in an office. And in two years I was an office assistant. That's what I did until I met my husband, the American soldier. At this time soldiers did not have a very good reputation. Girls who were going with soldiers were kind of—you would say—loose. My youngest sister had a girlfriend, and they used to go out dancing in nightclubs where American soldiers would come. And they had a great time.

So here I was, this good German. I was engaged to a German but found out—luckily, I guess—it was not the right thing. I gave him back the ring on a dreary November Sunday. My sister asked me to visit her girlfriend, Monika, in the hospital. Well, this Monika had an American boyfriend, and one of his friends drove him to the hospital. That was my future husband—we met at that hospital. I knew what little English you learned in school—a lot of words and grammar—but I really couldn't speak that well.

When the visit was over, this American soldier—his name was Stan—asked me if I would join him to play bingo at one of those clubs. My sister said: "Go ahead." Despite what I felt about girls who would go, I somehow, at that moment, was reckless. *Ja.* I said: "Why not?" He took me to dinner, and then we played bingo. It was all very exciting. After six weeks he gave me a necklace. And then he asked me if I would marry him. I thought: *Why not?* Deep inside I wanted to get away. I was always fascinated with America, you know, with the West.

I got engaged and married the same year Kennedy came to Berlin and made his famous speech: *"Ich bin ein Berliner. . . ."* I saw him on the street, and I almost could have shaken his hand. But I was always very shy because at home we really didn't speak up much. I was so fascinated. And I really liked the man. People at work said: "Oh, *your* president . . ." It was all so new and exciting.

I decided I wanted my oldest child to be born in Berlin. And it worked out that way. In 1965, when my son Ryan was six months old, we went to the States by boat, a military transport. The first station we had was in Georgia, and we stayed there for almost two years. My daughter Cecilia was born there.

Then we moved a couple of times within the States. Always on the East Coast. Maryland, New Jersey. I have only good memories of the military life. My husband was only a sergeant when I got married, and then a staff sergeant, but we did live comfortably, and the hospital care was always great. I didn't mind moving because I enjoyed seeing different places. So that was instilled in my children.

When my husband had to go to Korea, I could have moved in with his mother. But I decided to go back to Germany. This way I could make my promise good to my parents: "You will see the grandchildren." We had a nice year in Berlin. My kids grew up German. The language and all that. I guess my husband was lucky he wasn't sent to Vietnam. In Korea, at this time, there was really no fighting anymore. And I didn't even think he would get hurt because he was a radio operator.

When he came back, we were stationed in Pirmasens, near Kaiserslautern. So we stayed another four years in Germany. The children started school there. I enjoyed visiting my parents and sisters and relatives, and I enjoyed showing the children Germany so that they knew where I came from. But I didn't enjoy the way of living. I was so used to the way we were living in America, where it was free and open, and you felt good. In Germany you lived in an apartment. Every time you went shopping, you carried everything. Here we would take the car and have a big shopping day once a week. There you had to carry the children and little buggy up and down the stairs if you wanted to take them for a walk. Here I only had to walk out of the house. I guess we were lucky. We always lived in a house, and the kids had a big backyard to play in. There you had to go to a park. The convenience—it's what's so great here. Convenience, comfort, and just the way of living.

In 1972 we moved to Arizona. Since we were so close to the Mexican border, I said: "I'd like to talk to the people there." So I took all the Spanish classes I could. I always enjoyed languages. I hate to go to another country if I don't understand anybody or anything.

I've been in Arizona ever since. I stayed home with the children when they were growing up. I wanted to know when they came home. I wanted to know what kind of a day they had. I wanted to be there if there was trouble or if they needed somebody. When they were in high school, I got this restless feeling. You want to do a little bit more. So I volunteered at the library, since I'd always loved books, music, and paintings. When they needed more help, I got a part-time position there. I didn't want full-time because my kids were still at home. The library was perfect for me because I loved it there. I told my kids: "Choose a job you like. Nothing worse if you have to get up in the morning and say: 'I got to work.'"

There were a couple of old men who came to the library and who'd kind of say: "Well, you're from Germany. You know the Nazis. You know what they did." But that was about it. It was not that they were unfriendly to me, but they did let me know: *You're a German.* I think they'd been over there during the war. But mostly people would come in and try their German on me. And most of them would say they liked Germany, and that the people there were so nice.

Once I was working at the library, and this teenage girl, the stepdaughter of one of my coworkers, came in and said to me: "Are you a Nazi?" I said: "Why, no." Well, she said: "You're a German." I think I cried when she said I was a Nazi. So I said to her: "Just because I'm German doesn't mean I am a Nazi. I was a baby at that time. I really didn't have anything to do with it." Later on she apologized. Apparently in school they just had studied the Hitler years. But at that time it really hit me hard. I mean, she was a child, a teenager. Still—there are people who think that way.

• • •

My marriage didn't work out quite as well as I thought it would, and after a while we decided to separate. Stan went back to Germany for one tour and then to Panama. By that time I knew I didn't want to get back together. I had met Clifford, and Stan agreed on a divorce. When he was around, he was always invited to the children's birthdays. It's very hard to divorce, even under good circumstances. There's this guilt feeling. This way it was easier for the kids. I thought it was important for them to have a good relationship with their father. He spent Christmas with us even after Clifford and I got married. If he was in town on his birthday, we would have something for him. He would come to the kids' graduation, and afterwards we would be all at the house together. Clifford was great about not minding having him around. My first husband is deceased now. He died three years ago. That alcohol . . .

Clifford, too, is a very nice man. Happily married . . . yes, I am. I have been lucky in the choice of men, I guess. Clifford and my children have a great relationship. When Cecilia was in high school, I told her: "Go to college and travel if you can. See something of the world. Don't get tied down and get married." She decided to go into the army. She's a very good soldier. Luckily she went to Germany. That's what she wanted. She loves Germany. The coincidence—I came to America when I was twenty-four; she went to Germany when she was twenty-four.

My son Ryan is a computer programmer and analyst. I was happy when he found a job in Tucson. Luckily we have somebody close by, especially now that a grandbaby is coming. Ryan's dogs both have German names. One is Bismarck, which I could still handle. But what do you think he named the other one? Rommel. Rommel was a good German, let's say. He was not a bad Nazi. But I still didn't like it. I said: "Ryan, what are you doing? People hear you say that, and they'll think you're a Nazi with your German background."

And he said: "Mother, they don't think like that." Most people probably don't, but to me it's still deep-set.

You know, when you grew up, you really didn't think about the war. Because you were *in* those times. You just went from day to day. You only knew pieces. You didn't know the whole thing. It was just living. That's how it was. Even missing a lot of things—you didn't know because you didn't have them before. It's not like you were already a teenager when the war started. You just grew up with it from day to day and didn't really think of this terrible thing that was happening to Germany. You were just a kid.

Like I said, it's too bad that you forgot all those stories your father told. At first you didn't think about writing them down because everything seemed so normal. That's what everybody talked about at that time. You didn't think that you *should* remember.

Hans-Peter

Born: 1945
Age at time of immigration: 8

It's My Heritage—
Yet I Had No Say in It

Throughout my life I've had to work for everything, and I feel a little step ahead of everybody. I try to outthink future things that are going to happen. Planning and such. If you get shoved around a lot when you're young, you strive harder to make sure it never happens again.

I've been in the field of accounting since I graduated. I always liked numbers. I work for a small retailer in Maryland, and I'm fairly happy there. We have a mixed office with a lot of foreigners. The hard part is the interaction with our founder. He began this company from the ground up and never went through the school process. He's street-smart, and yet he doesn't understand. He thinks little of the so-called workers. I do a lot of things associated with human resources, interact with people and motivate them, whereas he will just say: "If they don't like it, forget it. They can leave." Well, that's not the answer.

He is not Christian. He's Jewish. I've worked with the man for eight years, and I still have an ingrained fear: *Heaven help me if he ever finds out I'm a German.* It's stupid. But it's there and it's alive and well. It's this big secret. Everyone else knows.

If my employer doesn't like the fact that I'm from Germany, he can fire me. I'm sure there's somebody out there who was fired because he's black. He might sue—but he's still out of a job. I have worked many times with Jews before, and I haven't run into that. My stepfather worked for a few and got along quite well with them, but he always said: "Watch out. If you don't stick up for your thoughts, they'll . . ." I don't know how to put this. They're somewhat aggressive, let's say, and they'll work on others, and if they can squash them, they'll squash them harder and harder—you, me, or anyone in general. I half-listened to my stepfather, but seeing things in action, that's really the way it is. Because my employer is abusive—not just with me, but with others. And if they lie down, he just becomes harder on them. It's strange—I'm living in a closet, so to speak, because my employer can influence my whole life. Although I've been working for this man for eight years and know him sort of inside out, that's one side of him I don't know.

Maybe he's lost family over there. . . .

I read a lot about the Holocaust in the library. I learned more from reading history than anything else. It was the most horrible thing I ever heard, read, saw. I felt horrible. It was awful. It made me mad that it happened. It's my heritage, but I had no say in it. I didn't have a hand in it, yet I live with the feeling. It was out of my control. And yet I feel that my family or friends of my family were involved or had to know somebody who was involved.

My stepfather served on the Russian front, and he said a lot of things about what the army was like in those freezing winters. But it really didn't seem a Nazi thing as much as an army thing. They were out there to fight. Hardly any propaganda. My uncle was with the *Luftwaffe* and got shot down in

Russia. They let him out in 1949. Once again, it wasn't a Nazi thing. It was more about life situations, how to struggle and survive while locked up in Russia. If there was no food, you would eat anything you could get your hands on, like grass and insects. He had this recipe—he made homemade wine that the Russians liked, so they looked after him a little bit. They knew a good thing when they saw it.

I don't know how much was in newspapers or on the radio in those years, or if it was word of mouth, but I'm sure they went through it a lot more than I did. I'm at the other end of it, the next step, so to speak.

My grandfather immigrated in 1924 to the U.S. of A. and brought my father along. So there are roots here. My father went home to Germany to finish high school, then came to Maryland again. In the early thirties he went to Germany, met my mother, married her, and brought her over. Until 1939 he had a successful business here in Maryland. Everything was fine. I'm not sure if he ever had his citizenship. I don't think so, because when the war broke out, he was locked up from 1939 to 1945. There are a lot more articles about Japanese who were interned. You hardly hear about German prisoners.

For some reason, my mother was not imprisoned. My father's first internment camp was on Ellis Island. Then Kentucky. Louisiana. They didn't leave you in one spot for long—maybe six months here and then six months there. In 1945 my mother and father were swapped with Americans who were locked up in Germany, and they went home to Germany. Everything was occupied in those years. I was born in Ravensburg, a French zone, in 1945.

My father was very strict and harsh. That's why I think my mother finally left him. He'd be sitting there having supper, and all of a sudden he'd start hitting me and my brother and my mother. You could see fists flying all over the place, and that was the end of supper. In those years it was accepted—a somewhat normal thing. Nowadays it would be considered abusive. It hurt. It seemed wrong. But at that age you don't know how to alter something like that. I would walk away from everything to this fruit orchard on our street and sneak in there with my neighbor, who was my age, to have some fruit.

My parents divorced in 1950. My mother met a civil engineer, and they got married. My aunt, who was very protective of me, thought my stepfather wasn't worth being my mother's new husband, and she just freaked. She kidnapped me, and I lived with her for three months while my mother was looking for me. Finally my uncle kidnapped me from my aunt. It was the middle of the night. My mother was waiting outside. She laughs about it now. It's something that happened and you can't alter it—just sort of accept it.

My stepfather had never been to America, but he'd heard a lot about the opportunities and how nice it was. I was eight when we immigrated to the U.S. of A. in 1953. We had a sponsor in Maryland, a few suitcases, sixty-four dollars in our pockets, and the shirts on our backs. We landed in the New York City harbor and saw the Statue of Liberty. It was a new experience. It looked exciting. At that age you don't know for sure yet why you're here.

When you immigrate, you become somebody else from who you were.

I'm sure immigration affects everybody involved. I was supposed to enter second grade, but because I didn't speak English, I was sent back to first grade. It was a Catholic school. If you spoke in class when you shouldn't have spoken, the nuns would hit you in the head with an umbrella. They had a lot of straps . . . leather straps. You had to reach out your hand, and they'd hit you on the hand. You learned pretty fast what you could do and what you couldn't do.

It was the most horrible environment while I was growing up because there was this anti-Nazi thing, and I experienced a lot of verbal and physical abuse. I guess students would let their mothers and fathers know that somebody from Germany was in school, and the parents would say: "Well, he's a Nazi."

It wasn't the kids' fault—they just seized the opportunity.

I feel a connection to blacks because I, too, have been prejudiced against. I mean, I wasn't a slave, but I came through certain things in my life. For me it was the initial years of this harassment—that you're a Nazi, and they throw rocks at you, but you don't know why—and that hurt. Blacks went through a lot, and so did I. I think we're equal. I don't look at them like they're lower than me, and I hope they don't think I'm lower than they, whereas I guess the average American would think otherwise.

I was sort of a loner, and between the fifth grade and high school I joined the Scouts. That did help me with social interaction. It was great. I love animals and nature. We used to sleep in the woods once each month. Some of the leaders liked showing you things, like what to do on a hike if a snake jumped out at you. The Scouts were a large influence, and I grew up with the theme, *Love your own brother and help others.* I really don't think negatively of anybody.

Soccer was the highlight of my youth. In Germany I'd played soccer in the streets with a tennis ball because we didn't have a soccer ball. Here the soccer club had a few Italians, a few Scots, but mainly Germans. So you not only played soccer but socialized. That always reinforced who I was—that I was not just a so-called American immigrant, but that I was really with a lot of other immigrants from Germany. We had the same roots. And we were here.

Meanwhile, each summer, we went to Germany. As my mother and stepfather got older, they sent me to visit relatives. There, between the fourth and eighth grades, I began to know some of what Germany was about. I saw how my relatives lived, and what they went through as far as reconstruction. I didn't meet Nazis. Hardly anyone said anything. It was like it had never happened.

I see these skinheads in Germany, who would like to rewrite history, and that doesn't make any sense to me. I mean, they're ignoring something that happened. That's really sick. For the sake of the victims and everybody, we should never forget. But we shouldn't have to hear it over and over again. Right now there are a lot of shows you can watch, like those on the First World War, the Second World War, or Vietnam. I haven't watched any of that for years. I just don't want to see victims hurt. My mother and stepfather feel the same way. There's a certain amount of history I would like to know. I don't think there's any right balance between knowing too much and too little—it's all in the heart.

I feel comfortable if I meet a stranger and say: "I'm from Germany." Now it's something unique. What has changed is maturity. It takes years to alter somebody's outlook on life. For me it was just easing up and accepting it and making something out of it that's useful. My mother and stepfather live about half an hour from here, and we see them at least once each week, but in the fifties and sixties, if I was in a restaurant with them, I'd feel horrible because they had an accent. And I'd be thinking: *Here we go again. People will look and say: "Hey, where are those people from?"* Being German was negative then, a horror, a black cloud.

In those years my mother was young and had a lot of energy. She'd grown up on a farm in Germany. She worked the strangest jobs just to make some money for us. I watched her in action as far as working hard, and I have the same work ethic. I was very close to her. She was a sweetheart. She loved animals, she loved humans, and she just went along with the flow. In the late fifties she was manager of a car wash. This little blond woman was nice to the black laborers, but she was firm.

I went to the local college and lived at home. In 1968 I

graduated. I felt strongly antiwar, and some friends and I went to Washington for a lot of rallies. I said to myself: *If I get sent to Vietnam, I'm not going to go.* Part of it was related to knowing a little bit about what had happened in Europe. Sending soldiers to Vietnam made no sense to me at all. I went through the physical exam and got classified as 4F. I had a heart murmur, but my heart must have been pretty good because I was still playing soccer. I had three friends who got drafted and left for Canada rather than serve. Six of my friends went to Vietnam, and three came back—one with a leg off.

In 1968 I went to work for a large company as an auditor, and they sent me to South America, Europe, Australia, Montreal, and the West. It began because I spoke several languages—German, some French, and a little Spanish.

I got married late—when I was twenty-eight—because I was looking to marry somebody from Europe. I felt that's what I should do. In 1971 I met my future wife. She's American. After we were married three months, I was sent to Germany, and she went with me. She also is a hard worker. She's working in a school system. She went to graduate school after she had the second child. Our relationship is great. I nitpick her, she nitpicks me. But in general, we're very solid. We have the same theories about what we expect from our children, and what we expect from each other. For me it means a lot to be compatible, rather than fighting night and day. We want our young ones to have more than we had. Not just material things. It's schooling, education. We want to be happy and successful and have a nice family.

Tracy is a junior in college, and Jennifer is in the third year of high school. I inherited a lot from my own father because I was very hard on Tracy. It began when she was seven and was fresh with her mother. I hit her a few times and screamed. A lot of that was from the old German feeling. I thought she should be a certain way, and that there was no other way. Later on you think: *That was really stupid.* We had it rough in her last year in high school, but when she was in her first semester of college, she flip-flopped completely and respected us. As she got older, we adjusted and became aware of who is who and what's what. With my second daughter, Jennifer, it's just the opposite. She was very friendly and outgoing and never hassled us with freshness, so it made it easier on us and on her.

I've seen a lot of that in friends—that they're really hard on their first kid. It's the same with my father, who remarried and had three sons. It's funny—with me and my brother he was very harsh, and with his next three sons he eased up and switched his whole self completely, which is a lot better for him.

When I was working in Mexico, I saw how precious freedom is. They swim across the Rio Grande or whatever for freedom. And I don't think it's just for material things. A lot of it is lifestyle. If you were locked up in Vietnam or still missing in action, what's your freedom? It should make you think. Let's be honest—there are a lot of things here in America that are nice and that we just take for granted. You can vote. And there's freedom of speech. If you didn't have freedom, you would know you didn't have it. In Mexico, we had warehouse men who were seized by the Mexican police—no questions asked. When electrodes were used for confessions, the men confessed to things they hadn't done and got locked up for fifteen years. Here you have at least some kind of system and laws.

Freedom to me means someone who wants to escape East Germany.

When I was in Germany with my wife, we saw these minefields and soldiers and graves of everyone who had wanted to leave East Germany. It really affected me, that risk of life for freedom. Over here we have the Fourth of July. What does that mean to people? It means you're going to be with your friends, celebrate with some beers and hamburgers. Is that freedom?

I have a lot of thoughts about the reunification. For this

wall to crumble in my lifetime was a highlight. It began with Russia shrinking down and letting up. My aunt has a son in Frankfurt, a lawyer who was always in the old East Germany. He said: "They don't want to work. They want everything handed to them for free, and they're not as hardworking as West Germans." I can't blame them, because they lived under the Russian system for so long. When I was over there in the seventies and spoke to friends, they said there was no food and they had to line up for bread. Then you open everything up and say: "Okay, now you're equal with us West Germans." I mean, they lived a certain lifestyle for X number of years and it's *not* the same. In some ways it's smoothing out, but they're still not where they should be. It requires a lot of money and jobs.

My wife and kids have other things in their lives, but I don't want them to forget. They know where I'm from and who I am. As my kids get older, they have more of an understanding of what really happened in the thirties and forties over there. It's important for younger students to learn history. I say to my family: "What happened was nuts, but it happened. Let's hope to God it never happens again."

When I was over there visiting, I saw a lot of foreign workers sweeping the streets and doing all the lousy jobs nobody else wanted. A lot of them had left Spain and Yugoslavia and found a new life in Germany. I don't think you can replace them because that society needs these people. Everybody wants certain work hours and certain lifestyles. Yet you got a lot of factions that would love to throw the foreign workers out, send them home. It's a situation with a lot of violence, and it could be the same theory all over again—that it's only for blond, blue-eyed Germans.

I hate to see it. It's like somebody would throw me out here because I'm from there.

Sigrid

Born: 1945
Age at time of immigration: 8

A Talent for Adapting

I think I can cope with almost anything.

When my second husband, Mark, died from cardiac arrest last fall, I wasn't sure how I would go forward because he had become an incredibly central person and focus of my life. I miss him terribly—there's no question about that—but I'm surviving. This is part of a very long history of doing this. It's who I am. It's a knowledge that because you've gotten through some incredible down times before, you will again. It's a core that is very solitary, that knows it will survive. It doesn't need a mother, and it doesn't need a father, because it didn't have either one of those.

And finally it doesn't need anyone.

I don't feel bitter about it. And it does give me a certain kind of strength. But sometimes I worry that I have an inability to connect intimately in that central part. When, all through your childhood, you practice not connecting because you'll bleed if you're constantly torn away from people, you learn how not to become attached. On the other hand, I couldn't have been more attached to someone I loved like Mark.

So I do know how to love.

My mother is a sad person. She was a real casualty of the war because she was a teenager when Germany was plunged into this darkness. So many lives—people with whom she was close—were permanently fractured. Marriages broke up, boyfriends and fiancés and brothers were killed, people had affairs and got pregnant.

When my mother was twenty-three, she was presented with a choice of either working in a munitions factory or as a secretary in the army. She was neither a member of the Nazi Party nor a sympathizer. But she felt she didn't really have a choice. So she went off into the army. In Yugoslavia she met my father, who was also stationed in Belgrade. He was married and had children, and they had an affair—a fairly common thing during the war. When it became evident that she was pregnant, my father and my mother discussed abortion. I'm not offended or hurt. I can understand. It wasn't like she knew who I was going to be and was trying to negate the possibility. Here she was, not married, pregnant, and in the middle of a war. It would be hard to imagine being a mother under those difficult circumstances.

I had an abortion when I was eighteen. The summer after my first year at Hunter College, I was hanging out on the Lower East Side in this Bohemian circle of artists and photographers. I was involved with two men. I became pregnant and didn't know who the father was. One of the men wanted me to have the baby and assumed it was his, but I knew he was just being very romantic and didn't seriously consider what it would mean. I wanted to finish college. I knew I was in a totally impossible situation to have a child.

Somebody got me the telephone number of a gynecologist in New Jersey. They did the examination and told me it would be four hundred dollars, an outrageous amount for me. They told me: "Go down the street and sit on a bench and wait. Somebody will give you details." About eight-thirty at night somebody sat down next to me and said: "Next Saturday take the so-and-so bus to Newark. Wait in the phone booth across the street from this drugstore." Around that time terrible stories were coming out about parts of bodies in the sewer systems from abortions, and I thought: *Oh my God, this will be it. No one will ever see me again.*

But I felt I had no choice. Friends loaned me money they'd saved from summer jobs, and I worked through the rest of my college career to pay everybody back. I took the bus to Newark and waited in this phone booth. Somebody came along in a car. I wasn't really that frightened. It's like something else kicked in, some other part of me. I was the first one they picked up, and then they went all around Newark, picking up girls. I was trying to cheer everybody else up. I guess I assumed it would be all right. We ended up in this apartment, which looked like a mini-hospital since everybody was wearing surgical outfits. It wasn't a back-alley abortion. I couldn't think of it as anything other than a medical procedure, not unlike an early miscarriage. This fetus was not a person in terms of personality or existence.

Years later I told my mother. She said: "It was the right decision to make. But if you had told me at the time, I would have been obliged to prevent you from doing it."

Apparently abortions were not easy to find in the late stages of the war in Belgrade, and my father assured my mother that somehow they would work things out. He was still in Yugoslavia when she was evacuated and ended up in this castle where pregnant women were sent from cities where bombs were dropping. She tells the story of this wildly romantic birth in the basement of the castle with the American army coming through the door. I was born midnight on April 1, 1945, Easter Sunday.

My mother became ill with an infection in her breast. She

was very thin, in a greatly weakened state, as many people were. I, however, weighed about nine pounds, so I'd clearly grabbed all there was to grab. She had to stay in the hospital, and I was moved to something like an orphanage. A woman named Ida used to visit and play with the children. She became very, very fond of me. She found my mother and proposed that she'd take me in until my mother was in a better position to take me back.

I lived with Ida for the first five years of my life. I was very lucky. She was wonderful. To whatever degree I have some kind of solid center has to do with Ida, because I knew she loved me, and I felt very wanted in that household. She not only took care of me, but gathered in children who were unable to remain with their families. Apparently she had been engaged to a German soldier, who'd fought on the French front and become involved with a French woman, who became pregnant. When Ida learned of this, she told him: "You have to marry her. That's the right thing to do." She was quite an amazing woman.

My memories of my mother are of this beautiful and magic woman who would visit now and then. I was always very sad when she left. Originally she couldn't have me with her because she was sick; later she had no way of keeping me with her because she was a domestic in the household of two American families who had come to Germany as part of the reconstruction. One family owned part of a shipping line; the other had come over with the Ford Foundation. These families would allow me to visit for vacations, and I became friends with the children. It was strange to visit these wealthy households, where my mother was the servant. Sometimes I'd eat dinner with the family, and she'd be serving the meals. It began to build a certain resentment that contributed to the later development of my politics and translated to a sensitivity for the underclass and working class, to a kind of an ideology and a socialist sympathy which remains with me to this day, a notion that equality and a kind of rough economic egalitarianism are really the ideal, that people should generally have similar resources available to them.

I went to law school because I wanted to use the work I do in order to pursue some of the social and political values that I hold. I feel good about working for legal services in a state-support center. Every state has one of these resource units. We do research and litigation support. I have a statewide responsibility for housing—that's my specialty.

But part of our budget for this year has been rescinded, and we're looking at substantial cuts. We don't know how they're going to play out. The direction from Congress has been that the cuts come mostly from the state and national support centers, and not from the field program. That seems fairly calculated to strike at the part of the legal services apparatus that does a lot of the policy and more of the impact work. So we're not only a central target, but we're a political target. It's clear that the conservatives know legal services programs will be fighting them if they want to do welfare reform and make changes in the social services structure. Getting rid of at least a part of legal services that does some of the strategizing along those issues makes a lot of sense.

I haven't translated it yet into a possible job loss for me. I'm the last attorney who was hired by my program. I've always felt absolutely sure I would have a job, and I'm a little shaky on that now. In all of the places where you would naturally turn to look for work, the work is not there. Just when I'm launching my son Jason into Columbia. So I don't feel in control of this right now.

I've always felt very much in control. Perhaps it's a mechanism I developed as a kid, a way of coping with a world that seemed to not be in my control. I tend to feel responsible for everything that happens—good and bad. There is a basic optimism that somehow things will work out, but this is the most serious job loss possibility I've faced in a long time. There has been a strong sense of shared pain, and I know people will try to avoid sending any particular person off. They'll try to make cuts elsewhere, maybe by people going into part-time, but if the cuts are large enough, there won't be any way to do it except lay people off, and I certainly will be one of them.

Somewhere I have half brothers and half sisters, this whole family about which I know nothing. That whole part of what goes into making me is a mystery to me. My mother didn't know very much about my father, other than that he owned land and farmed and had a family. When she didn't hear from him, she went to his hometown to inquire about him wherever people get registered. Germans are very good at keeping track of everybody. She found out that he had never returned from Yugoslavia and, in fact, had been killed.

My mother said maybe she didn't pursue my father's family because my grandmother was so distant from her own family. My grandmother was a rebel and despised what she called the bourgeois German culture. My great-grandmother was a very proper Victorian lady, and she was appalled that my grandmother wanted to be an actress. Within her class that was like going off to be a prostitute. My grandmother was well educated, loved music and literature and art. She was a very dramatic person, and half the time she frightened my mother into silence. My mother describes herself as a child, hiding under the table, being overwhelmed. She was three when my grandmother divorced my grandfather. There were a lot of family problems because my grandmother was pregnant and gave up the baby for adoption.

My family was small—essentially my grandmother, my mother, my aunt, and me. All women. My aunt was like my grandmother—demonstrative and theatrical. When I was five, my grandmother decided she wanted me to live with her. I had great affection for her, but I was sad about leaving Ida.

Life with my grandmother was intense. I grew up with an appreciation of certain high-brow parts of German culture that she was conscious of transmitting to me—the classical music, the writers, the poets. She'd listen to Beethoven's violin concerto and weep. She was not very nurturing, and nothing was ever easy—whether it was dusting or cooking. When she got migraine headaches, she would talk about how she preferred to be dead. I thought it was my job to encourage her to live and tried to become a very solid person, somebody she could lean on. She would say she had a very thin skin over her soul, that everything was magnified for her.

I wasn't afraid of her, although she could be very judgmental. When she was angry, she was totally rejecting. She didn't spank, but she was a great one for slapping me in the face, which I found humiliating. Mostly I had to sit in a corner. My mother and Ida never slapped me. From early on, I was conscious of trying to get by because I was always living in somebody else's family. This led to a certain kind of insecurity, but also to a highly developed sensitivity to what people around me expected. Sometimes I wasn't sure what I really thought or wanted. In order to survive, I felt I had to watch myself in the world. It's a female part of culture—how to be pleasing, how to be sensitive to what people around you want, and so I've always had admiration for people who will say what they think without fear of consequences.

In 1952 the family who owned part of the shipping line proposed to my mother that she come to America with them. They were delighted to have this elegant, cultured German woman as one of their servants. This is where I really resent the way in which rich people deal with the world. I was left with my grandmother. She said: "You can't cry because that'll make your mother sad. So you have to be *tapfer*—brave." I don't remember German very well, but I remember that word. *Tapfer.* My mother's parting gift was a stuffed little Steiff monkey, which I still have. For a whole year I was reduced to receiving letters and writing letters. When the family came back to their big summer house in Switzerland, I was able to spend some time there with my mother.

The family agreed I could come over to the States. These trips were made on their own shipping line, and in fact this is case number one against the very wealthy: they had my mother pay back her fare. She was probably making fifteen dollars a week, and they deducted five dollars for her fare. I think they did bring me over for free. Kind of generous. . . .

I felt like a foreigner in that I had an accent, but I felt like more of an outsider because I didn't have a normal family—a father and a mother. I attached no particular significance to being German and never felt really German other than as a historical fact. I couldn't live with my mother, but at least I would be in the same country. She paid room and board for me to Brigitte and Franz, people I'd never met, who came and picked me up. I remember the smell inside their truck—kind of strange. I didn't like it. They'd come to the States in the thirties and liked the idea of having a German friend for their daughter, Sylvia, who was my age. I felt protective towards Sylvia: she was an odd duck and didn't have many friends in school.

Unlike my family, they had a strong allegiance to Germany and a certain kind of low-brow German culture. We'd always go to those outdoor beer gardens where everybody drank like mad and played German music. They owned a hardware store in Connecticut, and we lived above the store. To this day I can't eat butter because I associate butter with that household. Butter and caraway seeds. I wasn't unhappy all the time. My mother worked forty-five minutes away. Most of her days off, she would try to visit. I very quickly—and this is part of my talent for adapting—learned how to speak English and started doing well in school and having friends.

Brigitte totally dominated the household and was always

complaining about Franz. It was obvious that she was somebody who was looking for something and hadn't found it and
was taking it out on everybody. She would pull my hair, but she
used to hit Sylvia with a spatula. What Brigitte did more than
anything was make me a witness. I didn't tell anyone. If I'd
told my mother, what could she have done? There was always
that notion of not making her sad. Protecting her. I never saw
her as somebody who could determine her life. She had absolutely no power. I didn't see it as her personal failing or neg-
ligence or lack of caring, but part of the woman's condition,
and this is where my feminism came from. For the longest
time her life was dominated and dictated by her employers.
Yet, there is safety in a domestic worker's life. You may have a
tiny room under the stairs, but you get to live in a fairly elegant environment, and there's good food. Maybe that security
was really what she needed all those years. It never occurred to
her to get welfare.

When I was a teenager, it was fashionable to blame your
parents, but I never blamed my mother. I was never angry with
her about this. Sad, maybe. The down side is that I had to see
her as a weak person in the world, and so I didn't give her
credit for the strength she must have had to survive on her
own. Maybe I've done this in defense. If I had thought of her
as being in control of anything, I'm sure I would have been
very angry. This way I couldn't be angry.

All I knew about the war from my grandmother and
mother had much more to do with our personal lives, our personal losses, family disruption, the death of my father, the
breaking down of their community. But we didn't talk at all
about the Jews or the Holocaust until I moved to Brooklyn
and encountered a Jewish community where people talked
about the Holocaust. For the first time I was confronted with
what it meant to be German in the context of post–world war,
post-Holocaust history. Most of my friends were Jewish, and all

of a sudden I became much more sensitive to and aware of what the history of Germany had been.

It could have been a more difficult adjustment in terms of people's hostility if there had been men in my family, but because it was just my mother and me, most of my friends' parents didn't see us as very powerful. I was extremely appalled by what had happened in Germany, but I didn't feel personally responsible. I hadn't even been born then. And I certainly knew my grandmother and mother were absolutely opposed to all that Germany stood for during the war. Both were willing to talk about it. I could ask: "What were you doing? Why were you not in the resistance?" They said they knew something was happening, but had no idea what it was and didn't feel they had much power to do anything about it. Like many people, they said they hadn't known about the concentration camps. I believe my grandmother and my mother. Once the war came, they were caught up in surviving. They simply were not that political. They were utterly appalled by what happened in Germany. I don't see anything in their character that would have any affinity with Nazism.

My grandmother was very dramatic, the kind of person who would confront anyone about anything. When she was outraged, nothing would stop her. One day she saw a bunch of kids throwing rocks at a synagogue, breaking the window. She sternly lectured them: "What do you think your Führer would think about this?" She didn't understand that this was precisely what Hitler was recommending.

Both said that the war took over their lives and that they were not aware of what was going on with Jews, other than that they were gone. I thought: *Well, where did you think they went?* But I've never been able to press them past what they're willing to say, in part because I see them as victims of the war. The stakes in trying to find out what was going on and doing something about it were very high. My grandmother told me this story about her landlord and his wife who were Jewish and disappeared abruptly. When he came back without his wife, my grandmother asked him what had happened, and he said: "For your protection, I'm not going to tell you," meaning he was afraid she'd let on she knew, and that it would endanger her.

Maybe I just never knew the questions to ask—but both of them seemed to view the war in a very personal way and not so much on the grander scale. I know they certainly would not be capable of being collaborators or participants. I could never say: *Well, didn't you see the stuff in the newspaper, those nasty, anti-Semitic articles and slurs and cartoons? What did you think happened to people when they disappeared?*

Maybe I haven't wanted to think about it.

It might have been different in smaller towns where everybody knew each other, but my mother and grandmother grew up in an urban environment. So I'm not sure things were always that clear. Maybe they moved around a lot. . . . I sound like I'm defending them.

Maybe I am.

Some people I've met in Germany are kind of ordinary people. That's the frightening thing—that this can happen in a very ordinary way. It lulls you into complacency to think it takes a certain kind of national character. We seem to have an enormous capacity to be mean and vicious to people whom we define as the other, and then anything is plausible. If you cannot do that, you're not going to participate. Whether you can find the courage and conviction that will allow you to battle it—that's another thing. And there's where you can't, unfortunately, expect people to be heroes. I believe most people are not heroes, and I'm not willing to fault somebody for failing to become part of the resistance because I'm not so sure how far I would go if it meant putting my life on the line. Those were life-and-death decisions. How many of us really have the courage to make those choices? You'd like to think you would be willing to go all the way for something you believe in, but there is just always a minority of people who can be that heroic.

It took quite a bit of heroism to be a dissident in Germany once the Nazis came to power. It wasn't as easy as in this country. At the height of the antiwar movement, we would march in Washington—it didn't take a lot of courage—but when Germans were openly dissident or disaffected, they could very well end up in prison or camps. Dead.

After I lived with Brigitte and Franz for two years, my Aunt Ilse decided I should live with her. After the war she'd come to this country with my uncle, who had been a GI in Germany. He was a marble layer, and first they lived with his parents, simple country folk, in this little town in New Jersey. They had an outhouse. Then they lived in a working-class tract housing development in New Jersey. I think my aunt started drinking so she could see the world in a more pleasant light. She'd grown up in a cosmopolitan world in Frankfurt, and she was unprepared for this country. She had enormous talents, and they wasted away. My uncle was totally in love with her. She was a seductive woman. Very lovely.

Since my grandmother was very lonely in Germany, she decided to come over, too, which was a terrible uprooting. She and I shared this tiny bedroom. Very difficult. My aunt and grandmother were similar in personality—high drama— and clashed often. There was constant tumult, and it became clear they couldn't live in the same house. My grandmother started working as a baby nurse or as a companion to older people. She felt misplaced, displaced. She hated the culture here, but she also never had great things to say about Germany. She might have been unhappy wherever she was. The humiliating way in which poor people get treated in this country rankled her. Germany tended to take care of people like her with medical care and some kind of state support. Here she had to apply for Medicaid. I remember her struggling with the social services bureaucracy, and it's ironic now that, as an attorney, I work at representing poor people and people caught in the welfare system.

My grandmother's last years were very sad. My aunt's, too—she drank herself to death by the time I graduated from college. With both I felt a real outrage at the world. My aunt had been stifled by the little town that didn't nourish her spiritually or emotionally, and with my grandmother the mental health establishment was responsible in part. My aunt's death was a terrible loss and may have plunged my grandmother into total depression. She tried to commit suicide by jumping in front of the subway. The engineer was able to stop the subway, but she was put into a big state-owned mental hospital. When I first visited her, she seemed a little disoriented, but okay. She should have gotten out. People were just warehoused there. I was appalled at the lack of care and counseling, but in spite of that, she was getting better. She was almost on her way out when she fell in the shower and broke her hip. As with so many older people, that was the end. She went into senile psychosis. A friend of mine, a psychologist, told me it's a kind of suicide.

When I went to visit her, this once incredibly proud and highly cultured woman sat in this chair in a restraint, just clutching humiliation, totally at the mercy of everybody, without any power to affect what was happening. Because for me the ability to control your world is so important, it seemed to be the worst that could happen to a person. I remember losing it and crying and accusing the nurses of having done this to her. As I looked into her eyes, I thought way back there I could see her. She died very soon after that. It was an awful death, and it haunted me for years. My mother felt guilty to some degree because she had desperately tried to keep my grandmother from moving in with her because she felt she would just get swallowed up again. I tried to tell her that was not her responsibility.

While I was still living with my aunt and uncle, my mother moved to New York City and started going to school to become a dental assistant. I must have always known that it was the goal to find a job and a place where we could be together. After she started working for a dentist, she found an apartment in Brooklyn, and I moved there in the summer of 1957. I was going into the seventh grade. The first year we lived together was loving and warm, but otherwise I felt miserable and lonely because Brooklyn was not at all like the small town in New Jersey, where I had friends and knew who I was. My mother worked long hours and often didn't come home until late. Weekends or late evenings we had a wonderful time, but initially I couldn't find my way in this huge urban community.

I felt I had to create myself in a way that I could be part of something, and the first guise I undertook was to be interested in clothes and boys, to wear makeup and do my hair so that I'd be popular. I always felt this person I was becoming was temporary—not somebody I would ultimately be. I knew I had interests beyond boys and movie stars and singers. My mother, of course, was appalled. She wanted her daughter to listen to classical music and read books, and here I was, chewing gum, teasing my hair, and developing a Brooklyn accent. That put a real strain on our relationship. I felt she had no idea what school was like, what the society into which I had been thrust was like, and that she didn't have a real world to give me. For a period of years I was very angry with her for not understanding this, and for not giving me a little room. When I began to make friends, I felt somewhat envious of people whose parents had a whole community in which these children flourished. And here were just the two of us. My mother worked in Manhattan, and so we really didn't have a community around us.

Initially she told me she and my father had been married;

but her maiden name was the same as her married name, and I dreaded having to fill out papers in school that asked for your mother's maiden name. She made up this elaborate story that she couldn't take my father's name because the marriage certificate had gotten lost. When I was sixteen or seventeen, she must have thought I was old enough to deal with this. She said: "We wanted to get married, but he was killed before he came back to Germany."

I remember walking down the street in Brooklyn and saying to myself: "Gee, I'm a bastard," and thinking: *Well, this is sort of interesting.* In New York City people had many different kinds of lives and family relationships. My friends weren't exactly jealous, but it was more interesting to be a bastard than to be an ordinary child of a married couple.

New York is such a conglomerate of cultures that it's hard to feel peculiar when everybody around you comes from somewhere else. I grew up without identifying with either Germany or America. Any part of politics I was involved in during the sixties was a very conscious internationalism, a notion of solidarity with other countries and cultures, a citizen-of-the-world approach, which sadly seems to be less possible these days.

My experience with boys in high school was unpleasant because boys' goals were to see how far they could get. Then they'd be totally disrespectful. I hated that whole world, but there didn't seem to be an alternative. At some point in high school I was able to discover a way in which I would not be lonely, and also be much truer to who I really was. That was through politics, student politics, the antiwar movement. I found a place for myself in that world. I began to meet people—including Jason's father, Sam—who respected other human beings, women, and were willing to connect with a lot fewer gains. Sam was also pretty active politically. He was the one who introduced me to Marx and Engels.

My friendship with him was always stronger than any

grand feelings of passion. Part of his appeal for me was that he came from this large Jewish family, who were very accepting of me. In some ways I married the family as much as I married him. Sam and I really never talked about me as a German—I think because I was so much of an antifascist and so political in a socialist or progressive way that I was never called upon to defend Germany.

I started working for a university-connected research foundation, doing editorial work. Sam and I were very active in left-wing politics and the early parts of the women's movement. The two of us were much of a mind about these things. I started graduate school, combining interests in literature, politics, and history. That's how I met Mark. He was my professor. We became good friends, though not lovers. Both of us were married—at that point pretty happily.

I was seven months pregnant when I went into labor, and the baby, a little girl, only lived two days. Oh, it was terrible. It was a baby Sam and I both wanted. It was the right time. I had been looking forward to having this baby. We were devastated. I've heard it said that the loss of a child either brings a couple closer together or pushes them apart if they carry their grief in separate ways, and that's maybe what happened to Sam and me. It took a long time for us to split, but that may have been some of the early seeds.

I didn't go back to graduate school. Friends who were lawyers were doing poverty law and prison movement stuff, and that seemed what I wanted to do. Sam and I moved to Los Angeles, and I started law school. That first year was pretty good between us. We lived in a kind of commune. He was working as a dental ceramist, making teeth. It's a good profession and very skilled work. Then he got laid off. I worked while I went to law school, but Sam wasn't finding a focus for himself. He also was becoming more conservative. Part of it was this backlash that some men in the radical movement were experiencing. Here they had been such good guys, in favor of integration, and suddenly there was black power and there was feminism. Where was their place in all of this? They felt they were being held responsible. Increasingly, the two of us collided on intellectual and political issues. Sam had very strong feelings for Israel, a kind of Zionism, and he resented a lot of the organized left who supported the Palestinian struggle.

It was difficult for him that I now had a profession, while he did a little here and there—nothing that gave him real satisfaction. I was thirty-two when I realized I wanted to have a child, even though it didn't look like our relationship was going to last. I still had warm feelings toward Sam. His family continued to be my family. He was one of the few people who knew my grandmother, my aunt, and in my world where I had such radical disjunction within the family, somebody who shared significant history with me was important. I deliberately set about trying to get pregnant. Sam was in on that decision, but later on people thought he shouldn't have left me when he did. It was bad timing, no question about it. I had always had these romantic notions of being pregnant and being together with someone. And so to be alone and pregnant . . . somewhere I must have felt doomed to repeat history. No one in my family ever quite made marriages work.

Even for Sam it wasn't easy. For quite a number of years he was not clear about what he really wanted. He loved Jason and tried from the beginning to get involved and take care of him when he could. He was always a part of Jason's life. We never really cut anybody loose from our lives. When we separated, his mother told me: "You will always be my daughter-in-law."

I was a single parent for a number of years. I wanted to have what other people had in the sense of *one* home, *one* family, *one* community, and I was conscious of not moving around with Jason too much. I found a community with other mothers and kids. Jason was part of a play group, and we did collective day care.

I felt the need to go home again, to come back East. A number of friends, my mother, and Sam's parents were on the East Coast. Mark was very much a part of my decision to move back. I had seen him once since I'd left for Los Angeles, and we'd had a wonderful long conversation about his life, my life. There was a way in which I connected with him that I didn't connect with anybody. He had that ability to talk to people and make them feel special and interesting. I wasn't thinking about him in terms of lover or husband because for all I knew, he was married again.

I called him a few weeks after I got back. We met for lunch, and he asked if we could meet for dinner. We fell in love—that quickly. Both of us felt we had found a real home in each other. Mark loved the idea that after ten years I had thought about him and had deliberately come back East to reconnect. Part of what made us work so well is that he was brought up by women—his grandmother, his aunt, and his mom—in the same constellation of women as I had been, and this had an effect on him in terms of his ability to listen. He was older by fourteen years, and he could be a kind of father for me in a sense of what you want a parent ideally to be—utterly and unconditionally accepting and loving you. He was the first person in my life who did that.

It's not that our life together was all easy. There were some rough times around his drinking and rough times around Jason's extreme dependence on me, but a lot of it really came together in the last years, and there was always this great, enormous love and real romance. Mark had stopped drinking in 1986, and Jason was much more self-reliant. Their relationship had grown to be very close and warm.

No death ever comes at the right moment. It was so unfair—some kind of big cosmic unfairness—because there were all the trips we were meant to take, and we had learned how to sit very comfortably with each other. There's just a big hole now at the center of my life. I don't have Mark anymore, but I have wonderful memories. It's not like he ever left us as a family, the way I lost Sam during the divorce. When somebody with whom you shared your life becomes a stranger to you, that's almost harder to bear.

It's going to take a really long time. I know I can manage and I know I can survive—but boy, those first few weeks, I didn't see why I wanted to. At that point, having Jason was very helpful. A kid his age might have been thrown by seeing that raw grief in somebody he always counted on to stay solid, but Jason didn't withdraw. He was there, comforting and supporting. He still needed me, and I certainly couldn't check out in any kind of way.

Sometimes when I look back, there is that sense of loss— my grandmother, my aunt, my first child. When Mark died, part of me felt like every time I turned around, there was somebody disappearing out of my life. Jason said Mark's death shook him in a way that made him afraid of what would come next. He was going through that similar sense of nothing being very sure in this world. Of course, the big scare then for him was that something might happen to me, and with a small family to fall back on, it was a scary prospect. Originally, he was talking about school on the West Coast, but after Mark died, he realized that for me it would be better if he could be closer. I'm glad he picked Columbia. It's about an hour and a half from here.

Jason doesn't see it as a conflict to have a German-born mother and a Jewish father. At this point in his life he's not particularly interested in either politics or history. For him that whole thing is sort of ancient and has nothing to do with him. Since my connections to his father's family are strong, he doesn't feel any kind of disparity there. Because of the particular people involved, it has all meshed for him in a very easy way.

Joachim

Born: 1947
Age at time of immigration: 9

During Hitler's Time You Would Have Been Shot for That

I just saw this film, *Europa Europa*. This boy was denying that he was Jewish. Look at all the people who denied that they were homosexual. I would have denied it. I have to be honest with you. Because I *did* deny it. Look, I denied it all these years, and *ja*, I consider myself fortunate that I can get away with it. I've heard the talk about people who are gay. Even the Jews discriminate against us.

I'm sure people at work know, but I don't talk to them about that part of my life. Every once in a while my bosses will drop hints. They'll say they didn't know their son's friend was gay, and that now he's dying of AIDS. I listen, but I won't get involved in the discussions. Twice in my life I lost people because I told them. The weight of the secret is that you're never entirely yourself in an environment where others are not the same as you.

I'm the county manager of a small community in Missouri. County managers handle day-to-day affairs of towns, such as police and public works and streets and parks and zoning and building. I like my work. Where else but in America could somebody immigrate and in a short time be a political leader? When I came to this town, it didn't have a lot of things. I had a vision, but I was only the orchestra leader, because it took the whole band to put this together. We built a new township building, expanded our facilities, and put our infrastructure in order, which included streets and sewers. People like this community because of the stability. Of course, everybody's saying: "That's because we have this good, strong German manager." They think that's all German orderliness and *Gründlichkeit*— thoroughness. I say: "That's a lot of baloney. It has nothing to do with Germany. It has to do with discipline." When people attach *"German"* to "clean and orderly," those traits come across as negative to me, and I feel a little strange.

I would like to create a better—or different—image of Germany than what people generally have. Those darker years from the 1930s to the 1940s don't reflect everyone in Germany. We're human beings like everybody else: we have the same feelings, the same strengths, the same weaknesses, the same aspirations. I want people to see us as human beings—not as the monsters that are evoked to this day in the news media and in the thoughts of people when they hear "Germany."

I try to understand what happened in Germany, why it happened, and how it could have happened. Unbelievable atrocities were committed. I agree with those who say: "Never again." We cannot help but feel ashamed for what happened in Germany, but I do not think people have a right to make us feel ashamed—those of us who were born after the war. I look at the pictures of my nieces and nephews. What in the world did they ever have to do with that? And yet this is constantly thrown into their faces: *Look at what your grandparents did.* No race wants to be responsible for what its ancestors did. It's exactly the way Jews were being discriminated against. They claim they called upon themselves the wrath of the Christians because they said to Pontius Pilate: "Let us crucify Christ. Let his blood fall upon us and upon our children." Are they saying that, because this kind of discrimination occurred to them all those years, the same should apply to Germans?

In our community I embarked on this one-man effort to have a partnership program with a German town. We communicate; we visit each other; students of theirs come here; students of ours go over there; businesspeople talk about ventures back and forth. What I like about it is how it opens up horizons for people who are generally not interested in anything but the little world they have. I try to instill in them that this little world doesn't exist. You look at the shoes you wear—they're not even made in your little world. Things you buy, things you eat, things you see on television—we can't live in that kind of a small world anymore.

My mother was a telephone operator in the *Arbeitsdienst*—voluntary labor service—during Hitler's time in power. My father was in the SS and was captured. They met when he returned from the war. We didn't see much of my father during our childhood because he worked in another town and wasn't welcome in my grandparents' house. When he did come, my parents would disappear for a while, but within hours they'd be fighting. My uncle used to say my parents got along best in bed, and after that was done, there wasn't much else.

I remember my parents pulling at each other's hair, screaming in pain. Neither of them would let go. Once my mother broke a vase over my father's head. They would hit each other. It was horrible. That all translated to us children because my father would not hesitate to use force. He once used a two-by-four on me. We had a tumultuous life, growing up.

Yet, holidays have stayed with me. Christmas we'd go to midnight mass, and then come home and have the *Bescherung,*

the giving of presents. Of course, preceding Christmas was St.
Nicholas Day, which was celebrated early in December. We
had to polish our shoes and leave a note in there about what
we wanted for Christmas. The following morning there usually would be nuts and candies and tangerines in our shoes.
To this day, when I eat a tangerine, I think of that.

In 1956, when I was nine years old, we immigrated to the
United States. I went to a Catholic grade school run by Do-
minican nuns in Washington, D.C. I had a crush on a nun by
the name of Sister Paul Joseph. She was not only beautiful to
look at—in those days just the nuns' faces were squared out by
their veils—she also was a beautiful person.

When my parents divorced, my father moved to Boston,
and my mother took me out of grade school and sent me off
to him by bus. My father was at the bus station in Boston; he
bought me a ticket and put me right back on the bus to Washington. Some pretty rough things happened to all the children—my brother Peter was the oldest, I was the second, and
then two sisters, Gabi and Agnes. My mother had a tendency
to strike out physically. Maybe we gave her cause to do that.
She would hit me in the head with her shoes, screaming: *"Ich
schlag dich bis du in keinen Sarg mehr passt"*—"I'll beat you till
you can't fit into any coffin."

The turmoil of my parents' marriage and divorce probably
did more than anything else to drive me into the arms of the
church. I thought I had a vocation, that God was calling me to
save the pagans in Africa by converting them to Catholicism. I
wanted to do something for mankind, and I used to think I
had visions, that I saw God in the form of Christ coming down
and beckoning to me. At age thirteen I entered the seminary
to study with an order of missionaries.

Three years later, when my mother took my sisters and returned to Germany, I was again alone. I guess I wanted to be
with them, and I was homesick for Germany—that was, after

all, my home. I didn't know if I had the vocation anymore. I left the seminary even though my father tried to talk me into staying and went to live with him in Boston. He had remarried. They got me into a Catholic high school so that I would still be in a religious environment. I had a roof and meals and the security of the church, but I didn't feel I belonged there. My father espoused a very disciplined and ideological path but didn't live by that himself. I looked up to him but was afraid of him. Instead of taking the train to school, I would hang out and see movies. When he found out, neither he nor his wife spoke to me for two weeks. He wrote to my uncle in Germany and made arrangements for me to go there.

Upon my arrival in Germany, my mother said: "You're not going to just sit around here." She had taken over her parents' *Gaststätte* and expected me to help. My uncle convinced her to let me start an apprenticeship in accounting. I had not been there six months when I received my *Einberufungsbefehl*—my induction order—into the German Army. To avoid interrupting my apprenticeship, my uncle tried to have me go as a volunteer into the *Luftwaffe*. But since I had several fillings in my teeth and a collarbone deformity—one is a little lower than the other—I was not accepted for pilot school. They look for the perfect specimen.

Surprisingly, I was accepted at the *Polizeischule*—police academy—which fulfilled my military obligation. I was with a group of men who were mainly talking sex, smoking cigarettes, or drinking beer. And I had lived in a disciplined environment in seminary: you got up at a certain time; there was prayer at a certain time. Don't get me wrong—I lived with my comrades, and we were friends. On weekends we would go out. I was always very outgoing and physically active. I won some regional awards for sprinting.

One day I received a letter from a priest in Washington, D.C., along with a newspaper article, describing a terrible accident in which my brother had lost his arm and leg and was near death. It was already seven days past the accident, and this was the first I'd heard. My father had never mentioned a thing. I rushed home to be with my mother. When she learned of Peter's accident, her first words were, of course: "Why couldn't it have been you?"

I heard what she said, and that was all. I never used to think about it. Considering all the times she and my father pushed me away, it wasn't an isolated incident. It wasn't the worst of it, you know? She probably looked at me as a loser. Still—that's not something you would tell your child. I don't think I need to forgive my mother that.

That situation with my brother caused me to go back into the seminary, and I entered an order in Bavaria. I still had a very strong belief in all the facets of the church. In retrospect, I've analyzed this strong pull towards the church. It gave me the warmth and security I wasn't getting at home, that sense of community, of belonging. While my parents kept sending me back and forth, the church was my real family, the only family who wanted me. Whatever anybody wants to say about the church—no matter where you went in the world, you had a home. Nobody else does that for you except the church. Nobody else has ever done that for me. The church always opened its door to me. I didn't need money—I just needed to believe and want to be there.

In the seminary, another guy by the name of Joachim— they used to confuse us all the time—and I were the only ones in this *Kursus*—class. You were not permitted to have a special friend. I guess they thought other things would go on. They used to tell us: "Where the community is not, is where the devil is." You know, I never saw the devil. But I think this friendship was more than just platonic on my part, and that was a beacon of what was to come in my life. I mean, nothing went on—it was more confusion than anything else, an unfinished feeling—but I'd always want to be with Joachim, do things with him. I felt maybe there was something wrong with the way I felt towards him. Why wasn't I feeling this way towards a particular girl? Once, when he showed me how to dance, I felt hot all over and thought: *There's something not right here.* I don't know if he was aware of my feelings . . . how deep they were.

When the seminary's funding was stopped, I ended up at his house with his parents. He and I planned to go to a seminary in New York, and he got his visa, sponsors, and was ready to be accepted into the school. When my mother promised to put in a good word for him with the rector of the seminary, I agreed to return to America with her. But she told the rector there was no way she would ever agree that a son should leave his family. She thought I should assist her, take the role of my father. Those words obviously didn't make the original proposal palatable for the rector. I cannot describe how much I hated my mother after that. But even though she deceived me, I wonder if what happened wasn't for the best since I had such feelings for Joachim.

But that wasn't for her to decide.

Since I was again on my own, I chose another community: I went to the U.S. Army recruiting station and became a chaplain's assistant for a Jesuit father at the military hospital. We were treating all these young men, who were coming back from Vietnam dispirited and demoralized, half of their bodies gone. How hopeless it was for many of them. The Jesuit father persuaded me to go back to the seminary and arranged for a discharge from the military, which proved to be a fatal mistake and haunts me to this day. It was a general discharge under honorable conditions, due to character and behavior disorders and suicidal tendencies. The Jesuit father had meant to help me when he set up an interview with a military psychologist, who asked me what kind of feelings I had about life and death. I told him I thought about suicide, but that I didn't think I'd ever do anything. Part of it was that I'd gotten involved with this guy who seduced me. Let me say this—I was willingly seduced, although I didn't know what I was being seduced into.

After I left the army, I traveled four months with a choral group. I think it was a cult: they watched you, and if you uttered the wrong lines, they would call you to task. But they weren't forcibly holding us there. We were a group of young people, all handsome, smiling—always smiling—and singing at colleges and military bases to convey a message of how God was good in people's lives. In between songs we'd get up and expose our own weaknesses publicly.

This group encouraged us to come clean with our parents. That's what their philosophy was all about—admitting your fault and then overcoming it. I went to see my father and said I wanted to tell him something about me that he probably didn't know, so that maybe we could understand each other. I also told him I had chosen not to partake in that lifestyle.

He said: "During Hitler's time you would have been shot for that."

I didn't think my father meant to say that *he* would shoot me. Comments like that come out of that criminal society. My father was well brainwashed by Adolf Hitler's lieutenants. Indeed, they did shoot and gas people for being homosexual. Well, my father knew what they had done to gay people.

I know now why this group had wanted me—to discredit the Catholic Church. I would not do that. But they kept insinuating that homosexual activity had happened in the seminary. They kept saying: "The truth will set you free." Well, *what* truth? *Whose* truth? When I didn't want to become a mouthpiece for them, they made me leave.

I was accepted into the Jesuits. There was intense spiritual training, and we also studied Latin and Greek and other subjects. Novices and scholastics were not supposed to speak to each other, except at appointed times. My sexual orientation was pretty well established, and even though I didn't want to get into that, I was drawn to a scholastic. I didn't look at it just as sex—I thought that it was more, that it was precious to give to somebody. But that was the end of my seminary days because I became so distraught over the deception. In the novitiate you have a novice master to whom you confess all your transgressions against the commandments and the house rules. Since I could not face the prospect of lying, I stopped eating to the point of total emaciation and was taken to a hospital. I was twenty then.

To give me peace and rest, they asked that nobody visit me. The novice master said: "The doctors cannot find anything wrong with you. What's troubling you?" I said: "I would like to make a confession." As I started confessing that I had this sexual relationship, guess who pops in? This scholastic. *Ja.* But the novice master was very understanding and absolved me. He probably figured I was so distraught because I really wasn't disposed that way. He misread that. What made me distraught was that I realized what I was and that I had to lie about it.

And this is what the lie did to me.

But what subsequently did me in was when those military records came. The church wasn't going to ordain a priest who was determined by the military to have character and behavior disorders. It was a milestone because it once and for all closed that career goal. I had no choice. That was the biggest loss—losing that home.

I went to get my seaman's license, ended up on a merchant ship, and got to see Venezuela, Japan, and the Philippines. Members of the crew purchased time for me with a prostitute in Venezuela so that I was able to experience that part of my sexuality as well. After seven months at sea I returned to Germany. When I got a job with the American military, I really let loose

on my alternate lifestyle. But I did not start having indiscrimi-
nate sex because I believed in sharing some kind of feeling.

At a private party I met an American soldier, Mike. Forty
Air Force people were there. There was more of that in the
military than I ever saw in the seminary. It wasn't even
covert—it was overt. The bar I used to go to in Frankfurt, the
Comeback, was full of service people until the Americans set
up a camera outside. Months later all these people who'd
gone into the bar were sent back to the United States and
given dishonorable discharges.

Mike and I established an affection for each other very
quickly. We ended up living with each other, and it was with
him that I ultimately came to Missouri in 1970. From then on
my life took an orderly transition. I sold shoes for a while,
then worked in a Laundromat until I finally got a job with a
bank. I started wearing suits again. I was always very good at
numbers, and I had a rapid and successful rise to operations
manager.

When my mother announced her arrival from Germany
and stayed with us, she asked me: "Where do you sleep?
Where does Mike sleep?" I didn't say we slept together, but it
was obvious. Of course, she insisted on staying longer than she
had planned. I knew what she was trying to do—destroy the
relationship with Mike. I remember Mike and me at night—in
anguish about the whole thing. I finally told her: "You cannot
stay." Years later my brother told me she came to him and
cried: "What did I do wrong?"

The first several years of my relationship with Mike were
good, and then he became jealous because he thought I was
seeing someone, when in reality he was. I would never do that.
If I'm in a relationship, that's where I am. I guess that's one of
the things in that lifestyle I detested the most—this lack of
monogamy. Mike and I spent as much time undoing the relationship as we had been in it. We'd move apart and then we'd
move together again—I don't know how many times we did

that. It was painful. After our breakup I went with a number of people until I met someone in 1976, and we established a relationship. That also ended because neither of us was mature enough. He has not had a relationship since, and neither have I.

I plan to retire in Germany. I see myself taking walks in the mountains around our village. I have no one here to spend retirement with. I'm closer to people over there—my nieces and nephews, my cousins and friends. Though I have friends here, too, the substance of the friendships is different. It takes so long to establish a friendship in Germany, but then it doesn't end that quickly either.

Most years I go to Germany twice. I make it a point to be there around Christmas. That's the hardest feast to celebrate without the family. Traveling for me is invigorating—the preparation for it and actually doing it. Next month my niece is celebrating her first communion. For Catholic Germans it's a big feast because the child is coming of age in the eyes of the church. I'm very fortunate because I have the luxury of coming and going as I please in either country. I can leave the negative things I don't want any part of. I think I'm multicultural, really, because I have been exposed to a variety of cultures and different disciplines. It has taught me how diverse life is. All the people I've met—whether German, American, Japanese, or Filipino—were all different somehow, their character, their upbringing, their orientations, their physical attributes; but then on the other hand, they were all the same. They're all trying to stay alive and probably try to do the best they can. Most people. Some are on self-destructive courses without realizing it. Some don't care.

I do believe there is evil in people. As a child, I didn't know about the kind of evil that is readily identifiable with my German heritage. We didn't learn about the Holocaust in grade school, and even when I went to higher educational institutes, there was a muffled silence, a maddening silence. Maybe people were shocked, afraid. Maybe people didn't know or want to know. Maybe people didn't want to be reminded. When the Wall came down, I listened to a *Bürgermeister*—mayor—tell me horror stories of how they were treated under the Communist regime. All of a sudden nobody could find all these people who had perpetrated these evil things. They were all victims. Right. I thought: *My God, this is what happened after the war. Nobody did anything.*

But my father, to this day, sings the glorious praises of that era. He certainly doesn't talk about the Jews in a flattering way. He says the same thing the Nazis said—that the Jews are responsible for all the evils of this world. He was in the SS *Panzer* Division, and he proudly shows his Iron Crosses. He belonged to these groups that harbored Nazis. That's where they'd get together, sing old military songs, talk about how they lost the war because of Jewish treachery. It's ridiculous to believe that. What do you tell a man like that? He's seventy-two years old. You don't argue with him about those things. I laugh about it even though I should cry. But then I think: *It's horrible that there are people who think like this.*

A lot of people in this country don't speak highly of the Jews. It's unbelievable when you hear them say Hitler didn't get enough of them. I tell them: "You've got to be kidding! How can you say that?" And then this racial bias that people have here. I was at a table last week where people were talking about niggers. I usually ask: "What did you say?" hoping they'll think about what they said, but when they repeat it, I say: "I don't believe you said that."

I guess I should also be calling my father on it, but I don't want the discomfort of having a brawl with him. He'd probably call me a name. *You fag!* He's done that already. I don't want to deal with that. See, I don't live that life publicly. I think it's a deeply personal thing. My expression of my intimate feeling for another person is nobody's business. On the other hand, I cannot even share that person with people around me. So there is a double-edged sword here. In my family it's not a secret, but except with my sisters, I never discuss it. This weekend I was really annoyed with my father. After he had a couple of *Schnapps*, he kept referring to my sexual orientation in an insulting way. Everyone laughed, but I didn't have the guts to tell him: *Why don't you shut your stupid mouth.* Because it would have gotten worse. He would have really gotten into a rage. He doesn't leave it alone. But he's my father. There's a limit though.

He did admit for a while that he shouldn't drink. I started down that path when I first went out and saw that people liked me more when I had this freewheeling personality, when I would just drink and be merry and dance and kiss everybody. But you cannot always be drunk, and I didn't like waking up the next day with a hangover. Now I hardly ever drink, and I don't need to.

There have been moments in my life when I reached a really low point and didn't know what to do. As recently as a year ago, I wanted to give up. I didn't know what that meant, *give up,* but I just didn't want to do it all anymore. You get tired.

I don't know if I'm normal or if there is such a thing as a normal family.

I have rosary beads hanging right next to my bed that Pope John Paul blessed when he was in America, and I have medieval pictures on my wall of altar scenes from Germany. Yet, I don't pray anymore. I used to pray, think, and meditate on God, coming to communion with him or her. We don't really know God's physical makeup or gender makeup or whether he/she even has a gender.

I was involved in Dignity, a national group of gay Catholics, until they hit a radical streak. Even though they kept aspiring to be part of the church, they would do things to distance themselves. I consider myself still a Catholic—not a practicing one, but I was baptized one. As far as the liturgy is concerned, I'm probably a conservative Catholic. There has to be some discipline in the faith. You can't just have everybody say: *This is what we should believe.* The Catholic Church remains a vibrant organization in spite of all these challenges. If the church is based on faith and teaching, someone has to maintain those teachings. Again, maybe it's that part of me that's looking for a home. A number of my fellow Dignity constituents and I have started going to this Jesuit church here.

I guess I could be complacent and say what happened in Germany could never happen here in America. But I'm not so sure. Because it's already happening. That's frightening. I think of what the right-wingers are doing with AIDS politically. They're such a phony outfit. I call them the phony right. I've not had to deal with that kind of discrimination because I've not openly admitted to my sexual orientation. I'm fortunate not to have any of those characteristics usually attributed to gays, even though they are stereotypical. I mean, some have a lisp or move their hands a certain way. I've even felt uncomfortable being publicly seen with a companion. When we would stand in a theater line, I'd see hundreds of eyes just shouting: *Those faggots.* But then sometimes, when I would be a little bit tipsy in an environment where people didn't know me, I'd act outrageous right in the middle of the street, kiss a man on the lips. It was almost like baiting fate: *What are you going to do because I did this?*

I have a network of gay friends. But I haven't been in a relationship since 1980. That's probably why I'm still alive. I've lost a lot of friends. People I've been intimate with are gone. Mike died of AIDS complications a couple of years ago. I've not tested in any way HIV positive. I must have done something right. I don't mean to put on a moral hat, but I chose partners for whom I had feelings. I wanted more than just that orgasm.

Now, if I could have that ideal relationship where you

could be independent and still be in a relationship . . . that would be nice, but I haven't found that, nor am I actively looking. I've come to the conclusion that my life the way it is now is better than being with someone. Because I've been through that so many times. Even short-term relationships . . . I don't want that pain anymore. That's probably why I didn't buy a house and surround myself with pets. I've had pets and they died. People say: "You're making yourself immune to any kind of feeling." That may be so. A way of protecting myself. But I'm not going to go after anybody.

I invest a lot of my life in doing my work or thinking about it. I also like to play as hard as I work. I'd rather do physical exercise than watch it on television. I enjoy playing around with my computer. And I'm glad I can choose when I want to be with friends. Still, I think of my life as somewhat not complete. I think about it a lot. I think mostly about not being here, but being in Germany with my sisters. And I think about our village. I want to go back to the past more than to the place. I also realize that can't be, so I try to live life every day, and take what comes, and overcome what I have to.

Kurt

Born: 1946
Age at time of immigration: 6

Am I the Product of a Rape?

I don't remember much about the orphanage in Germany.
I remember helping push a milk cart up the hill one day and having a milk can slide back and smash my little finger. I remember being one of many kids and not getting enough to eat. I remember what a treat it was to get cut-up chunks of liver and mashed potatoes. I remember a large wooden train at Christmastime that you could sit on. I remember eating sand and getting worms and being punished for it by the nuns.

I have been so starved for attention.

The attention was punishment.

And I would rather have that than none.

I was adopted three or four times before I was finally placed in America. I would be taken out of the orphanage, put into a home, and then wind up back in the orphanage again. The worst part about it is that I don't know if I was sent back because I wasn't wanted or because something went wrong in the relationship. I didn't find out that I'd been adopted several times until four years ago when my parents gave me my passport, the adoption papers, and my old airline ticket. I didn't even know I had a German passport.

Some things are very vivid about coming over here. I was awakened in the orphanage in the middle of the night and told to get my things together. I had a little wooden train, a pair of *Lederhosen,* a white shirt, and high-top shoes. I remember a train ride along a river and an unbelievably large train station, which would have been Frankfurt.

I have looked up on a map where I think I'm from. I may have the wrong Frankfurt, but if I look at the maps for 1945—about the time I would have been conceived—Frankfurt was as far as the Russians advanced at that time. And I have funny, high cheekbones and somewhat squinty eyes which point towards Slav or maybe even Russian heritage. From the paperwork, I have no idea who my father was.

People have asked me if I don't want to find out more about my mother or see if I can find her. I spent many years telling people—and telling myself—that she didn't love me enough to keep me. So why should I care? As I've gotten older, I realize that circumstances in postwar Germany were such that, probably, it was a pretty big sacrifice on her part. Probably, it was the best thing she could have done. I have my mother's name, but I haven't got the foggiest idea how to go about finding out where she is. The curiosity has always been there, but I manage to put up enough barriers. The barrier now is: *I'm forty-eight years old. It's unlikely that she's still alive.* I'm afraid I'll find out my mother is dead, afraid it will end another part of my life that I never had any part of. Still . . . it's a fantasy to hang on to.

What was my mother? Was she a normal woman who was a victim of war? Was she just a streetwalker? Am I the product of a loving relationship? Am I the product of a rape? What am I?

Part of me doesn't want to know.

• • •

Six years old, and they put me on the airplane by myself, a Pan American clipper with an upper and lower deck. A little circular stairway from top to bottom. It was neat. The stewardesses let me run around, and I got to sit on the pilot's lap. Apparently, I was a cute little kid.

My adoptive father met me at the airport—that was the first time I saw him. Took me to eat. I put mustard on everything. Got introduced to ice cream. Ate ice cream like crazy. You don't get ice cream in orphanages. When I got to my house in the Midwest, I got out of the car and walked to the front door. And there was this great big boxer standing on her four legs, all excited. She licked me in the face, and I went screaming back to the car. I never did bond with my parents. I don't think I ever got close. It was always a stilted, "Give your mother a kiss before bed." That type of relationship.

I had terrible dreams, spectacular dreams, over and over again, of lying on the ground in some sort of gully with a large cat, either a tiger or a lion, on the range above me, getting ready to jump on me. I also had horrible dreams about someone in uniform pushing someone out of a window. It had something to do with a home I was placed in at one time—that part I do remember. I didn't just make that shit up. At six your imagination isn't that well developed.

Since I didn't speak any English, my parents took me to an old lady's farm. She spoke German and English. That fall I spoke English well enough to go to school. I don't remember being teased about an accent. I lost it completely. My ability to blend in as an American might have been different had I spoken with an accent. I was extremely bright as a youngster. Very high IQ. All the time I was growing up, I wanted to be Frank Lloyd Wright. I loved playing Frank Lloyd Wright. I wanted to be an architect. Then somebody told me you had to be a draftsman for some ungodly number of years before they let you start doing your own work. I think that's what put that one under. I've always been into instant gratification.

My parents made some mistakes. I'm sure I did, too. I was pretty bad for a kid, actually. My mother had a collection of mother-of-pearl-handled knives, forks, and spoons on display. I used to steal them, dig in the ground, and lose them. Eventually, she figured out they were gone. They'd ask me if I'd taken them, and I would stand there, bold-faced, and tell them I hadn't. I did a lot of little stuff like that.

My father used to back me into a corner and punch me in the stomach. That was his discipline: one real healthy shot to the stomach, so hard I couldn't breathe. Any time my parents were really mad at me, they'd say: "You could still be in an orphanage in Germany." God only knows how many times I heard that. Sometimes I'd say: "I wish I were." Sometimes I'd feel they didn't want me. A lot of times I felt I wasn't as good as my brother. Because he came from America, it always seemed they liked him better. Now that I'm older, I understand that when you raise somebody from an infant, the bonds are closer. I resented that. I don't think I ever got the attention that an infant does. I craved attention, and I tried to get it at school, either by doing real well or being bad. I did a lot of self-destructive things in my life.

First time I ran away from home was when I was nine or ten. I had horrible handwriting, and my parents used to make me sit and practice handwriting in the summertime. One day I got mad. I got eight miles away. Not bad for a first time. Running away was my reaction to almost everything I didn't like. My father promised me I would get a car when I was sixteen. When I didn't, I hitchhiked to Florida. Got myself a job working in a motel. The fellow in the motel befriended me and had me doing really crummy work. Eventually, he found out who I was, where I was from. One day I picked up an extension phone and heard him talking to my parents. I found out when they were coming down to get me. It was hilarious, because the day they came, I was walking up the street and I saw them drive by the other way.

I hitchhiked up to Georgia. Stayed five or six days. That's the first time in my life I've been so hungry I was begging. Actually walked into a drugstore and asked the fellow there if he had anything I could do to get money for some food. And he did. That man was very nice. Then I stayed in the Salvation Army. After I figured it was long enough for my parents to be gone, I hitchhiked back to Florida. Unbeknownst to me, they had gone to the police and filed for a runaway. The police got me within a day. So I wound up in a jail for a couple of days. My poor parents had to drive all the way back from the Midwest. I thought for sure they were going to be very angry. Turns out they were typical parents: just relieved that I was okay and glad to have me back. Gave me use of a car when I got back.

I stayed home, and outside of a few bouts of going out and drinking beer with the kids, I was pretty good. By the time I was in high school, I was sick of hearing about how smart I was and how much better I should be doing. My IQ is supposedly in the 180 range. I didn't graduate because I muffed somebody's algebra exam. I just didn't bother. Didn't study. Goofed off. This was a class I could get As in if I wanted to. Last day of school they had an assembly for seniors to practice graduation. It was a traumatic day for me. They called out the names of all the people who were going to graduate and had them sit in front of the auditorium. I was sitting in the other section all by myself. The only one.

That afternoon I packed a suitcase, stole a bottle of my father's Canadian Club, and stuck my thumb out. Hitchhiked to some place in Colorado. A fellow picked me up and gave me a ride the rest of the way to the West Coast. I was a little worried. I thought maybe he was gay because he let me stay in his house. After a couple days he said: "Do you know anything about construction—building homes?" So I lied and said: "Sure." He was putting an addition on his house, and I worked for him a couple of months, putting up drywall and doing that kind of work for room and board and a few dollars.

I called my parents and got them to send me the money I'd saved up in the bank. With some young people in the neighborhood I got pretty heavily into drinking and a little bit into drugs. I found out I didn't particularly care for drugs. When the house job got finished, I was getting pretty broke.

The only time I contacted my parents was if I needed something, which was seldom. My mother was a staunch Baptist, who disapproved of the way I lived my life. But for years and years, no matter what happened, my father was always happy to see me. When I went back to the Midwest, I would first go to my cousin, and she would tell my mother and father that I was back. They hated that. I think I used to do it to make them mad and to somehow make them pay for whatever kind of trouble I came home for. They fixed me. Left my brother four times as much as me.

I decided to join the army. My whole idea of getting in the service was to go to Germany, see where I was from. The recruiter promised me I would go to Germany. So naturally they sent me to Texas. After a month and a half I found out that I was not suited at all to military life. Apparently, there's a part of me that isn't *that* German. So I went AWOL. I deserted, basically. Ran away again. They caught me and sentenced me to six months in the stockade. But about that time they figured out that I might be a little bit off because I was saying: "Fine. You can put me in the stockade. I'll get out in six months. As soon as I'm out, I'm off again." After I talked to some army psychologist three or four times, they finally released me on a medical discharge under honorable conditions.

I've been a salesman all my life. I'm good at it. But in the back of my mind are fears that I won't succeed. *You'll fail. You could have done a lot better.* It's been like that all my life. And yet I'm a good salesman. I'm a damn good salesman. I've been married six times. Can you imagine what a selling job that is?

I made a lot of money. Needed a lot of money. I was paying more in child support than most people make. My relationship with my kids is absolutely horrible. I do not miss them. I can honestly say I have no more feeling for them than I would have for a puppy. Actually, I probably might have more for a puppy. I've never tried to understand it. I know that I know how to love. I know that I know how to care about people. I know how to hurt when someone else hurts. But I don't have paternal feelings in me at all. The few times I do talk to my kids, I feel awkward. And I just want to get off the phone as quickly as possible.

I have to turn it on and off when I'm a salesman. I call it a little switch inside. Even during some bad periods—when I come in hungover, or dead tired, or grumpy, or sick—I have a little internal switch I can turn on, do my job. When the customer is gone, I turn it back off again. I have to be nice to people all the time, no matter what. It is hard. And because I have to do that on a daily basis, I'm real selective about whom I talk to in my personal life.

When I was a used-car manager, the new-car manager and I were close friends. But he came up with some rather tasteless jokes: "Kurt's lampshades break out in prickly heat in the summertime." "Kurt's the only guy I know who has showerheads in his living room." That was the closest I've ever come to having anyone even tease me about being German. We're not a very funny people, actually. I hardly know any German jokes. They make jokes about Polacks, about Italians, about Mexicans.

Customers have to like you. That's the most important thing. The other most important thing is that they have enough confidence in you to believe you know what you're doing. Very poor people to do business with are doctors, lawyers. Because they are so full of self-importance that they think everybody owes them something for nothing. I won't even wait on an Oriental. They always want something for nothing. They ask how much a car is. You say: "Nine thousand dollars." They go: "Ha ha ha ha! I give you six." *Six! Get the hell out of here!* I hate waiting on what we call dots. Indians from India. The dot on their forehead. Hate them for two reasons: they smell bad, and they do the same thing the Orientals do. Never offer you a fair profit. Certain cultures, used to bargaining for everything, come to this country and try to bargain unreasonably because they don't know where to stop.

Never had a problem with blacks. Hated Jews. I mean, cheapest people in the world. Buy the consumer guides and tell you how much your car costs and how much they will pay you. *No.* Nobody tells me how much I'm going to sell a car for. I determine that—not the customer. *Out!* The Jewish people as a people—with some exceptions—are horrible to do business with.

Sometimes I joke—not very well, either—and then I always hate myself. Because then I see or read something. I've read everything there is to read about the Holocaust, World War II. Trying to find out why Germans, as a people that I love, let themselves be led like sheep. I have some understanding of it. I could never understand it totally, but then I wasn't there. Why we allowed ourselves to degenerate to that status. To burn books. To put up with that kind of shit. I love books. I mean, books are my best outlet. Under normal circumstances I read a book a day.

As a race we were pretty damn smart, but we must have been pretty damn stupid to let that happen. I always wanted to go back to Germany just to see and talk to people and find out how much they actually knew. There's been a lot of TV stuff done about it. They all claim they didn't know. I mean, they all were real blind, didn't see the smoke, couldn't smell it, couldn't see the trains going through town? Blaming the Jews for all their misfortunes. Sort of infuriating.

I have to admit I can't understand a race that would let itself be loaded into cattle cars and shoved off to ovens. The
same people that went to Israel and fought the British and
Arabs. One of the best fighting forces in the world. Piled on
boats, fled the country, gave up everything. You wonder
whether that's strength of conviction or if there isn't some in-
herently stupid gene. How could people be that gullible?
"We're going to relocate you." *Yeah.* "Meanwhile, let me have
your suitcase." "Put an armband on you." If somebody came
and threatened me, they'd have a hard time getting me. It's
that simple. I'm not a sheep.

As a people, Germans have gone through a lot of strange
things. Having some wacky little short Austrian take over a
whole country . . . It's absolutely amazing how he engineered
it. Makes you wonder how people can do that. Then you start
watching the way things are going in this country. We're going
to legislate ourselves into the same position. I watch what's
happening with our gun laws, and there are some interesting
parallels. In the thirties, Hitler wrote a long paper about dis-
arming the citizenry prior to taking control of the country.
Then you pass laws to control them, making more and more
things illegal. We're doing it here. I'm a very avid gunner. I
can shoot three shots into less than an inch at a hundred
yards. I like guns as pieces of intricate machinery. To take
them apart and put them back together. To polish your skills
at being able to shoot that one-inch group.

I'm not a survivalist. I'm not a skinhead. I'm not a neo-
Nazi.

I'm not particularly politically active. I voted the first time
this year in twenty-five years because I'm tired of watching our
liberties being taken away. There are intelligent people in this
country who are listening to all the different reasons why we
should outlaw guns. But these same intelligent people don't
pay any attention to history. Karl Marx wrote about it. Lenin

wrote about it. I find it extremely hard to believe they can shove this whole gun control thing down our throats. The only people you're going to stop from having assault weapons are people who would obey the law anyway. Stop and think about it. Is a criminal going to let a law stop him? *No.*

People either don't think, they're brainwashed, or they have this natural fear of guns. A gun can't kill. A gun can't kill anybody. I can put a loaded gun on this table, and if neither one of us picks it up, it will never hurt anybody. It can't do anything by itself. It needs a person. It needs a human being. It needs our temper, our repressed desire to kill. Without that, it can't kill.

I can kill you with a fork, break this glass.

Seems every time I got into a relationship with someone— if it got very good and things got going real smoothly—I would do just about anything to jeopardize it. Impulsively spend money. Run up bills. Drink a lot. I think there's a little mechanism inside me that used to figure out what button to push to really make somebody mad or want to leave. And then I would push it. I was pretty smart that way.

My first wife was a waitress. She claimed I got her pregnant, so I wound up marrying her. I came home one night from work, and she was gone, running around till all hours on me. So I left her. That was one of the few I ever left. The child wasn't born yet.

I met wife number two at a party. She had just graduated from college. Moved in with her and her parents, which at the time was very permissive. She got pregnant. We got married. We had a daughter. We were married for a couple of years. Lived in a house trailer. I started fooling around. One day I came home and she was gone. I was pissed off! I dusted her. I blew her off. Very low period in my life. Lived in a shitty studio-type apartment, where the sofa made into a bed. You go out and drink for a long time, and then you stay home and feel sorry for yourself.

I met some girl and took her out to dinner one night. It was pretty funny. There was this absolutely drop-dead gorgeous hostess. So I proceed to get my date drunk. While she was in the bathroom throwing up, I got the hostess's name and address. I wound up marrying her. That was number three. A very hot and cold relationship. We wound up having four kids—the two she already had, and then I had two more with her. We were poor. I mean, kids will drain you. Things were going smoothly, but I started drinking heavily, and my partying got out of control. My wife finally said: "You have to move out."

I wound up meeting some other woman and living with her for two years. She was eleven years older than I. All this time I was working in a car dealership. One night this young lady came in looking for a car. All the salesmen ran in the other direction, saying: "She's by herself. She's going to need to bring a boyfriend, a husband, a father, somebody who can buy a car." I said: "Okay, I'll fix you guys." I sold her a car and checked her credit—obviously for financing. She had her own house and was making thirty-some thousand dollars. *Good prospect.* I called her up and asked her out. Got married two months later. Agreed not to have any children. Doesn't she get pregnant? She was on the pill. I'm still paying child support for that kid we agreed not to have.

When my two sales managers hired this real pretty girl, I told them: "You're crazy. You can't hire a girl that good-looking for the showroom. It's just going to cause trouble." I was right. I married her. That particular time I thought I was doing everything right. I think I was smothering her. We were married for about a year and a half, and then she did one of these: *I love you, but I can't live with you,* and moved out. I was very much in love, and that was the most painful breakup I ever had. Started drinking real heavy again. I finally went and got some real good therapy. He put me on sedatives because I was pretty torn up. He asked a lot of questions that nobody had bothered asking before. Getting out all the things about the orphanage and having been adopted before. Family background. The way I grew up. We found out one of the reasons I got married so many times is because I kept rejecting relationships. Possibly going back, way back to the orphanage time.

This wife's my sixth. My sixth and last. I met her through a friend of hers. She's taught me to like some things that she likes. She's learned to shoot and to ride a motorcycle. We're very happy together. Once in a while, we get angry with each other for some dumb thing, but it doesn't last very long. I almost like myself. Turned out to be a halfway decent person. As a husband, I know who I am: I come home, I clean up the kitchen, I do the dishes, I cook, I help clean the house. I do more than my half or better. I'm working real hard at making this work. At this point I have to. I don't feel I need to push her away. I don't feel threatened by her. I don't feel she's going to leave. I don't feel I have to leave. I hope it sticks. Shoot, I'm not getting any younger. God forbid something happens with this. Then what do I do? I'm forty-eight years old. I can't do this again—I really can't.

I don't think anybody can do anything to me that I haven't already done to myself. Put me in jail? Shoot me? That's been done. Take my money away? That's been done. I have very few fears left. The only thing I'm afraid of is something happening to my wife. That's my only fear right now—this horrible fear of being alone.

If you take a pad and put the good things on one side and the bad things on the other side, I didn't do too good. I really didn't. I'm not exactly a shining example of the super race that I came from. I have never been to Germany. I've wanted to go, to see the Germany that I came from. Very frankly, I've never been able to afford to go. I've always been a little bit proud that I'm German. I'm also a little bit proud that I'm a naturalized American. People think it's neat that I came here from Germany, neat that I was adopted. I don't really think of myself as anything but American, but somewhere along the line I think of myself as somewhat of a German. I'm very orderly. I'm good with numbers. I attribute that to being German. I'm curious about machines, weapons, airplanes. I tell myself that's a German trait.

The Germany I was born into in 1946 was the Germany of World War II. I was *not* a product of postwar Germany. I was a product of Germany at a time of war. The war had not ended. *No.* The only part that ended in 1945 was the hostilities. The Russians and the Americans were still struggling over lines of demarcation. The German people were just learning to deal with occupation, and the occupiers were just learning to deal with being occupiers. The American and Russian soldiers were just coming down from the four-or-five-year high of killing and fighting and being lucky to be alive.

I am literally a survivor of World War II. I didn't have to live through it—but I lived through the aftermath. Being from Germany has an awful lot to do with what happened to the rest of my life: being in an orphanage, being bounced around for years, being unloved. Some of it still affects me almost every day. Those first six years—they set a pattern for how I managed my life up till about three years ago.

I'll never have the self-confidence that my skill sets should provide me with. It's very hard to overcome darn near forty years of deliberately doing things wrong to avoid pain. It's been havoc. You run from relationships so *you* can determine when the pain comes rather than having it come as a surprise. You control the timing of the hurt. You know it's coming, but if you can control *when* it's coming, you have at least some degree of control.

Every once in a while I have dreams that I can will myself to fly. Not like Superman. I have dreams where I have enough brainpower to overcome gravity. You can send for the white coats now! I'm serious. I haven't had these dreams very often lately, but I still have them once in a while where I'm able, just by thinking, to come up off the ground. Oh, it's a great dream! I just wish, I really wish, I could do it.

They could put me in the New Jersey Home for the Totally Fucked. One way or another, I think my brain has been pretty badly scrambled. Usually by myself. Or perceptions. Sure, it scares me. I have wanted to quit. Often. I've wanted to run away. There have been periods of self-doubt, self-criticism, and self-loathing when I've contemplated giving up. I've attempted suicide. I've got a nice, neat bullet hole to prove it. Ironically, I bought a Walther P-38 German World War II weapon and shot myself with it. In the side. Right straight through. I missed. Somehow, my brain took over and didn't let me get myself in the heart. I was aiming at low in my chest, but when I pulled the trigger, I moved it.

After I shot myself, my parents took me to the VA hospital. Believe it or not, a panel of seven or eight psychiatrists determined that I was a sociopath and that I have absolutely no conscience whatsoever.

I laughed at them.

Marika

Born: 1941
Age at time of immigration: 22

I Need to Survive Again

I tried to be the good daughter and do what's right. But
deep down is a very deep distrust. My mother wanted a boy.
She kept a diary when she was pregnant, which she let me
read after I had my first child. She was a horsewoman, and I
apparently was very much alive and kicking. She thought this
was just going to be a great horseman she was raising in the
womb. She was so disappointed when I was born, and she
could not bring herself to accept the fact that I was a girl for
the longest time.

She told me this—sort of laughingly. I was still a child.

For three weeks my mother would say to the nanny, "I wonder if *he* is still asleep. Do you want to check on *him*?" Until the
nurse finally said: "You need to get used to the fact that you
have a little girl there."

This rejection stayed with me for the rest of my life. I felt I
was second-rate, and I turned into a sickly, sullen child who
became aloof. My mother didn't get it, you know, what children need. When my son was a year old, she visited in Amer-

ica. My son was not an easy child: he would bang his head against the wall or the floor—terrific temper tantrums—and my mother said to me: "You know, Marika, I can really understand your disappointment in this child. I went through the same kind of thing."

But I was happy to have him.

My grandparents and parents were hardworking, successful. When I look at pictures of the way they lived—hunting parties and orange trees, leather wallpaper and crystal chandeliers—I see real luxury and elegance and a sense of having arrived. My mother went to a finishing school, where she learned how to manage a big estate. They had a lot of servants. Obviously, when the war started, all of that changed, and everything fell apart in Germany, especially in those parts in the East.

I once found a bookmark at my parents' house. It was parchment, and on it in beautiful calligraphy it said: *Meine Ehre ist Treue*—My honor is loyalty. I thought my father had given this to my mother—a true sign of love. I was so disappointed when I found out it was a Nazi slogan. They all had to swear allegiance to Hitler with that kind of sentence.

From what little I know, my parents did not think too much of Hitler and his consorts. For example, they did not greet each other with *"Heil Hitler."* My mother did not join the *BDM,* the female version of the Hitler Youth. When all the women were parading in their uniforms with flags and marching bands, she had to walk by herself at the end.

My father stayed out of the war for a long time because he did not believe in that effort. He said: "I need to be in Germany and help grow crops to feed the population." He wanted boys to follow in his footsteps, take over the farm. He employed about 150 people and founded a private kindergarten for all the kids on the farm—very progressive, in that sense. He also built an air-raid shelter for everybody. The planes that came from Britain—getting ready to bomb places like Berlin—would go straight over our farm. A lot of my memories are of confusion, anxiety, fear of being grabbed in the middle of the night and running to the air-raid shelter.

In September 1944 my father got drafted, went through basic training, and hated every moment of it. He got sent to the front in Czechoslovakia, got shot in the arm, and was overjoyed. He said: "If that's all it takes, I can now go home and plant my crops." When he was taken to a British internment camp, my mother didn't know where he was.

Things really became chaotic toward the end of the war. My mother took in a lot of wounded people—refugees and evacuated people from Berlin. That part of Germany was going to be Communist, and people were trying to get her out so they could divide it up and make it state-owned property. When she refused to leave, they put her in jail. I remember having a temper tantrum because I wanted to see my mom. A child knows very little and feels afraid. In any case, my mother came to her senses in jail. We moved westward. My sister was still in diapers. We were two and four years old. That trek through bombed-out Germany lasted a long time . . . from one friend and relative to another, not knowing where we'd go, if we'd ever find my father again. Wherever you went, you weren't wanted. You were just a refugee.

I remember walking over a bridge in Bremen and seeing smoke and craters and debris . . . all these things you see in the movies. Slowly, we made our way west. Walking. And trains. Being in some sort of cattle car. And under trains—just as in the movie *Germany Pale Mother,* where the mother is under a train with the child. When my mother tried to get the two of us under the train, we were incredibly afraid of falling from the crossbars onto the tracks.

By that time the Russians had come in—or somebody like Russians in uniform. I remember being in a car with my mother. Outside stood one of these soldiers, barking commands. Since we always heard, "The Russian is going to come," I asked my mother if this was *the Russian*. To me, he was *the Russian*. He showed up in some of my nightmares later on in various disguises, hounding, pursuing, threatening me. *The Russian*. Much later I had a dream of being in an empty room on the second floor, and *the Russian* showed up outside the window, getting ready to come in and get me. He didn't have a face. It was only this figure, this threatening body in a uniform.

After I was ten, I had to ride my bike to school, and I often was afraid of being assaulted. Our generation is scarred for life. We were all shaped by this fear that is unnamed, probably transferred from grown-ups, who were afraid and unable to explain to children what was happening. It shows up in your dreams. I had another nightmare where *the Russian* was sitting by the side of the road in uniform, twirling a knife on his index finger, looking at me as I was coming with my bike. This one had a face. I hate to tell you—in my memory, it happened to be a Jewish face, the stereotype Jewish face that a lot of people identified.

The anti-Semitism that bothers me a lot was never clearly stated. I think a lot of Germans, not just the people in my family, are anti-Semitic. You grow up with it, and it's an unspoken condition. I don't know if that will ever go away. Even now I get very upset when I have conversations with my mother, because over the years I've tried to educate my parents. I've given her things to read, and she'll give me an example that "something was in the Jewish character," or "this was typically Jewish." As if it were a justification for somebody like·her to generalize that way.

We as Germans have lost all rights to make statements like that. I do not want to hear that from anybody because these kinds of statements don't have any kind of validity. It doesn't matter to me that there are Jewish people who may make Jewish jokes. *I* don't want to listen to Jewish jokes. I work very hard to overcome this blatant anti-Semitism I was brought up with. It's part of my education in this country, part of the Americanization of me, that I've learned to be more tolerant of other people's beliefs, of other races. Less generalizing about the Germans, the Americans, the Japanese, the Mexicans.

It's part of the reason I left Germany—that intolerance and arrogance and this impression that I was brought up with that people like us were better than others. I really reject that now. For example, I was not encouraged to play with certain girls in my school because they had Polish names. It's so stupid. Living in isolation, I was hungry for friends. It was a matter of class—not a matter of accomplishment, intelligence, or good qualities. It was not a matter of money, because I grew up in absolute poverty, but always with the idea that you can do better than that. You *are* better than that. I've very much tried to overcome this. I don't know how much I succeeded, because there are times, still, that I have to fight this certain arrogance in me as a German.

My mother, sister, and I ended up in a town by the North Sea with my father's sister at the end of 1945. The first time I saw an orange was in that town when a whole box of oranges washed on shore. They told me oranges were wonderful, and I wanted to taste one. It was full of salt water.

My mother learned to tend sheep and milk cows to make herself useful. She felt unwelcome and didn't know where my father was. She still has lots of bitter memories. *You have nothing—you are nothing.* This whole idea of loss—loss of home, of livelihood—this unsettled state of being, of being displaced, creates a deep sense of insecurity in people. At least it did in me. Insecurity about the future. You never know what is going to happen, even if things go better. You don't know if this is going to last.

My father got released from the British internment camp after close to a year. He had developed some illness like rheumatoid arthritis, and they couldn't treat him. Since the camp was in northern Germany, he decided to call his sister, and it was my mother who answered the telephone. That was the most wonderful thing that happened to my family in those times. Of the people I grew up with and went to school with, I'm the only one who had a father. All other fathers were gone and lost—missing in action, killed in the war, died in prison, died from illnesses due to the war.

This image will be forever in my mind: my father getting off the train on crutches, completely bandaged up. It was April 12, 1946, two days before my fifth birthday, and he was just so happy. He always reminded me that two days before my birthday he came home—just in time for my birthday. I wanted to be close to my father. I adored him, I idolized him, I loved him. He was distant—not very emotional. His mother died when he was very young, and he just didn't have that kind of nurturing himself. He was an emotional cripple. He was nice, congenial, caring in practical ways—but not affectionate, not loving.

My relationship with my parents is very complicated. Both ways. And the relationship between my mother and my father was also very complicated. They were married for fifty-three years, but they weren't very compatible. My mother was twenty-two when she married my father, and really naive. She was very much in love with him, but she was full of insecurities and never felt he really loved her. For one thing, he never told her. For a while it was like "Well, that I married you—that should tell you." She suffered from that all her life. For my father a lot of things were unspoken. The last ten years of his life were almost unbearable for my mother, but she stuck it out because she'd made that vow.

After we spent some time by the North Sea, my father found a farm to rent. We all worked on the farm, even as children, after school. To keep us entertained, my mother would tell us stories about the olden days. They always began with the word *früher*—before. "Before the war . . ." There seemed to be this division between our daily life and memories that my mother wanted to relate to us. The two didn't seem to have much to do with each other.

Our little farmhouse had one room with a fireplace in the middle. One part was for humans; the other part was for the animals. It was primitive, at the end of the world in a nature preserve on a river. Idyllic, but completely isolated. For my mother it was almost unbearable: she'd grown up with servants in uniforms and white gloves, and here she was on her knees in the fields, trying to clear them from weeds and bugs. My father adjusted more easily because he was basically an optimist; he also didn't have to deal with the day-to-day hardship of the children, the cleaning, the people who moved into our house because they didn't have anyplace else: my grandparents who'd lost their home, uncles of various kinds, and refugees from Silesia. Some of them helped. At times twenty people lived in this little farmhouse and bunked in the attic that stored grain. Also rats and mice.

We children didn't have rooms of our own. From the time my brother was born in 1949—I was eight—until 1954, I slept between my parents. I hated it. I could not move left or right. My mother probably was using that as some type of birth control. She had given my father the heir he'd always wanted, their little crown prince who was supposed to follow in my father's footsteps, and she didn't want to have any more children.

My father had a childhood friend, a womanizer and drinker, and at the same time a well-loved, competent physician. One night he got drunk, and they put him into my father's bed. Of course, I was there. And he didn't know what he was doing. He turned over and started some sort of molestation. He didn't get far because he was too drunk. I was probably lying very still, thinking: *I hope this will pass.* The next thing I knew, he turned to the other side and threw up.

• • •

When my mother had been on the farm by herself in East Germany, one of the wounded people was a young man, Franz, who'd been close to an exploding mine and had lost his hearing. Though he wasn't useful in the war effort anymore, he was a good worker and had learned to read lips. Toward the end of the war Franz came running to my mother, very disturbed, and communicated that an empty railroad car had shown up at the farm. He yelled: "There's this railroad car with the sign AUSCHWITZ on it." Since he'd been on the front, he must have known something. My mother said: "I don't know why you're so excited." She had no idea. I believe that because it rings true to me.

He knew.

She didn't.

Franz also showed up at our farm in West Germany. He was a great hero of mine. To get to the village where I went to a two-room schoolhouse, I had to be taken across the river in a boat. My father did that. The winter of 1947 was harsh—lots of ice and flooding and snow—and that boat got loose. Franz jumped into this ice-cold water and got our boat. He was secretly in love with my mother. I don't think she was in love with him—she was in love with my father. When it became known in 1948 that she was pregnant with my brother, Franz went into the attic where he lived and hanged himself. Nobody told us what had happened to him. I remember a wagon . . . a horse in front . . . and I remember straw and something on it leaving our farm.

Something terrible had happened, and Franz was gone.

My mother was very distraught. I remember crying. To my mother, crying is a sign of weakness; you never let anybody see that, and you don't tolerate it in others. Especially not in me. And I cried easily. Franz was buried in a cemetery, and she took care of his grave for a long time. It was a sad and confusing time.

I was probably twelve, picking beans with my grandmother, when she let it slip out that Franz had hanged himself. I said: "*Oma,* what are you saying?" And she said: "Oh, I bet I wasn't supposed to say anything." You know, part of this silence: *You have to keep it from them.* But you don't really. You make it worse because what you imagine as a child is often a lot worse than reality.

My parents only talked about selected things and left out a lot. It always came down to how much the people had suffered, how much better it had been before the war, and how much worse off they were now. This idea—*we're really in bad shape, but it used to be better, and who knows what's going to happen in the future*—was very important to me. I don't know how much they knew about the war. I didn't think there was anything my father was hiding. When I said "What did you do in the war?" he would tell me about basic training and that he'd made some friends, about the internment camp and how he organized lectures. He never talked about anything that was serious or painful or controversial.

My mother mourned for the good old life. As time went on, less and less was said about those times before or during the war. Things were too busy: looking to the future; making a better life. They wanted to put all of that behind them. Very quickly. And not much was said in school. It wasn't until I was in my late teens that I understood a little more about what had gone on and read books.

Without saying anything, my mother let me know that sex was a shameful, taboo thing. We always were made to wash our hands first thing in the morning in case we had touched ourselves down there. In me this kind of fear was so strong that I never did explore myself and never did learn how to climax until I was well into my thirties.

The other taboo was the suicides in my immediate family. My godmother killed herself and nobody talked about it. My mother's brother killed himself. He'd spent four years in Siberia and he'd come home a broken man. And my grandmother, who was eighty-five, completely healthy and sane, felt she had lived a long life. She systematically divided her possessions and wrote farewell letters. She probably still had some cyanide, the way a lot of people had after the war—just in case the Russians came or in case they'd get raped.

These things were all kept from us. In my mother's case, it's a matter of controlling people. When you keep information from somebody, it's a way of asserting your power. My mother was a real master at that: "Children are better off not knowing."

Once I became interested in boys, nobody was good enough for my parents. That became a great source of conflict. I turned openly and secretly rebellious, lying, going off with a boyfriend. But my mother was always a step ahead of me, a lot sneakier than I was. She was very violent. I got beaten with a riding crop so that I had big welts on the back of my thighs. It was her temper. It was her frustration. It was her helplessness. It was her fear. My father did not beat us unless she told him to do it. It was awful . . . embarrassing actually.

She was quick with a fist . . . anything . . . a hairbrush. And she would threaten me: "If you see this boy one more time, I'm going to take a shotgun and you won't be able to creep anymore." And I believed it. *Ja.* She was a physically big woman with a man's shoulders, the waist slim, a hunter's daughter. If there was a rat in the barn and she had boots on, she'd stomp it to death and grind it into the dirt. We shot a lot of rats. We'd go to the chicken coop together, she with her shotgun.

Once she went out in the hall and got her gun from the rack. I thought she was getting ready to shoot me, and she said: "No, not yet." But this idea that, if I misbehaved one more time . . . I was pretty scared. She was unpredictable. And if I ever had notions of telling anybody about it, it was, "Don't soil your own nest."

I got very sick emotionally. It manifested itself in physical illnesses nobody could diagnose—hives and eczema and allergy attacks—and I got sent from one skin doctor to another. I was taken to the hospital with palpitations and hives all over me. I was almost incapacitated for several years. Once my mother said: "Maybe that's all the evil coming out of you." I have never forgotten. This idea that you are an evil child—I don't know whether I believed it. I may have thought there was something to it. But I think in the back of my mind there was a tiny voice—it got tinier and tinier—that said: *It ain't so.*

I had eczema until I was twenty-two and decided to go to America. It was the best decision I ever made. I went to my professor, a Jew who had spent quite a number of years in America, and he gave me the addresses of a few people. I got accepted at this small college in Wisconsin. My parents didn't give me any travel money. They weren't exactly against it, but they didn't see the sense of it. I got a travel grant.

America was the great liberation. I woke up and was reborn when I came to America. Those skin diseases cleared up. It was psychological. After being an outsider all my life, I felt accepted right away by my professors, by the other students who took me home to meet their parents. I could not believe that there was actually a large group of people who could be so genuinely accepting of me, nurturing me in subtle ways. I've had more wonderful, interesting conversations because I speak with an accent. People want to know where you're from, and they tell you their background.

My dorm room was very bare because I'd come with a suitcase. One day some of the girls distracted me: "Come on over to the Student Union, have a coke . . . listen to some music." After an hour I came back, and they had redecorated my room with peacock feathers and maps and posters.

My first two years in America were essentially the happiest years of my life. I became a different person. This shy, withdrawn, self-conscious little speck on this earth became a person. I still have problems with self-esteem, and I still have the feeling that I have to prove myself in big ways, but I'm a lot more outgoing. I discovered that I can be funny . . . charming . . . that people are generally interested in what I have to say or how I feel.

My first year in college we were studying Kafka. I felt uncomfortable and nervous. I was very aware of what the Nazis had done, and of how much that played a part in my feeling guilty as a German, even though I really didn't have anything to do with it. But that feeling was there. And it's completely irrational. Not healthy and not entirely sane. I don't know why I feel that way. I do know that people who are younger definitely do not have that guilt or shame to live with.

Of course, when I was still in Germany, it wasn't that much of an issue. But by the time I got to America, I felt there was something not entirely positive about being German. I don't have much emotional connection to Germany anymore. Once my mother passes on, I probably won't go back. I've been very happy as a German in America. To be an outsider in Germany is not a good thing. Having been a refugee there, I know what it means to be spat at or discriminated against.

Here people appreciate you. Right away there is a connection that is friendly and open. I've lived here for thirty-one years, and I lived in Germany for twenty-two. I am probably very German, with certain German characteristics and the strong German accent. I'm German by passport. But I feel much more American now than German. I have a hard time separating the two. It's me—and part of me is American.

An administrator at the college fell in love with me and wanted to marry me. He was a fascinating, intelligent man, and I learned a lot from him, but it was difficult to live a normal life with him. He was an alcoholic, and he was very abusive. Perhaps if you were beaten as a child, being loved also meant getting beaten up. I didn't tell anybody about it. It was long before times of shelters, women's groups, TV programs about domestic violence. The few times I carefully sought help, my attempts were squelched, and so I stayed—much too long.

You live with this hope that if you make things right and if you don't make any mistakes and if you love this person enough, things will get settled down, change for the better. But I recognized after a while that things wouldn't get better. He did not like the fact that I wanted to work. He hated my friends, my family. He wanted me all to himself. And when my son, Andrew, was born, he was very jealous. I thought many nights that I would not wake up alive. The beatings were that severe. My son—for the first six years of his life—witnessed far too much violence and discord. Yet, I didn't know a way out because everybody I consulted, including lawyers, said: "You'll get sued for willful desertion." "You'll lose your child." "You'll lose any kind of support."

I got more and more withdrawn. At the same time, people admired us and thought we were just the most glamorous, accomplished couple—elegant, dashing, exquisite cars, interesting trips, wonderful stories to tell. . . . We built a house together on a lovely piece of property with a view, and I thought I would spend the rest of my life there. I put in a vegetable garden and flower beds, put a lot of love into the decorating. We presented this beautiful picture. Inside, I was dead. I can look at photos of me now and see in my eyes this scared, sad woman, who had so much potential and was trapped. No support. No friends. I hid the bruises.

Finally, it got so bad that I thought for sure that I wouldn't survive. My husband had bought himself a gun and he'd joke to people that he was going to do target practice and then try it out on his wife. Eventually, I got out. Then, of course, I had to go through a year of living in an apartment with him banging on the door, screaming and yelling. My son and I lived alone. We had a pretty good time together, and got our life back in order. I have a little piece of paper Andrew wrote in first grade. It says: *I live in a better house now.*

My life has turned around in such a way that I can now talk about it. I don't want anybody to think: *Boy, she must be really stupid or masochistic to have stayed there.* It would have been better if I'd left earlier, but I didn't see the way out until the time I went. I've made my peace. I can look back and say: *This was part of it. I've learned from it. I'll never let this happen again. Ever. Nobody's going to mistreat me or trample on me ever again.* And it's something that I've had to go through to learn.

I'm not angry. Anger is not something I want to feel. I very consciously do not want to be angry. It's more sadness or feeling sorry for the guy. Although it's difficult to recognize that there was somebody who had so much power over me. *Ja.* But then my parents had a lot of power over me, too.

I learned from my childhood and from that experience not to mistreat my child. I made a conscious effort not to repeat the mistakes my mother made with me. Not only did I plan and want this child, I made it quite clear in my mind that I accepted it whether it was a boy or a girl. When he was born, it took a day or two before I felt comfortable enough to hold him. He seemed so fragile at first. But it didn't take long before I had a close relationship with him. I tried not to punish him unnecessarily, not to be unreasonable with him, and to love him the way he was, hoping he'd turn into a happy, self-confident child.

It didn't happen that way, but I tried.

I know now that the conflict and anxiety in me and in our home carried over to him. From the time he was about one year old, he started punishing himself. He would bang his head against the wall. When he was two, I started taking him to a child psychiatrist, even though Germans think psychoanalysts are evil shrinks to be avoided at all costs. She observed him playing with toys, and she told me he was sensitive. Even then I didn't feel comfortable telling her what was going on in our home. When I saw her again after the divorce, she said: "I wish you had told me. I would have understood much better what Andrew was going through."

He saw a lot of violence against me that he couldn't understand. I would run out of the house and he'd run after me, screaming because he thought I was running away. But I was trying to run away from the horror. He saw too much. Real scars there. And even though I tried to protect him from that, it's still real. He still lived with it.

He told a friend: "My father beat my mom and broke her body. He broke her body."

Luckily, I got married again, to a man who is kind and tolerant. James was happy to help me raise Andrew. They would go and see these movies that I don't like to see, like *Raiders of the Lost Ark,* get a few kids together and have pizza or go camping. We put our family back together. The first years in school were quite happy for Andrew. The teachers liked him and said he was a unique child. I was so proud. I thought he was on the right track. You know, when you're still full of hope . . .

The four years we had together were peaceful and quiet. When we left the area, I cried for months because I was so depressed. But my husband needed to move on. I've been wondering if for Americans moving is a much more accepted way of getting ahead. This loss of your home—I don't know if I'll ever get over that. I very much want to be settled, and I suffer about leaving behind friends and a house where I've lived. It probably goes back to the original loss of our family farm, leaving under horrible circumstances. And some survived, and some finally got to our place, and some were lost forever.

I felt very guilty leaving Andrew behind in boarding school. At the time it seemed like the right decision, but it was probably a mistake, even though his own father was there.

When Andrew turned thirteen, puberty started and all hell broke loose. He was rebelling against the neglect from his father. In all the years, Andrew spent one whole week with his father on a vacation. The rest of the time he was with us. Our lives always revolved around his schedule. I would go to Germany with him, send him to Germany, or we'd go on trips together. But his father did not care about that very much. This kind of rejection is very difficult for a child.

Andrew got into drugs when he was about fifteen, even though we had talked openly about the dangers, and once that happened, he was pretty much lost to us. I still kept trying to reach him even after he got arrested. He felt so bad. He said: "I don't deserve to come and spend Christmas with you." And I said: "You're our son, and we would like you here, and we'll spend Christmas together." That was the last time I had a good conversation with him.

I tried to figure out why he was so angry and rebellious, and I reached out to him no matter what he said and how offended I got. I tried to show him in daily life that man and wife can get along. My present husband and I are very kind to each other, affectionate. We talk quietly about how to handle things. There is no arguing, yelling, or throwing of dishes. Sometimes we may disagree, but we settle that with reasonable words. That didn't seem to make much of an impression on Andrew. He had a hard time controlling himself. Once he took a knife and went through several layers of bed covers, quilt, and mattress into the wooden part of a platform bed. I took all the knives away from him. I was very afraid of him. There were times when I wondered . . . you know, you read about kids like that killing their parents when they're asleep in bed.

James felt terrible because he knew how much I was suffering, and I felt very helpless. Until two years ago, when we still were behind Andrew—writing, calling, making sure that we knew where he was—I thought things would turn around for him, that he would come to his senses and with graduation and his probation being over, get into a direction where he would find a job and settle down.

Once he severed his ties with us, I kept waiting to hear from him. During holidays especially because they always meant a lot to him . . . Christmas, birthdays, Mother's Day. But after a year or so, you don't wait for it anymore. It was very difficult for me, but I pushed it out of my mind as something I would think about later. It's really sad. You bring this child into this world, and you really want it and spend all these years trying, really trying your best, loving him and caring for him in significant ways, making sure you do things right. And then to lose him . . .

It's not that he died, which would be terrible enough if you had to deal with the death of a child—lots of people have to do that—but not knowing what's happening to him.

If you let yourself, you fall apart, and you don't want to do that because you want to live. It's not going to help him if you fall apart. It's not going to help him if you worry a lot. It's not going to make things better to torture yourself. I mustn't let it get to me now because I have a job, I have a house, I have to survive. I am happy that I survived. I mean, I could be dead like Nicole Simpson. It was that kind of relationship with my first husband. And I need to survive again in a different way.

My life now is fairly orderly, but my son is missing. For the longest time I did not feel the need to find out where he was. I had a vague idea that he was in Maine, where he was last seen. I thought: *Maybe he's settled someplace working. He just hasn't gotten very far, and so he doesn't have anything much to report about. Eventually, I'll hear from him.* In my heart I always knew he's still alive or I would know about it. I would know somehow.

A few months ago James found an address in Maine through a computer program. We located Andrew, but then he bolted again because he was probably afraid that it wasn't we who were looking for him, but the police. Now it's almost more difficult for me to accept that I don't know where he is and what he's doing. *What's he thinking about? Does he even remember? Would it even occur to him that—if he were in really bad shape—he can call us and we can get him?*

There are times I wish I had certainty one way or the other, including that I would know if he were dead because then I could really, really grieve for him. Right now this grief is very undefined. It's the uncertainty that's much more pronounced, not knowing what's going on with him, and having dreams that he's come home and I'm just overjoyed. He seems healthy, but when I wake up, I have to confront this horrible fact that he isn't there. You dream that he's still little and you can hold him, or that somebody tells you: "Oh no, he's not in Maine. He moved on to so-and-so and he's doing such-and-such and don't worry about him." Or you have this nightmare where he's lying in the gutter or in some doorway, hungry, sick . . . broken bones, broken nose . . . teeth knocked out. I keep thinking about his teeth because we spent so much money on having them fixed, thousands on braces, and once all of that was done, he had such a handsome smile. But he wouldn't smile very often. Only when he was caught unawares. I keep thinking about that.

I don't know if I'll ever see Andrew again. I don't know what he's thinking. I don't know if his mind is gone. I would very much like to talk to him, and if not talk to him, perhaps just see him to see that he's okay.

That he's still alive.

When I was baptized in 1941 at my parents' home, things were still the way they used to be in the old days. It was in June or July—a lovely day—and my whole family was there. A movie was made of that, three or four minutes at most, jiggly black and white, not focused very well, but it tells me a lot. Everybody's very elegant in tuxedos and evening gowns even though it's late afternoon. I recognize cousins and aunts and uncles and grandparents and my father and my mother. What is significant to me is that my mother is walking with a friend, both in their splendid evening gowns, while I am held by a nanny. My mother is not holding me. To me that is almost symbolic. Here my mother is walking with a friend along these garden paths that are beautifully raked. And everybody is seen. Toward the end the nanny comes. And I'm in *her* arms.

Heinrich

Born: 1939
Age at time of immigration: 14

Playing in Bomb Craters

We had a dog, a German shepherd. His name was Nero. Good watchdog. One time he just bowled me over, chasing me and licking me. That dog loved to dive into the cold water in early spring when the ice was breaking, chase those floating chunks of ice as they were drifting down the river, and try to drag them back to shore. That dog was actually drafted into the war. And he was killed. My parents got an official notification that he died with honors.

I hate to think what that dog was being used for.

I was born in Malapane-Antonia which originally was Germany and now is part of Poland. My parents could speak Polish, and as a child I could understand Polish but not speak it. There was a bit of strife and conflict, the ethnic type of separation. Yet at the same time, Germans married Poles, and Poles married Germans. It was a small farming community. Huge linden trees shaded everything. We had fruit trees in front. When you came into the front yard, the first thing you saw was the *Misthaufen*—manure pile. We had a couple of cows and goats and hogs. It was not a large farm but enough to sustain us. In the woods behind us, my mother used to gather mushrooms, big *Steinpilze* and *Pfifferlinge*—boletes and chanterelles. Blueberries. And of course, the fruit off the trees. Dry the fruit and mushrooms. Preserve everything. She lived off nature and had a medicine for everything. Now I see many of her characteristics in my daughter. She also gathers wildflowers and weeds.

My dad enjoyed being a pattern maker. He made the molds for a steel foundry. Yet he had to go as a soldier. He felt he didn't have any choice. So he sort of went along with it. If you did not participate in the Nazi and Hitler activities, it was off to a concentration camp. It was unfortunate how one person could create a movement that dragged so many people in for no benefit at all, except perhaps to build one person's ego.

I have vague recollections that there was a war, that my father was in the war. I found out from my mother that I had a brother, who was also off in a war. He was born in 1925, fourteen years older than I, and he was taken up by the Hitler Youth movement—the camping, the games, all that hoopla and rah-rah. At that time, being impressionable, he just thought: *Hey, this is fun. This is great.* He was put through engineering-type schools, worked on diesel engines, and repaired submarines. That's about the extent of his involvement. He didn't do any fighting.

I didn't grow up with my dad in the way typical families would. My mother and I lived with her parents by the Malapane River. I remember her saying that my dad was going to come home on leave. All of a sudden there he was. That's how I knew I had a dad. Then all of a sudden, there was my brother. When he and my dad came home on leave, they went fishing every now and then at night. When I woke up in the morning, northern pike and eel would be swimming around in this big bathtub.

Winters used to get very cold, always such a dry, cold, powdery snow. You could hear crunching under your feet. My dad made a pair of short, wooden skis for me. Since we didn't have any hills, I would go to the top of our manure pile and ski down from there.

We were working in the field the summer of 1944, and all of a sudden everybody was scurrying. My mother grabbed me, and we ran into the drainage ditches. I heard: "Air raids, air raids!" The war had started to turn, and our area was getting bombed. The Allied forces were trying to destroy the steel factory where my father used to work. During peace time that factory had produced machinery, but of course once the war started, they were producing armaments.

In February of 1945 we were notified that the Russian front was advancing. I remember soldiers coming through— German soldiers—going west already. Some were wounded, bandaged up. Somebody woke us up one night and said: "It's time to go. It's time to go!" I was bundled up. My mother and her sister packed a few belongings. Everybody had one of these little hand-drawn sleds that kids used to ride. All kinds of people were walking along that road heading west. I remember the crunching snow. The sun had just come up. God, it was cold . . . bitterly cold. German soldiers were walking. We hooked our little sled to a horse-drawn sleigh that had wounded German soldiers on it. They'd haul me up on top so I wouldn't have to walk. I'm not sure how many days went by. I remember seeing dead people alongside the road. Dead horses.

Somehow we managed to get onto a freight train. They had wooden bunks set up in there. Everybody was just packed in. I don't know if that train had been used for transporting soldiers, or if the Nazis had used it for transporting Jews to concentration camps. I kind of doubt—knowing how rotten the Nazis were—that they would have provided bunk beds for Jews.

We were sleeping in bombed-out airports. No roofs. At times I was awfully hungry, yet something always seemed to appear. You really had to depend upon each other in order to survive. We arrived south of Berlin in the spring of 1945 and decided to wait things out. Everybody was hoping the war would end. We were getting bombed at night, strafed during the daytime. Whenever the sirens sounded, we all went into the basement. In the evening people went around checking all windows to make sure they had blackout blinds with flaps on the sides so that the bombers wouldn't know where the buildings were located. In the morning it was time to pick up the bodies. They would dig big graves and put thirty, forty people in there because they couldn't dig individual graves fast enough.

In the daytime we would go out in the woods and try to get some firewood so we could cook. Fighter planes would strafe the roads and people with wing-mounted machine guns. You'd take cover in whatever ditch you could find, under a tree. I was going on six, and I couldn't figure out why people were trying to kill each other. I was totally confused, and I remember crying quite a bit. My mother would hug me and try to comfort me by saying: "Let's hope it'll end soon."

Berlin was catching the brunt of it. At night you could see this eerie reddish-orange glow on the horizon. After these bombing raids huge craters would be left, where rainwater or natural groundwater would collect. We used to play and swim in those wonderful holes. Frogs would be in there, little tadpoles that we caught. You just enjoyed life at a different level, made do with whatever was there. Maybe it's survival where—given the minimal life support—you didn't expect any more.

That spring we heard artillery fire real close, and next thing the Russians came. There wasn't that much shooting going on, but an awful lot of looting. A soldier dragged my mother off, and my aunt held me tight, clutching me. A while later, when my mother appeared again, she was crying. So, based on that, I take it that he probably raped her. I never did ask her because there were certain things you just blocked out. I remember she kept saying: *"Abwaschen"*—"Wash." From what

I understand, a lot of women went through a similar thing.

Now we were under the Russian occupation. There was a great amount of hatred for communism, even though we had been bombed by the Allied forces. We were suffering more as a result of that—yet the hatred was for the Russians. After the war ended, we found out through the Red Cross that my dad was in West Germany. We started heading west in early fall. We walked in a long column of people, as far as I could see. Bundled up, shivering. Some people had hand-drawn carts. There was no color. Everything was drab. Like looking at a black and white movie. So desolate. Everybody downtrodden. I don't know if there were Jews.

My mother kept saying: "Yes, your father is safe. We're going to be united again." At times we were really hungry. I remember my mother and others working on this huge pile of potatoes, sifting through, trying to pull out the good ones and discarding the bad ones, or cutting whatever good parts the bad ones still had. Making some communal meals. I'm not sure how many days went by. One time, as we were working our way west, there was a swimming pool. It was empty, of course, full of junk, but we had fun sliding down the incline toward the deep end.

We crossed the border and wound up at my dad's sister's in this little town, Dassensen, population 800. My father was captured by the Allied forces and escaped. He said: "I didn't want to go into a camp. I knew my sister was nearby. I worked my way to the woods as close as possible." We had no idea where my brother was. My father was overqualified for working at a carpenter shop, but any kind of work was better than nothing. One of the things he was very good at was precision. "Do it right the first time, otherwise you'll have to do it over again." Later on in life, when I was designing data-processing systems for banks, I was always being nagged: "Hey, this has got to be done faster. I don't care if it's not right the first time. Just get it done." That was very frustrating.

The three of us lived in one room. No plumbing. Just cold running water with a sink. The typical kind of farm dwelling. My parents were hoping the Russians would have to relinquish the area that was ceded to Poland. My dad always wanted to go back there, but since our farm had been destroyed, they both felt that it wouldn't be worth it.

The town was Lutheran, and we were of course Catholics, definitely the minority. The tiny schoolhouse had two classrooms. I was always a good student, very attentive. I prided myself on getting good grades. I had precise, crisp handwriting. I was good in math and loved geography. The only thing I couldn't do was sing. My mother would work in the fields, and I used to help out, leading the cows around. One time a stupid cow stepped on my foot, and I was in agony. Fortunately, the ground was soft enough to give a little.

Eventually, my father got a job seven kilometers away in the bike factory, Heidemann Werke. He used to ride his bicycle there. If the snow was too bad, of course, he'd have to walk. We got some bus transportation. We were always being referred to as *Flüchtlinge*—refugees. And that hurt. We were looked down upon, and there was a fair amount of tension. The refugees didn't care much for Hitler, but the people whose home was in Dassensen thought: *Ja, Hitler . . . Hitler was doing the right thing for Germany*. They hadn't lost anything. All the land, the farms, the buildings were still theirs. So they didn't really suffer as a result of the war as we, who had basically lost everything.

I was feeling adventurous and a little cocky: *Hey, I've been through a lot. I've seen a lot more than you guys have*. I was small, and the bigger kids, of course, used to pick on me. Since we were considered refugees, there was that much more reason to pick on me. My only form of defense was to run away. That's perhaps where I developed a lot of speed and was good at track. One bully I couldn't keep off my back. My dad threatened him, but every time he got a chance, he got a hold of me.

Finally my dad said: "We've got to stop this. Why don't you go on out. I'm sure he's going to find you. Just run back home." Sure enough, I just barely stepped outside, there he was, chasing me. Right into our yard. My dad was waiting behind the gate and beat the living daylights out of him. From that day on I had peace. Now that I look back, it's sort of funny. It's not really the way you want to resolve problems, but maybe at times you have to get somebody's attention.

We found out that my brother had been taken prisoner by the British and put into a POW camp in Belgium. In 1948 he was released. He had little black scars on his back from working in the coal mines of the camp. It was so hot in the mines that they used to take their shirts off. They got scarred by falling coal or from brushing up against it. And the black still remained under their skin—the strangest-looking thing.

My parents never talked much about what my dad had done in the war. But from what I understand, he actually did some of the fighting on the eastern front and in France. He did not pride himself: *Oh yes, I was a German soldier,* and, *Yes, I fought for Hitler.* This is what Germans were supposed to be— proud. My father didn't care for Hitler at all. So there was a certain amount of silence. You just didn't talk about the war in the open.

But one of the things that made a deep impression on me—and it's still with me now—is that one shouldn't take advantage of somebody else. Hurting others was not in your own best interest. My mother would say: "Look what the Nazis and so many Germans did. Then it backfired, and they in turn were the ones who got hurt." Anytime you take advantage of another person, you're going to start developing distrust, hatred, and everything that goes along with it. Sooner or later it's going to develop into open conflict. And this whole thing about race in terms of: *You shouldn't trust. Certain races are worse than others.* . . . To this day I don't know why strife has to be there between one race or nationality and another one.

One time we were at another refugee family's apartment. They had an official, published album with pictures of soldiers and artillery pieces and dead people and bombed-out buildings. German soldiers with rifles were standing at the ready, and there was a bunch of civilians. On the backs of some coats was the Jewish star. When I asked my parents about that, they said: "Well, *ja*, those were Jews, and they took them to concentration camps." That's all they said. I still didn't understand anything as far as concentration camps were concerned. I just remember there were *Juden*, but my parents never said anything hateful about Jews. There was just sort of a skepticism in terms of how they viewed them. A lot of bartering was going on after the war, and quite a few Jews were coming through, selling things like cloth. My mother was a fantastic seamstress, and she would buy or barter material.

I remember her basic values in terms of saving and working for things, preserving things. It's something that is still in me now. I don't buy anything on credit. If I don't have the money, I don't buy it. Though I consider myself more American than German—multicultural, really—I am proud that I am of German origin because that upbringing taught me a lot of valuable things that I still believe and practice. *You do have to work for a living. You have to save your money.* And this thing about working together, living off the land.

Whenever possible, my parents helped each other out. They were very close—not the lovey-dovey-cushy-type thing you'll see around here. It was a mutual understanding. Sundays we used to go for walks, gather mushrooms or firewood. My parents used to tell me how important the woods were, how much life you can get out of them. In the fall the beechwoods would give off these triangular seeds—*Buchecken*. We used to eat those and also make oil from them. My dad and our landlord grew sugar beets, which they sold for making sugar. They actually made *Schnapps* from the sugar beets. My parents also had this huge glass bottle in which they made rose-hip wine. My dad, of course, made all the furniture. When my parents died, they still had that original furniture.

My dad died in April of 1969 in my mother's arms. He fell asleep and never woke up. My mother was very distraught. They'd done so much for each other, leaned on each other, making up for the lost years they'd had during the war, the separation. My mother apparently took the tablecloth as they do in Germany—lean out of the window and shake out the crumbs—and lost her balance. When my brother got there, her head was crushed. She was bleeding and couldn't see anything. She died six weeks after my father's death.

We used to get care packages from my aunt and uncle in Chicago. My aunt had met my uncle in Malapane in the early twenties. He was a butcher. After he came to the United States to work for a cousin who had a butcher business in Minnesota, he proposed to my aunt by mail. That's how those two got started. He opened his own little butcher shop in Chicago, and they added some groceries. One of the things I really loved getting from them, believe it or not, were the cans of Spam. I loved to read and was getting these Western magazine-type novels. I was hearing all these stories: *Oh ja, money grows on trees over there . . . you don't have to work. . . .*

They were trying to sponsor my family to come to the United States. We went through the formalities and interviews at a processing camp near Hamburg. It turned out my dad had a hernia and needed to have an operation before he could come to the States. After the operation we reapplied, but the immigration quota had already been filled.

My aunt couldn't have children. She and my uncle thought that perhaps my brother would want to work in their business. But he fell in love with a girl in Dassensen and decided to get married and not come to the United States. Now it was down to me. I was thirteen. My parents sat down with me and encouraged me to go: "Here you have a somewhat uncertain future. You'd have to start from scratch. Naturally, we'd help you, but you would probably have a better future in the United States." It was implied that I would go into my aunt and uncle's business. Even at a young age I was very adventurous. I said: "Okay, I'm going. I can always come back." About the only thing I really wanted to take along was a *Mundharmonika*—harmonica.

My parents signed a notarized letter: *We agree with the immigration of our legitimate child . . . Heinrich . . . to the United States of North America. We are aware that we may not get a visa at a later time. . . . Our relatives don't have children and want to accept our son . . . as if he were their own child. . . .* All of a sudden it came time to say goodbye. My mother gave me a piece of dry rye bread, the heel. She said: "If you get seasick, eat this. It'll make you feel better." I wasn't going to get seasick.

She stayed behind in Dassensen, and my dad took me to Bremerhaven. The passenger liner was called the *Neptunia*. Man, was I excited. I raced through that ship, trying to see what was there. I saw my dad in the crowd and came back again. Next the band starts playing *"Auf Wiedersehn, auf Wiedersehn . . ."* and all of a sudden we just cast off, and I was waving goodbye to my dad.

The thing that was running through my head mostly was: *Wow, what's going to be waiting for me over there?* I remembered my parents saying: "You can always come back." That eased my mind, but I cried. But then of course there was all the exploring. I made friends immediately. I was in a cabin with bunk beds for nine or twelve people. We went up to England. Picked up more passengers. From there to France. Up to Ireland. That's when we got into some rough seas—waves higher than a boat. *Ach.* Practically everybody was seasick. I ate that rye bread and got over it. When we went by that Statue of Liberty, there, boy, I had some real, real hard gut feelings: *This is going to be a land where we can be free.* I cried as we went by. We all threw our coins at the Statue of Liberty.

It was November 4, 1953. People were being called off the

boat in a certain order. I just had that one suitcase. Of course, we had to unpack everything. This guy from the Immigration and Naturalization Service saw my harmonica and said: "Play me something, just anything." Here I was in the process of going through immigration, playing my harmonica. All of a sudden he started applauding. The people around started applauding. And he was just all smiles and said: "Welcome, welcome, welcome."

I arrived in Chicago on the train. I had a picture of my aunt and uncle, and of course they had a picture of me. We walked out of the train station toward this car, a 1950 black Roadmaster. I had never been in a car like that before. And in Germany you didn't have all the traffic and lights and horns and skyscrapers. We got to their house. I'd never seen wall-to-wall carpeting and hot running water. They had a real TV and refrigerator. It was just total ultraplush everything . . . like walking into a dream.

I liked my aunt and uncle. They were friendly, open. My aunt's English was worse than my uncle's. They spoke German to each other. They associated with the German-American club where everybody spoke German. But they pushed to Americanize me: "After three months we want to stop talking German with you, and we want you to speak English only. Some people don't like Germans over here. When we take out your citizenship papers, we want to make your name as American as possible. We have to Americanize you now." I didn't know any better at that time. In essence, they were my parents now, caring for me.

My aunt was very much like my mother. Very kind, very tender. Perhaps not quite as forceful and outspoken as my mother. Because my mother had gone through the war, she had to exert herself a lot more. My uncle was the forceful one, playing the typical man's role. He would not let her drive. My aunt resented that. He took care of all the paperwork. When he finally died, I had to teach her how to take care of checking accounts.

My aunt and uncle sent me to the Catholic school. Nobody had ever seen a foreigner before. Since I played soccer, I was quite the hit. They had American-type football here. As soon as they found out how I could kick the ball, oh, everybody wanted me on their side. I was ahead as far as math and all that other stuff was concerned—that came to me easy. The only problem was English. Every place I went, I had this huge dictionary in my pocket because I was constantly trying to communicate.

Since my uncle felt that I was imported from my mother's side, he wanted to have somebody from his side in the United States, and so he brought one of his nephews over. Martin was two years younger than I. We had a major falling out after my aunt died. He did not like the way the will was set up. Some money was left to my aunt's cousin, who had taken care of her. I felt the cousin deserved every bit of it. Martin felt he and I should be splitting it. I was the executor of the will, and I basically told him this was the way my aunt had wanted it, and that I was not about to challenge inheritance laws. If he wanted to, he could do it on his own, but I would not help. That was the last time I ever heard from him.

Our house was in an Irish-Italian neighborhood. The people on one side spoke with a heavy Italian accent. Wonderful people. On the other side we had Irish neighbors. Their daughter turned out to be my first love. Across the street we had another Italian plus a Jewish doctor. A wonderful guy. But here again—this is perhaps where that old German heritage comes in—my aunt used to say: "Well, they're Jewish." And she said it sort of quietly. When I tried to dig a little bit deeper, she said: "We don't talk about that." The doctor and I got along just fine. Well, looking back on the war and the concentration camps, here was this wonderful guy who was Jewish, and here was I—German.

What went on in Germany didn't make any real sense until I was in the States and started finding out in school about the concentration camps. I heard about documentaries, saw live footage. Any sort of ethnic cleansing—I mean it's absolutely absurd. It's ridiculous. Like what's going on in Serbia. It reeks of Hitler or Nazism all over again. Perhaps the world does need some ultimate policeman or police force—if it could be kept honest enough—to establish freedom. Like what the United States has done in Kuwait and is doing now in Haiti. Not have a person terrorize and control others. Royalty and the British crown and all that, it's just a bunch of crap as far as I'm concerned. The kings, the queens . . . they're just a bunch of self-appointed dictators.

The thing that really tore me up was when I saw the first pictures of the American flag burning. It's utter desecration. I've always felt very proud of this country. But I think this country, at times, is way too liberal in terms of freedom of speech. Those extremists are hurting other people's feelings. Quite frankly, every time I hear about Richard Butler and the Aryan Nations having free speech, it sends shivers up and down my spine. It's sick what we are allowing to happen. Now you're hearing that a lot of neo-Nazi activities are taking place in Germany again. It scares me that there are still younger people who are falling for that. If, let's say, Germany were ever to get itself into a situation like it was during the Hitler time, and if I were called upon to put them down, I would do it as an American, even though I'd be fighting against Germans.

At times, when people found out I was from Germany, I heard: "Oh yeah, Nazis." How can I really be responsible? As a child born during or after the war, you should not be held responsible for what your parents or other Germans did. I can understand where, if you were Jewish and had a family member die in a concentration camp, you would say: "You're responsible." But I would very strongly defend myself against that—not physically, of course. I know I had nothing to do with what was going on there. And as far as my parents were concerned—I mean they were in the war, they were part of it, but they really didn't have anything to do with it. They just went through the motions because they basically had no choice. And my brother was taken in by all the hoopla and brainwashing and was too young to know what was really going on.

We all need to remember what took place so it is not repeated, but at the same time, I don't think we need to continue using that as a crutch. The descendants should not be held responsible. In other words—this is something that happened; now we're going forward. We have to make that separation. There should be some form of forgiveness.

Right after I came back from Vietnam, I reestablished the relationship with my brother on a mature level. A lot more bonding took place then. We talked about Vietnam. I felt justified in going to Vietnam, due to what the Viet Cong were doing in terms of taking over South Vietnam. I hated communism. It's not that I hated the Russian people, but I have hated the Communist ideology. I helped set up an army supply system in Saigon, so I was not really where all the gory fighting was. We constantly had to be on our toes because there was a lot of sabotage. You didn't know whom to trust. The Vietnamese robbed us blind and then resold the parts on the black market. We had a slush fund. If we couldn't find a part in our own supply system, we went out there and bought the part because it was ours to begin with. In the heat, bodies decomposed rapidly. I remember that stench when they brought missing soldiers back in body bags. We were all within the same compound. I imagine that's probably what took place in some of the concentration camps in terms of the smell of decomposing bodies.

When my brother visited here in 1984, he didn't really talk about the gory stuff that we now know took place in the concentration camps. I've never probed him about that. He was not close enough to know what was going on. Perhaps he also found out more when he saw the documentaries. What my brother is saying primarily is: "I don't understand—now that I look back on it—how I could have done that, how I could have believed in what Hitler was trying to do."

But what was actually going on was not available to them. Since he was primarily in a mechanical facility, he was not all that close to what was going on. He only knew that he was going to be trained as a mechanic. And that he was going to have a good future in Germany.

Beate

Born: 1942
Age at time of immigration: 29

Small Talk

When I lived already in the States, I asked my mother: "How did you deal with the question about so many Jewish people having been killed?" And my mother plain old said: "I cannot believe it. These atrocities are impossible." This is how she dealt with it—she just ignored it. However, she must have known something because in 1945, when we were in refugee camps, we were deloused. We obviously had lice. Our hair was cut very short. Maybe it was shaved—I don't remember. We had to go to a community shower with wooden planks and things on top for water to come out. My mother was scared to death that it wouldn't be water, that we would get gassed. She must have known at some point. This was never discussed. Years later, when my aunt visited us and wanted to see the concentration camp in Dachau, my mother went with her, and that upset her very much.

Basically, there was a huge silence about the war years when I was growing up. We happened to get to World War I twice in history class, and then there was the summer break.

Once in a while, little excerpts were mentioned about how it was under Hitler. I must say my family was very apolitical, more concerned about family and survival. My parents probably listened to the war news a lot, just to be informed. They were pro-German because we were ethnically German, but it wasn't a total identification. My mother listened to the BBC, and that was plain old forbidden. One of my early memories is of speeches on the radio—they must have been Hitler's speeches—and my mother getting worked up. It was too much for her.

I guess I'm glad I didn't grow up in the Third Reich because I don't know what I would have done. I'm scared to think about it. I think many people just tried to live their daily lives and were not very concerned with politics. And there also is this tremendously effective way in which Hitler could use many of the—what I would call—general characteristics to his advantage. Who doesn't want to hear: *You are wonderful. You are the chosen people. You are great.* Even if one is mature enough to say: *What is this nonsense?* On some gut level, it worked. It works here in America with advertisement, with positive reinforcement. People had children for the good of Germany or worked in factories for the good of Germany, not thinking that for the good of Germany might mean for the bad of many other people.

I think in tremendously evil, genius ways Hitler did use the feelings of superiority and loyalty. Loyalty for me is very important. I have a hard time with loyalty versus knowing better. If you give your word, you do it—even if you don't like it. For example, would I have gone to Vietnam, or would I have been a draft dodger? I don't know. Though it was a ridiculous war— totally unnecessary like all wars—I would have felt awful about everyone else going there and being killed, while I would have just taken off. I would have felt I should be there. I think Hitler used this loyalty. People did go—not so much for Hitler, but for their neighbors, their friends.

I have seen movies in the States. In Germany they were taboo when I was growing up. We would never see Leni Riefenstahl movies. I forced myself to see them here because I wanted to see how this was all done. The Nazi regime was an indoctrination of a very strong sort, and for me Catholicism was an indoctrination of a very strong sort. I used to be a devout Catholic. If I think about it, I cannot believe it. My friends ask: "How could you not question?" And I tell them: "That's part of the indoctrination. You obey. You do not question. And the better you obey, the better person you are." Certain beliefs in Catholicism are just ultimate. *That's the only way. And all the others are wrong. Poor souls.* That's crazy. It took me a long time to start questioning at all, and then it took me an even longer time to think that some of the rules are just inhuman. Yet, Good Friday I still go to Catholic mass—not for religious reasons, but for memory.

I have a very difficult time dealing with the Holocaust. I think there is a collective burden in our generation because it is just so tremendous, so horrible. On the other side, I must say that we have this *Gnade der späten Geburt*—the grace of late birth. It's an easy way out. I don't have to really deal with it as long as I try not to do immoral things in my life, and do in my little ways what I can do. I believe that strongly.

One woman I worked with was Jewish. We became friends, got along really well, talked about a lot. She told me once: "I like you although you're a German." But I knew how she actually meant it: *Some people have done horrid things to us, but I don't see you as some people. I see you as a human being. You had nothing to do with it.* But it came to my mind that there is a shadow of a collective guilt. At the same time, I feel it is not my personal guilt, and there's nothing I can do. I feel a lot more guilty about not being able to help in Africa or in Haiti because it happens right now, and we do nothing. All the violence in the States, and we do nothing. I would compare that with the Holocaust. I'm not thinking of how many more people were killed there or how few are killed here—that's not the point. Horrendous things are happening right now, and we do nothing. Horrendous things have happened in the past, and many people did nothing. And that does not belittle the Holocaust. It was horrible. It's beyond any description.

I was born in 1942 in a big village in the Carpathian Mountains where my ancestors had lived since 1300. The town had a Slovakian name, Handlova, and a German name, Krickerhau. Most of the people were German farmers, and there was brown coal mining. The population of Slovaks lived somewhat separately. My parents were ethnic Germans but technically Czech. We are called *Karpatendeutsch*—Carpathian German. My family always considered itself German, probably more so than people in Germany, which is quite typical for people in any foreign country. We spoke a medieval German dialect, which I still speak, a mixture of languages very similar to Yiddish. It's a wonderful old-fashioned dialect. I cannot say any small talk in it.

There were actually many German settlements all over the East of Europe. People had come there to be given land for agriculture. Around the fifteenth century it must have been a feudal system. People stuck pretty much to themselves as a German ethnic group. There was not much intermarriage. From what my parents told me, the Germans there were pro-German and anti-Slavic, since Germany seemed to become bigger and better—at least until the war.

My uncle enlisted in the German *Wehrmacht*—armed forces. Later he was a prisoner of war in Nuremberg. He actually has a lot of positive things to say about the American prison camps. My father was never in the war. He was a good family man, and it wouldn't have occurred to him to enlist. There was a lot of partisan activity going on. People actually got along quite well, but for political reasons they had to be against each other. The word partisan was a household word.

It was always *"die Partisanen, die Partisanen,"* and it was always bad. Some of my relatives actually got shot by Slovakian partisans, but my father was warned by some of his Slovakian friends to hide. He hid in the attic for some time, waiting for the German front to occupy that region of Czechoslovakia.

I must have been one and a half when the Russian front came close to that village. I remember listening to machine-gun fire. I wasn't told what it was, but everyone was very afraid. This probably had a lot to do with the fact that—despite my positive outlook on life—I am fearful of things I don't know. As soon as I know what they are, it's okay.

Towards the end of the war, there must have been German soldiers, Russian soldiers, and partisans in the village. My mother told me a Russian soldier came into our house to see what was going on. She was terrified he would either kill me or—I don't know. It ended up that he gave me a glass of canned pears or cherries that he'd probably stolen someplace else.

In January of 1945 the whole village was strongly urged to leave. We were *evakuiert*—evacuated—from the war zone and sent to the Sudetenland, which was occupied by Hitler. We were supposed to be more secure there. But some of the men stayed in town to defend the German country there against the Russians and the Slovakian partisans. These must have been the best weeks of my father's life. He told about it later on. He had solidarity with all the other men—what we now call male bonding. I don't think he ever had a rifle. I am sure he never shot anyone. They just had a good old time although it was war. They made sausage. It sounds awfully flippant, but I'm glad he had this time. I think he felt important for the first time in his life because he was doing something for his Fatherland.

Later on, he joined us in the Sudetenland. My brother was born there, and I have vivid memories of families being together, kids having a good time . . . but some danger was out there which I couldn't identify. It was not in the family. In the fall of 1946 we were put into cattle trains with all our belongings and shipped to what was called *Heim ins Reich*—home to the *Reich*—Germany, in our case to a small town in Bavaria. The two main classes there were *Einheimische*—natives—and *Flüchtlinge*—refugees. I was the *Flüchtling,* the underdog. So I know exactly how that feels—being different. People spoke a Bavarian dialect. It was the same language, and yet it was a different culture. I was embarrassed that we ate bell peppers and garlic and poppy seed, which was unknown in Bavaria. I was supposedly very sensitive and also carried around an awful lot of aggression. To a certain extent I still do.

We received one room from the city for the whole family of five in the *Kreisleiterhaus,* a word that was taboo and didn't make sense to me. People changed the subject when it was mentioned. Years later I realized that a *Kreisleiter,* district leader, must have been the political official for the city and the *Kreis* in Nazi times. And it was his *Haus.* He probably did not survive. And then the word disappeared from the vocabulary. One of the war criminals, Ilse Koch, was in a women's prison about twenty kilometers away. People said she used to make lamp shades out of human skin. I was too young to realize what that meant. I just knew she must have been a very bad person. Once in a while, people mentioned: "Oh, this would not have happened under Hitler." It was kind of hushed. "There was more order."

The different social classes played a tremendously big role. My father was a shoemaker, and that meant we were lower middle class. My mother was somewhat more educated, but she did not develop her own life because she felt she couldn't outgrow her *Stand*—class. She was modest and did not want to achieve anything that was not proper the way she saw it. She was also in a very traditional woman's role, working for the good of the family with my father, whom she actually loved very much. But the price she paid for it was depression. However, through her religious beliefs, she could manage to snap out of that again and go on with her life.

As a girl, I had my dreams, which were not very concrete. Mainly I wanted to get out of the poor, simple lifestyle of my parents. They helped us there, too, did the best they could. It was the old saying, *"Ihr sollt es besser haben"*—"You should have it better." I'm really thankful for that. My driving force was reinforced by them: *You are going to make it. You're going to show them that you can do whatever has to be done.* And the only way to do that in Germany was through education.

One time I went to a woman doctor who was around sixty. I was so impressed because I saw that she had found her place. She was very serene, and she did her job the best she could. I thought: *I would like to become like this. To just live and do your best and not be so worked up about it all the time.* But to become a physician was out of the question—mainly because I didn't dare. There were limitations from my family, but if I'd had enough energy and willpower, I could have done it. Since I was interested in natural sciences, I became a *Chemisch Technische Assistentin*—research assistant in chemistry. When I was twenty-one, I moved to Munich and worked in research labs at the university. Much later I realized that my main goal had been to marry an appropriate man. Appropriate meant better educated than I was. Marry up, basically. Other men were just not interesting—I couldn't talk to them.

I was in a Catholic youth group for girls. It was wonderful. I felt accepted. I also liked my work. However, there was some nagging feeling: *Is this all there is?* I felt unhappy, not fulfilled. And I became older. The goal to find an appropriate husband didn't seem to work, but I was at least realistic enough not to just marry for marriage's sake. I thought: *Well, maybe go one year to a foreign country, have some other experiences, see something of the world and have time out to reflect, to rethink what you could do with the rest of your life.*

That was an important decision. I'm happy I did it. I spoke some English, and the United States was the only country where I could get a job in my profession. I was twenty-nine when I went to the States in 1971. I quickly met the man of my dreams, who was not the man of my dreams after all. He was the classic American Western man, the lone Marlboro Man who comes into town, does his thing, saves everyone, and goes back. But what that really meant was that no one—particularly no woman—would ever get to that soul. Neither of us knew the other person. I expected an American man with a European soul. I was used to European men, with whom the emotional catering role was much more equal, and I didn't want the traditional role of catering to a husband. He had this image of the good, loyal German women who cater to their husbands and don't ask many questions, little ladies who are put on a pedestal and have to be helped. However, there's a twist to it—the little ladies do all the work and run the house and work with the children independently. Like frontier women, they do that quietly and don't exchange much with the man.

And it just did us in. It was too painful for us both. I loved him very much. I still love him, but I cannot live with him. We were married for fifteen years. It's tragic. We have one daughter, who is a very troubled teenager. When she was little, I had a certain litany of German children's songs I'd sing to her every evening: it started with *"Schlaf Kindlein Schlaf," "Guten Abend Gute Nacht,"* and *"Hänschen Klein Ging Allein."* I also told her the classic Grimm *Märchen*—fairy tales. We hid Easter eggs and let her find them. That was a lot of fun. When she was little, we dressed up for German *Fasching*—carnival—and walked around the house in costumes. I think she still remembers.

I had to fight a lot against depression, which I'd inherited from my mother. I only had three options: I could go home, commit suicide, or live. Suicide I considered slightly because I felt miserable and had anxiety attacks; my pride forbade me to go back as a loser and say: *I cannot handle it in this country;* and I learned to rely on my own resources, which I did not have to do until then. With the help of friends, I realized that depression is aggression turned against yourself, and that I had never really dared to tell myself: *I am angry. I can't stand this.* I always thought: *I probably deserve it. I'm not supposed to be angry.* And the realization that it's okay to be angry because you have definite reasons to be angry—that did it. That got me beyond the depression. I'm still prone to it, but I have learned to work myself out of it consciously.

I also had to come to grips with my family history, what roles were played, and what my parents had gone through. While I'd come to America on my own account, they'd had no say when they were taken out of their surroundings. I also learned more about the history of World War II, because I was far enough away to come to grips with my culture and my tradition. People who are out of their familiar surroundings are forced to define it. If you never get out, you don't have to define it.

I must say I never felt discriminated against as a German in the States. I felt people respected me more for being German, and I felt uncomfortable with that. It was the same as feeling badly as a refugee: I had nothing to do then with being discriminated against; and I had nothing to do now with being particularly promoted just for being German. It's ridiculous.

I remember coming to the States, being stuck in a hotel because the airplane had motor trouble, and eating dinner at a round table with about fifteen people, most of them American. I don't remember what was said, just my reaction to it: *Why don't these people say anything? Why do they only say phrases? They are far away, behind their masks. There must be something behind there, but I can't recognize it.* That was my first encounter with what I later on called small talk—a name for the whole system of not interfering with each other.

I find it fascinating how the United States developed a system of communication which is an entity within the language. Everyone can talk to everyone in a nonoffensive way. There is no cultural need to express yourself in other ways than small talk. You do not need to be confronted. You stay with your phrases. If you are a master at that—and we all learn it and we all have to do it—it's functional. The United States mastered small talk because people from different backgrounds came together in one country and somehow had to be able to deal with each other *without* the past. It's present and future—not past tense, which I see as traditional.

That is not meant to say that in other languages so-called small talk is not done. It's often done in formal situations where you do not necessarily have to say: *I don't like this food,* or, *This could have been better.* Behind some of it is just politeness. But there are other factors involved. In more traditional societies, like where I grew up, you build a reputation slowly, and you can draw on that. This is why poor, noble people still had high status and the *nouveau riche* did not. In a modern world where people—at least in theory—can rely upon their resources and efficiency to rise to the top, small talk is one of the means through which it can be achieved. You are more able to fulfill your dreams than in a traditional society. On the other side, you cannot rely on anyone else because you are on your own. You cannot talk down to someone you may need next week.

Small talk has another side which I find to be very negative in bringing up children because they are hardly ever told, particularly by society, that this is not right or acceptable. Of course in your job you are never told directly if you are doing well or not. It is all covered and couched in small talk. One example of that is the old joke where you go to work in the morning, your boss greets you, grins in your face, says: "Hi, how are you?" "Fine." "You are fired."

I must say, small talk is a dangerous way of dealing with each other. It's useful and practical, but there is a human component missing. It's safe, it's sterile—not human. I do not by any means want to say that many Americans are only able to talk small talk. That's not true. People, if they want to, can say more things personally. It will take a little longer. People will be a little more careful. That's all right. People all over the world have the same concerns, the same problems, the same pains, the same emotions. The question is if you want to put emphasis on that, or if you want to put emphasis on the shape it takes to express it.

I'm not saying all small talk is negative. But it has the disadvantage that, as a foreigner in particular, you have to find out the nuances—what is being said, and what is really meant. For example, I stumbled—like many other Germans—over the famous *"Hi, how are you?" "Fine, thank you."* They are polite phrases to fill in gaps which eventually can be overcome, but don't have to be overcome. Of course, being freshly imported from Germany, I'd say: "I'm not so well today," or "Yes, I'm feeling fine because I had this and that for breakfast." People all of a sudden would look a little strange, and I'd think: *I guess they didn't want to hear that.* This was a new code, a new culture, a different form of dealing with others.

But now I have this small talk that I use exactly as it's being used in society. I use it to protect myself in professional situations. I don't say any value statements if I don't want to. I control with small talk—it gives you a way out, which you would not have in Germany, where people are by culture allowed to be more critical than in the United States. When you make a statement, the other person makes a statement back, pushes the ball back, so to speak. In America, if your statement is too outrageous, no one will bounce it back. It sticks out like a sore thumb, and you come across as intense or pushy because the dynamics are different. So you have to hold back.

I think the healthiest people here are the ones who can easily switch from small talk in business situations to intimate talk with their friends. But I also know people who can only do small talk, and those are the ones who end up, at best, in therapy. My daughter avoids any kind of confrontation because she has never learned it. She always ran away from it, and she sees me as the pushy mother who wants to connect, to talk. I can see how annoying that is to her, but she doesn't know what she's missing either. And there's nothing I can do. I'm sad about my daughter because I cannot reach her very often.

After my divorce I said to friends that my idea of a wonderful relationship would be a male friend who lives in a different house. And actually I got it, for the last four years. I'm delighted—it's exactly what I can deal with, what he can deal with, and what we both like. We both are open about it and make jokes about it. His mother is the child of Polish immigrants, and his father is from a many generations Anglo family. So he has seen both ways, and he combined them somehow. He traveled a lot in his life, and he just plain old tells me, "I can deal with European women usually a lot better."

I can see why. For him it is more on a gut level. I had to deal with it intellectually to see what was really going on. If I had gone to Mexico or India, I would have expected society to be very different, but coming to the States, I was under the illusion that many people are of European extract and therefore thought like Europeans. And that of course is not so. I feel I'm kind of on the border. I feel quite comfortable in American society because I know now what's going on, and I feel comfortable in European society because I *still* know what's going on. American society is technically open. It's functional. It's easygoing. In Germany there are many restrictions. *"Man tut das nicht"*—"One does not do this."

I'm glad to be here in the States because you have many more options, and no one will criticize you for doing or wearing certain things. There are rules in public, but you have a lot more freedom as a person. Basically, for the last ten years I've been just myself. If people cannot handle it, it's their problem. People say: *Oh, that's just the way she is.* I think Americans are more tolerant or just ignore behavior that is a little bit outrageous. In Germany outrageous behavior would be questioned. So again, all these things have two sides. Some of it is positive, and some of it is potentially dangerous.

Gisela

Born: 1943
Age at time of immigration: 4

The Making of the Beast

When my son, Terry, asked a couple of years ago if it would be okay to find my father, I said: "I think you should. It's your right." My issue with my father is my issue. My son's needs are his own. From the day he was born, I felt Terry belonged to himself, that he was mine to shelter and to expose to the world, but not mine to control or own. My son wanted to learn the Truth. With a capital *T.* The one Truth. I said: "Sometimes we don't get to know the truth. That's what soap operas are made of."

Terry traveled in Europe and visited my aunt and uncle. The gossip from the family was that my father was still alive. And furthermore he was a concentration-camp guard. My son called me up in the middle of the night: "Why didn't you tell me all of this? He was a Nazi. He was a concentration-camp guard." I reminded him that I had told him, but he'd been too young. I said: "I'm not so sure it's something to get excited about, that he might have been a concentration-camp guard." My son's response was: "But you don't understand. This is history."

He went to the town where he'd been told my father, Horst, lived. Turns out he is this man's only grandson, and I am this man's only offspring. Terry asked Horst what he had done during the war, whether he was a guard in a concentration camp. Horst's wife—I think his third wife—burst into tears. They didn't want to talk about it. I can understand that Horst would be afraid of being misunderstood. He's over eighty now, and that generation is so different from us in terms of openness.

My son tells me he learned that Horst tried to write letters. There's some big mystery about a letter . . . who wrote first, who said what. Well, who cares? Stories always get mixed up. That my father abandoned me—that's the thing that matters to me. This notion of abandonment . . . I don't think it is peculiarly German—it is peculiar to children of war.

What my father did in the war really doesn't have anything to do with me. For some reason I can be understanding about that. What kind of a husband he was to my mother doesn't have anything to do with me. What he was not, as a father, has a great deal to do with me. If he did horrible things in the concentration camps, I consider him just as much a victim of the times as anyone he might have victimized. People are victims of circumstance. I've carried the lessons of the Holocaust: *What is it in a human being that can change that person into a monster?* You do have to ask that question. You can't get away from it without repressing a great deal.

I get irate about people in their comfortable lives, looking at history, judging people who supposedly did heinous acts, and assuming they would have behaved differently. We don't—any of us—know how we would behave in a situation until that situation hits us right between the eyes, and our children and parents are involved. Germany is not the story. It's what's in the heart of the individual human being. I will not accept or acknowledge the presence of an enemy.

No person is my enemy.

Each person is me.

Whatever happened in Germany is not isolated to Germany. That's what gets me so riled up. Yes, we have to study it. For many years I watched everything I could on the Holocaust. What happened in Germany is happening all over the world. This minute. And we're turning our backs on it. That we're a continent and an ocean away from Bosnia is no excuse. We know it is happening. We could have an impact, but we choose to live our complacent lives. I'm beginning to think that the nature of violence is inherent in the human being, and that we're never going to get past it. But the problem I've seen in the literature is that it is looked at in terms of Germans and Jews. And I would like to see it looked at on a larger scale. If we're emphasizing a larger humanity, maybe that's what needs to happen to heal.

But because it goes to the bone, the marrow, I can't apply that to my relationship with my father. He doesn't know the impact he had on me by not coming for me. He should have fought harder to find me. I could have been a prostitute rolling in the gutter, for all he cared. Why didn't he come find me?

My son learned that my father came back from the Russian concentration camp and went to my mother's parents to find us. He was told that we had gone to America, that we were happy, and that he should leave us alone. These are all soap operas. My son said to me: "How would you feel, Mom? You've been in a war, you've been in a concentration camp, you find your entire family has divorced you and left, and you've lost everything."

I would have moved heaven and earth to find my child.

I've never pursued meeting my father. I had an opportunity to connect with him at one point, and I refused it. Anger.

Just plain, garden-variety, neurotic anger. I know what's going on. I'm intelligent enough and well read enough to know that the most healing thing is to meet the enemy. That is head stuff. In my heart I'm in pain. I think he should get on a plane and come here and see me. I think he should send me flowers. I think he should telephone and write. I think he should demonstrate that it's important enough. I don't feel hatred for him anymore. I feel sorry he's apparently still tormented. Since he can't talk about the past, he's still tormented by it.

I imagine my father was very much like Rhett Butler—tall and dark and dashing. A real *Poussierer*—flirt. He must have been some number. My mother couldn't believe he was interested in her. I'm fascinated by this story. I find it colorful and intriguing. My mother married my father by proxy, as was common at the time. He was in Russia. The day of their marriage occurred after my conception. I was born in 1943 in the middle of an air raid.

I didn't find out what my father did in the war until recently. My mother is extremely open about everything. According to what she knows, he did serve in a concentration camp in northern Germany for a period of time, and he didn't like it. Whatever that means. *"He didn't like it."* He asked to be transferred to the war in Russia. It seems to me, that's a credit to him. Because if it was a horrible concentration camp, and he didn't like what was being done to the inmates, then it was a big deal to be transferred to the Russian front because it was very dangerous. I have no notion of my father's soul, his spirituality, or his humanity, but he was accorded the transfer and he did fight on the Russian front and became a prisoner of war in Russia.

I have very few memories of childhood. I read somewhere that can happen when a child moves around a lot. I'm also intrigued by the notion that I might have repressed uncomfortable things. My mother tells me—I'm very suspicious of this—that I had no concept of the war, that I was not aware of air raids and the horrible things going on. That I was a happy, golden-haired child. And that when we were in the air-raid shelters, I spread joy and laughter. I cannot believe that a child of two or three could be immune to the tension and suffering. My grandfather tells about the American bombs that would light up the sky like a Christmas tree. You could see everything for miles.

Some of my memories, my mother says, are dreams and *Quatsch*—nonsense. "How could you remember such *Quatsch*? It never happened." But children very rarely make up things such as I remember. What's more likely true is that I mixed up reality with something I didn't understand. In the basement of my grandfather's house—where potatoes, coal, tools, jars of jam, and spare parts for bicycles were kept—I thought I saw my aunt hanging from her ankles and stripped bare, bloodied up as though somebody had plucked at her. My mother said: "Oh, that's nonsense! Of course that never happened." And it probably never did happen. What might have happened is that I came upon a rabbit carcass in the basement—we raised rabbits in the backyard, and one of the ways my family survived the war was by eating those rabbits—but why I mixed that up with my aunt, I'm not sure.

My mother barely appears in my memory. She tells me she had tuberculosis. She was sent to a family farm out in the country. My grandfather and grandmother raised me. My little dog was killed in front of my grandfather's house. His name was Foxle. A big, army-green truck drove up with a black face driving the truck. And he ran over the dog, broke the dog's back. The dog was crying in the street, and I couldn't help it. At that time Germans weren't allowed to have any weapons. I'm told—I don't know if I saw it—that my grandfather put the dog out of its misery by holding him by his hind legs and slamming him repeatedly against a wall. That probably tells you why I'm an animal rights activist.

My grandfather was a member of the armed forces that Hitler called out in the end when Germany was doomed. My mother tells me that this regiment of old men and little boys was asked to go to war. One little twelve-year-old boy was crying: "I don't want to go to war." And my grandfather said to him: *"Geh heim, Bub"*—"Go home, boy. We're not going." Some people might say: *Sure, that's the story that's told,* but I believe that of him. It's the kind of thing he would have done. He was a very generous man. Mother said she couldn't keep a diaper or a *Schnuller*—pacifier—in the house. He gave everything away. But I think that's the kind of story you don't see in the movies. All you see in the movies is the bad German.

I don't know if American movies portray Germans that way because many of the people who produce movies are Jews. It's quite valid that Jews want to tell the story of the Holocaust, and if they can produce or direct or create a vehicle to tell that story, certainly that's what they have to do. Maybe that has to do with the fact that for people who are in their seventies and eighties it's in the marrow. I know people who have the numbers stamped on their arms. How can I ask them to have a balanced perspective? But as people get younger and further removed from the pain and the loss, then it is more possible to be objective, to look for a balanced picture.

But I can't ask that of anybody who's been in the middle of a situation. I mean, I can touch that just a little from my own experience. Don't ask me to be reasonable about my natural father. If people are really close to the pain, they have to tell their stories in any way they can. There are many stories to be told. And we have to look at all of those gathered up together and come to our own conclusion.

A story I'd like to see explored is one my grandfather used to tell about a chemical bomb that was dropped. The bodies were so shriveled and burned black that they couldn't be identified. My grandfather and other Germans shoveled these bodies into a truck and buried them unidentified. I'd like to see Americans look at what they did in the war. I mean, how many Americans know that chemical bombs were dropped during World War II? The Americans weren't blameless either. We have stories of soldiers coming through the town and raping the women, and it didn't matter if the soldiers were French, Russian, German, or American.

War makes monsters out of everybody.

When the war was over, the American forces moved into the bank across the vacant field from my grandfather's house. The soldiers could look across to my grandfather's house with the fecund garden, the fruit trees and berries and sunflowers and rabbits and walnut tree . . . everything growing . . . and these two beautiful, young women. One of them was my mother, one my aunt. My mother was in a lounge chair, recovering from tuberculosis. Naturally, the young soldiers crossed the vacant field. As soldiers, they were able to hunt, and they would bring venison and bread and food that helped my family survive.

Some of these men wanted to marry my mother, and one of them became my stepfather. He told my mother he wasn't going back to America without her—that was his proposal. My mother wasn't really sure if she was in love with him, but her family told her that was because they spoke different languages, that he was a good man, that she should marry him. She went through divorce procedures from the German father, presuming him to be dead, and married a man she hardly knew. My stepfather adopted me, and at four and a half, I was whisked off to a strange new continent. The marriage was difficult. My mother was not accepted by his family, and he didn't know how to raise this little German girl. He was either an absent father or physically violent.

Some little boys called me "Nazi." My mother tells me this. She says I cried. A neighbor lady scolded the boys and told their parents what they'd done. I have no recollection of that.

They could have called me anything. They could have dunked my pigtails in the inkwell. Little boys are horrible to little girls. I didn't know what a Nazi was. All I knew was they were calling me a name—and that made me cry. But it didn't tap into any cultural history because I was too young. There were other taunts. I mean, the little girls did terrible things—that's what kids do—not because I was German, just because I was a wimp. I was a little good girl. Little German girls are raised to be little good girls. It took a long time to stop being a good girl, and I resent that. One misses a lot in life by being a little good girl. Cinderella was a wimp.

My mother always told me stories about my German father that made him seem less than desirable. She had found a ring in a box and a bank account. He said that the ring belonged to the widow of a fallen comrade, that he and his comrades had opened a savings account on her behalf. It was my mother's suspicion that he had a wife in another port, so to speak. She also told me he hated to hear me crying. He'd run out of the house. The one positive thing I was given was a photo album with pictures of me as a baby. Around me, he had sketched a *Himmelbettchen,* a bed with veils for an angel. He had written poems to my mother and to me. Somewhere in my growing up I must have had a hazy recognition that there was more to the man than the negative stories.

When I was about twelve, we were stationed in Germany for four years, and I went to an American army school. In high school we were shown black and white films of the concentration camps. When we came back to the States, we lived in Iowa. From that time forward I was in America except for a couple of visits to Germany. When I was seventeen, we learned for the first time that my father was still alive. Some petty bureaucrat came to the door and asked my mother if she had a daughter, and if the daughter was still living. The government agency had received a communication from my father, inquiring as to my status because he wanted to deduct me on his income tax.

Son of a bitch.

Now, at nearly fifty-two, I feel more compassion for my father than I did when I was growing up. But unfortunately, I really needed to understand the story of my father and the absence of a relationship when I was a young girl, contemplating dating, marriage. His abandonment has affected my relationships with men tremendously. It has cost me loving relationships. I had an affair with a man who was married for a long while. But other than that I keep coming back to not knowing how to relate with honesty to a man. I'm not comfortable with them. I don't trust them. My mother says I'm looking for excuses, that I'm blaming whatever happened in my life on the past, that I should forget, move on.

I pursued a career as an actress. Actors are butterflies, shimmering in the light. Now I realize I wanted to be one of these glorious, fascinating, wonderful people so that my father would realize what he had missed. My mother admires prominent people, and so I wanted to be famous. Older Germans often are impressed by people who are *berühmt*—famous. I gravitated toward acting because I love language. This is something people from any foreign country have in common. You try harder to absorb the language. Acting was a way to convey ideas and emotions and change the world.

A key changing point in my life was when a prowler came into my bedroom. I woke to find a flashlight flickering around my bedroom. The worst part is that an hour later, when the police finally did come, they didn't even dust for fingerprints. They patted me on the head, figuratively, and said: "Well, everything seems all right. There's no evidence of any problem. Go to sleep." I didn't sleep for years after that.

Around that time, a man killed nine nurses in Chicago. It

was the first I had ever heard about vulnerable women and mass murder. Then two stewardesses were beaten bloody across the lake from me. I had always been a totally airy-fairy, afraid-of-nothing person. You could find me on the docks at midnight, too naive to realize there were dangerous elements in the world. And then the prowler came into my life. For the first time I realized I could die. Shortly thereafter, I married a man in uniform. I married the whole U.S. Coast Guard. I wanted the father figure. I wanted somebody to take care of me, to fight my battles for me. And the man I married was able to do all that. He would get into a fight with someone in the middle of an intersection. He took me away from the stage. He saved me from all of that.

Once my child came into my world, he was everything. I didn't want to take any time away from him. To be an actress receded more and more. I began to pick up my paint brushes again. I sold some portraits and drawings. Invariably, no matter whom you paint, people become beautiful as you get to know them and begin to translate the planes of the face and the light in the eyes. You try to capture the personality and the spirit. It doesn't matter what they look like—they're almost always beautiful by the time you're finished.

I quickly realized the marriage was wrong, but I was raised by a very German mother, and the role modeling I got was that you don't throw a marriage away immediately. Not only do you try harder, but it's the woman who makes a marriage work. Oddly enough, years later, when I began to have some confidence in myself as a human being, I divorced my husband for his protectiveness. There wasn't anything wrong with him. I just didn't need those qualities anymore. My divorce was more successful than my marriage. My ex-husband and his wife live only five minutes away from me, and my son always had access to them. We kept things focused on Terry's welfare, and we now have a fairly decent human being as a result of his being raised by three relatively reasonable people.

• • •

I went into paralegal work. Instead of having to work in a civil-law firm with contracts, I got assigned to a serial murder case. My belief was that the death penalty was wrong, but that maybe it was appropriate for some people like Manson. The worst of the worst. I had to research this tremendous body of literature on the death penalty for the closing argument.

Let's face it. The death penalty was used during the Holocaust. Whatever powers were in place in Germany ascribed the death penalty at random, ad hoc, at liberty, to a creature someone decided was not worth living. What happens in a human being who looks at someone else who's alive and says: *You are less than I. You don't deserve to live. I can torture you. I can hurt you. I can kill you.* What causes that?

If you can do it to Christ, Schweitzer, all of the people that you'll study in the human rights literature, if you can do it to the least of these, you can do it to anyone. If you can give the death penalty to an eighteen-year-old, if you can put a twenty-one-year-old away in prison for life, then part of you is kin to those Nazis who separated themselves from the Jews, from the intellectuals, from the homosexuals. If you create a distance between yourself and an other, then you're moving closer to the ability to do what the Nazis did.

In studying people who committed murder and who get the death penalty, I've learned that there is a very long history that goes into the making of the beast. You have to go back into the family, the circumstances of their lives. From the time they were born, they were brutalized in one way or another. It's very rare that you find a person on death row who's had a good, easy life.

We can look back very complacently at World War II Germany and say: *Well, they should have done this and they should have done that.* Because it's far removed from us in time. Centuries from now people will look back on us and say the same thing, that we've failed to solve our problems in an intelligent, compassionate manner. Killing somebody is a very easy way to end the problem. But the problem is still going on because people are still growing up in adverse circumstances that turn them into insensitive, unfeeling creatures. I bet if you studied the histories of people in the concentration camps—the guards, the murderers, the people carrying out orders—you would find that they were not exactly raised to be sensitive people.

The fact that I come from German history, the Holocaust, German culture, probably has a large effect on my philosophies today. The fact that I'm a card-carrying member of the ACLU, the fact that I work against the death penalty. If you come from a background that's comfortable, you don't perhaps have as much stimulus to think deeply about human rights and atrocities. Whereas, if you come from a background such as I do, at some point something kicks in, and you begin to think how that impacts you, whether you share in the guilt, and whether you need to do anything as a result of coming from that background.

As far as I'm concerned, I feel no guilt whatsoever. I told my son and his Jewish girlfriend that they should feel no burden for what happened before them, that their burden is to always be very conscious in the world, to be aware and sensitive to atrocities of all kinds. My son was uncomfortable telling his girlfriend about his grandfather. He said: "Well, Anna's family are Jews from Poland." And I said: "But you're not responsible for what I did, or for what your grandfather did, or for what anyone did. You're only responsible for yourself."

I've had a healing gift, which is the friendship of Jews. It's as though we're wordlessly creating bridges. Hitler, the Nazis, the sympathizers, tried to create a master race and subjugate other races. By becoming friends with or intermarrying with those people the Nazis wanted to subjugate, we're thumbing our noses at the Nazis. The laughter, the humor, the love, the bridging the gap foiled those people who wanted to create a thing that is evil. It's the very best way that we can overcome that.

The story of the Jews has been told. But I believe the heritage of the perpetrators has to be looked at also. There's a victimization there, too. Research and literature are beginning to discover that German offspring of the war have that same survivor guilt that Jewish offspring have. *Why me? Why did my grandfather have to starve? Why did my mother have to suffer? Why am I comfortable? And what do I have to do to earn the right to that comfort? How can I honor my family?*

You can't know the truth unless you know both sides. It's important to tell the story of the Jews, but it's also important to know the story of the perpetrators.

Jürgen

Born: 1945
Age at time of immigration: 3

Why Should So Many People Come and Change Our Culture?

I'd like to be married to some reasonable woman. I had no problem dating in the recent past, but now it's a lot harder. They're either too young or too old or not attracted to me that much anymore. So I feel a big push now. I've got to set my priorities and work in that department.

Looking back on the Debbie situation, I think I was just too damn unsettled and self-centered. Wanted everything perfect. Escaped from the potential responsibility of marriage. Debbie was such a doll—the perfect woman. We were together three years and went to this marriage counselor because Debbie wanted to get married. I didn't. We loved each other, but I was inventing all these excuses why we were ultimately incompatible. It was a bunch of malarkey. The counselor said: "Hey, there's nothing wrong with Debbie. It's you. You're just too inflexible."

These counseling sessions gravitated toward the German connection. It was like a psychological investigation. I didn't think there was really any relation to it. It was overwhelming. I said: "To hell with this." Anyway, Debbie and I broke up. It was nice to the end. Very nice.

In three other instances the relationships grew very close, and then the subject was: *Why are we still on this honeymoon? Let's get married.* Of course, the relationships broke up when I didn't go through. I wasn't ready if the queen of Sheba had come by. But I think that's past history. I'm over that hurdle. Maybe the German connection colored some of that, but I hate to rely on blaming the past for something I can certainly change if I develop a serious sense of purpose. Now I'm willing to settle for a lot less.

It's becoming a major issue for me—not being connected. Most of my friends are married. Some of them are having children.

The records indicate I was illegitimate, born a Catholic from a Catholic mother near Bremen. I think my mother came from a shoemaker family. There are maybe some relatives in Munich. I guess those were trying times. The Allies were approaching, and things were collapsing in wartime Germany. Records indicate my mother had some reluctance to give me up for adoption. She lived near a Catholic orphanage.

I treat my adoptive parents as my biological parents. They adopted me from that orphanage when I was three. I was selected, one out of many. My father, a U.S. Army lawyer, had an interesting history of investigating war crimes at Nordhausen and Dachau. He was involved in the denazification program. Both Mother and Dad learned German and befriended many German citizens, particularly some well-known industrialists. Anyway, they stayed at some of their very nice homes. Mom was kind of a collector. She had beautiful Meissen plates. German antiques. She didn't rip off a lot of these castles like so many others did over there. She got them fair and square. They were gifts. Of course, the barter system . . . So they did very well.

We had a German maid there, and Mom said I rode on her back all the time while she scrubbed the floor. It sounds very sexist now. My parents said: "Call her *Oma*—grandmother." I was very sensitive to loud noises and to anybody raising an arm quickly. I guess those are negative things about the tail end of the war or the orphanage.

I have a vague recollection of crossing the Atlantic in late 1948. Seeing a man who hadn't washed his face serving us food. This really surprised me. It turned out he was a black man. My parents thought that was real funny. And I guess it was.

Since I wasn't picking up English rapidly enough, my parents just stopped speaking German with me. I did have a very funny feeling for a long time, repeating English words. But really, in kindergarten, first, second grade, I didn't have a language problem. I related to kids and played.

Many times my parents and I would go to movies, and they'd hold my hands. That was very nice. And at kind of a late age, seven, I'd sometimes sleep with my parents in their double bed. They were very affectionate, very touching and warm.

I was about eight when they changed my name to Jürgen—after Grandpa Jürgen, who was Swiss. Mother was a second-generation Swiss. I didn't like the name. I thought it was odd-sounding—Jürgen. I adopted the name George for myself. *George slew the dragon.* Mom went along with calling me George in a playful manner. I outgrew it in a coupe of years. By the time I got into sixth grade, I was back to Jürgen. Gradually, I liked the name. My original name, Franz, does not have any kind of emotional connotation for me.

I didn't know I was adopted until sixth grade. It was just like one day Dad said: "We picked you out in an orphanage." The implication of that never really affected me. Except one time when kids were teasing me that I was adopted. So I never said that again to anyone but close friends. The idea of any German heritage was really beyond my understanding or interest in elementary or early high school. I was in the habit of saying: "Well, I'm from Wisconsin." I don't know where I picked up the idea that it wouldn't have been correct to say: "I'm from Germany." My parents never wanted to broach this subject. I wanted to, but I didn't feel they encouraged it at all. I don't know why.

When Dad died in 1988, I found out I was illegitimate. In sixth grade I had asked who my father was, and Dad had said: "Your father was killed by a German submarine." Did I ever wonder? Oh sure. Definitely. But I purposely did not get into this. I never looked up my origins because I wanted my parents to feel that I was completely their offspring.

I know nothing about my birth mother. Ever since my parents passed away, there's a need to find the root connection, to search for the biological birth mother. It's getting pretty late in the game, of course, but it's becoming increasingly important to me. I've got the money, I've got the time, but I don't have the language. It's just inertia. I've got to get off my duff and learn German. I find it very difficult to learn it. I'd like to say: *Hell, I'll just give somebody ten thousand dollars and guarantee they'll do it.* But I'd hate to do it that way. A friend of mine, who is German-American, wrote a letter to the *Standesamt*—registry office—in Löhnhorst to trace where my birth mother is. I never sent the letter. I don't know why.

I'm perplexed at my increasing interest in the G & A experience. German-American. I don't know how three years of living in another country can have so much influence on your middle age. It wasn't until ten years ago that I gave it a lot of thought and started taking some language classes. Five years ago I joined a band and a *Schuhplattler* group—a Bavarian folk dance group. I like the social aspects, but I also like the idea that it's a connection to G & A things.

This German-American organization is fascinating. A cultural heritage group. We went to Germany four years ago. In Munich I tried to look up my mother's name in the gigantic telephone book. I couldn't find anything. I had this need to make a pilgrimage to Dachau because Dad spent a lot of his time there. I got to see this gate where it says: *Arbeit macht frei*—Work liberates. I thought I'd get this spiritual experience because my father, after all, had been there. And you know, I didn't. I just felt flat. I mean, a lot of horrifying things happened there. . . . But at least I went there.

We took a rural road through Oberammergau. Then a week in Burghausen, which is south of Passau. Since we were just across the Salzach River, I really had a need to see where Hitler was born. Not to honor him. It wasn't a pilgrimage. But I was curious to see the environment this terrible tyrant had been born into. The locals certainly didn't make it a landmark. There's nothing available. It's not a tourist spot. When I found this church off the beaten path, I had this overwhelming feeling of sadness as I went down into the basement. They had this small engraving to the fallen at Stalingrad. I thought that was odd—in the middle of nowhere in Austria.

From seven until about age thirteen, I had this recurring severe nightmare. It was vague, like something was after me. . . . Darkness. I'd get the hell out of my parents' house. Sleepwalk. And then I'd get out of this trance and come back. Fortunately, they left the door open. I've related the nightmare to my origins. There would be a clock ticking. Usually when I was ready to go to bed or relaxing. It would get louder and louder like it was going to explode out of my brain. So I'd run into my parents' room and sleep with them. That was a very frightening experience. Only very recently have I gotten over a dread of the dark and being alone.

Sixth and seventh grades were a period of turmoil as far as these nightmares. I was an omnivorous reader, and one time when I was reading this encyclopedia, I saw these Greek masks. Like comedy and tragedy. I went upstairs and hid under the bed. Dad came up, and I had such fear of him finding me. Fear of Dad. Or something. And he was never cruel to me, never beat me. But then when he said, "There you are," everything was fine. And I slept.

The final straw was when I went into my parents' room, and there was something haunting, horrible about this dark room. And I've slept with my parents in their bed. We've had such wonderful . . . they were very close to me. So I couldn't understand this. It bothered me a lot. I went right through the window. Opened it and jumped from the second floor. Fortunately I went through the bushes. I went to a neighbor and said: "Gee, I just had to get away from that house."

I told Mom and Dad: "I got to go see a doctor about this. This is crazy." So they took me, and I told the doctor. I was worried. He said it was just growing pains. I guess that helped. No explanation really, but he said: "Well, Jürgen is perfectly normal."

I looked up to my parents. I really respected that they'd chosen me, that it wasn't an accident. There was a lot of love and affection, and maybe not enough discipline. Basically, I was pretty spoiled. When I'd fly off the handle, Mother would say: *"Langsam, langsam"*—"Slow, slow." I could manipulate one or the other if I wanted a new toy. Pull a tantrum. I didn't use it too often. Dad would blow up. When I was really bad—like throwing rocks and beating some kids—he would finally give me a spanking.

Outside the confines of adults, I was a holy terror. It must have been 1949 or 1950 when I was running and saw a little red wagon. I picked it up and threw it down the stairwell outside this garden apartment. A woman started running after me in a rage. I ran straight to the safety of the house. Mom was there. And she gave me a lecture. But my God, throwing a wagon down a stairwell? Why the hell would I do that? Looking back now, that really bothers me and shows that I was a destructive little person. But all our friends remarked how obedient, what an angel I was.

I'm not quick to anger now, really. I'm not a violent person now, but I was pretty violent when I was little. I was embarrassed because I was so big. In fourth or fifth grade, I was always picking a fight with another bully or somebody bigger than me. I just had to be dominant. I was a little JD at thirteen. Juvenile delinquent. And I had a penchant for rock throwing. I remember my mother crying in front of me because I was going up to juvenile court, just crying. And she got me crying. Instead of hitting me, she hit her fist and bruised it badly on the wall. That cured me. I was a good little boy after that.

I had my own room in sixth grade, and I remember putting up a sign: GERMAN GENERAL STAFF. I don't know why in the hell I put that up. I went through this phase. That must have really hurt and mortified my parents, but they didn't tell me to take it down. They were cool . . . very tolerant people. They had no ill will toward Germany or German people. I was the only kid on the base bicycling around with this German World War II helmet—a *Stahlhelm*. Everybody had army helmets and was playing cowboys and Indians or soldiers. I wish I had a picture of me then.

About that time I discovered Dad's documents on his war crimes investigations. A lot of very grisly photographs. Living skeletons. People after they'd been beaten. My parents probably knew I'd seen them, but they didn't say anything. Maybe this is why my mother said: "We'll watch this film together on TV." There was this big documentary called *The Twisted Cross*. It was about *Kristallnacht* and the persecution of the Jews and the rise of Hitler from the Munich beer halls. I recollect the clarity of it all . . . these thugs running around German streets and beating up on people. It was horrifying. I was awestruck, watching this thing in silence with Mom. She never lectured me or suggested that Germans were bad. She just simply had me watch it.

In college I was a student of history. I like the Jewish culture. I'm dating this Jewish woman now. It's basically the German-Jewish culture that made Germany what it is. Although the Jewish people are pretty standoffish and separate. Yet the German Jew in the nineteenth century, early twentieth century, is exemplified by Marx, Freud, Einstein, and a lot of others who made such an intellectual and cultural contribution in the German lands.

It was such a great nation. It's just too damn bad Germany lost all that land. And maybe rightly so. It's a little unfair, but that's the legacy of that horrible, dark regime of Nazism. There was so much inhumanity and barbarism. I wouldn't want to see it arise again anywhere in this world. It's really a pity the Nazi regime came up.

Germany has such a unique place in history. In my quiet, dark moments—years ago—I thought a lot about that period of time and caught myself in some weird, weird thinking: *Gee, if I was an invisible man and I was in Berlin, I'd be killing all the Russians.* . . . Never Americans, but Russians. Just weird stuff. That's out of my mind now.

That time fascinates me because I was, in a sense, the tail end of it. I'm proud of the German eagle—the Nazi eagle— on my birth certificate. They've crossed out the swastika underneath the eagle. I would really like that to appear because that's part of the bad heritage. However, that's what destroyed Germany. I feel sorry, you know. I think I feel a little guilt. I don't think I would have this feeling if I came from Ireland. After all, Germany was very aggressive in two world wars. A lot of people died. So there's a little guilt. I imagine it's more extreme for people who lived there as adults. I see a fainter connection if you were born after the war.

I was involved in planning the German-American Memorial in downtown Washington, D.C., near the Washington Monument. There are plaques in the ground about German-American friendship. Reagan was pushing it with Kohl, and I'm glad to see it. But only steps away is the Holocaust Museum, which of course blames Germany for the whole thing. It should be titled People's Inhumanity to People. The Holocaust is a very recent example of that. I mean the Catholic Church, American Indians, Russians against the Jews, Chinese against their own population, what the Arabs did to the blacks . . . So it's a little too narrow. It bothers me. I'm quick to anger when somebody talks about all the horrors perpetrated by the Nazi regime, when there are a lot of examples of other countries. So you can't say that Germans are uniquely predisposed in making it bad for other people.

I've developed into a Germanophile at this point. I feel it's a neat connection that I've got the genes of one of the most advanced cultural nations the world had ever seen up till the early 1940s. On the other hand, I like to think I'm American, too, because I grew up here. I've been deeply immersed in American culture. School system and friends. American parents. Hardly any connection with Germany at all. I feel pretty plain down-to-earth American. What the hell—the Constitution says I'll never be president of the United States. It's unfair. I've gone and sung the American anthem. I'm pro-American. I think it's basically the greatest country in the world.

I'm a German-American in terms of immigration, and I'm proud of that. This is a nation of immigrants, and I think I can be free to accept my brief German connection—a very important connection early on—and be proud of it without having a person say: "Well, you're a German." I'm not going around publicizing my heritage. You've got to be careful whom you speak with. I learned early that it can come back to bite you. Sometimes veiled prejudices are in the air if I talk about my German connection. Somebody might use that negatively, in anger. Then I feel a cultural gulf, a separateness.

After Mom passed away in 1991, a good friend of mine said: "I've always wondered something about you, Jürgen. You just don't look like your parents. Are you adopted?" So I said: "Yeah." It bothered me when he came up with that. It's this feeling that maybe you're not a true American. He started asking me a lot of questions about it, so I gave him minimalist answers. But then he used it against me when my heating system went out. I can afford a heating system, but I wanted to see how it is in the winter without any heat. All these welfare people complaining, and here I lived without heat and got up and put on my suit and tie and went to work. But it wasn't socially acceptable. My friend got really mad: "It's probably some connection with you being a war orphan." It bothered me that he used this war orphan statement to get at me. That's one of the reasons I don't publicize it. Because it'll come back.

I work for the federal government. Security and safety issues. Basically, I'm kind of a Republican, conservative and not ultraliberal. I wouldn't say I'm a racist. Some of my best bosses were a black woman and a black guy. I'd do anything for them.

The emphasis throughout the government and corporate world now is cultural diversity. You dare not talk about Captain John Smith or Pocahontas. Or about the Founding Fathers. Our cultural climate is really, really changing. The positive aspect is that you have Black History Month or Hispanic Heritage Week. But now the Equal Opportunity Office is opening it to everybody, and November is going to be Cultural Diversity Month. Last year at work they had someone represent Oprah in a make-believe interview. Everybody enjoyed it. You plan it, and then go up in front of the audience. This year they're going to have a Jewish guy, a Levi Strauss, you know, the jeans. It's well balanced—about three-fourths blacks, some American Indians and Orientals. They're all nice people.

Anyway, they invited me to be Beethoven. I told them I'd like to tell them a little bit about German immigration. Because of the war and because so many people lost loved ones in the Holocaust, it just wasn't good to say you're German-American. There was some undercurrent. Now it's getting a little more acceptable. So I got my work cut out for me. I'll wear an old tuxedo or something. I'm delighted because this shows the German-American experience a little. You have people out there who have no idea.

Opening up to cultural diversity has positive effects in the United States. More of a melting pot rather than a collage of different cultures. But there is a lot of concern about illegal immigration and the change of our culture. Things are getting out of hand. Because I'm an immigrant, I have a little prejudice against the change in immigration. You had to be sponsored by somebody here. Not come in and go automatically on welfare. You also had to have some needed profession. Be a contributing member of society. Maintain the northern European heritage. But that's all changing. And it's hurting America. That's what makes me mad. Why should so many people come and change our culture? Europeans don't have preference. Now it's Orientals and Hispanics. It bothers me going to a 7-Eleven and having to work to have English understood.

So I guess I do have a kind of a prejudice toward other cultures. Individually, I'm not prejudiced against anyone. Although I don't think I could marry outside my culture. If I can't talk about what I grew up studying—John Milton—and where I grew up, and objects that I was surrounded with, like early American or German antiques or porcelains, just the whole European cultural experience and the American white experience, then I feel a little uncomfortable.

Two years ago I was dating this blond girl, pure Russian. Two Russian women have been in my life. I got a feeling they're all high-strung and want complete obedience. These women always wanted their own way. They had high champagne tastes and lifestyles. One always wanted to go to fancy restaurants and plays—heaven forbid occasionally to McDonald's. I can basically afford it, but I have a midwestern upbringing with middle-class tastes.

I think it's funny—considering my feeling about the Russians in World War II—that I was dating two Russians. None of this German connection really mattered. I have nothing against Russian people, believe me. They were as bad as the Nazis. Or more so.

Basically, I'm all alone. You know, I can do just about anything. Because I'm pretty free. I never really get lonely very often. If I don't get married, you could say it's poetic justice for every woman who wanted to get married when I didn't. So I'm getting my punishment.

Katharina

Born: 1947
Age at time of immigration: 10

When Germans and Jews Can Talk

I have a number of Jewish clients. I work really well with them and they with me. There is a range of how much sharing a therapist will do with a client, and I tend to be on the more open end of that range. My Germanness plays an important role when I work with Jews. It has to be acknowledged. We have to understand that we understand each other through that. Over and around and through that. I see this Germanness as a thread that runs through my life—every aspect of my life. Sometimes you see it and sometimes you don't. It weaves in and out. It's a part of all the work I've done, a part of my choices. It's hard to separate out.

I have not brought it to the surface before.

When I know somebody is Jewish, that needs to be out there. I want my clients to hear that from me and not discover that in some other way because that would be a betrayal of trust. They need to have the choice of working with me or not working with me. I don't think it would be an issue if I were Italian.

It is an issue for Jews to trust Germans. I'm thinking about a particular client I have right now. Her being Jewish is the very prominent part of the work she needs to do. If somebody can be very Jewish, she's very Jewish and proud of it, but she also feels the weight of that. She understands me, and I understand her because I have similar feelings about being German: it is both—the source of wonderful gifts to me, but also the source of pain. That's how we know each other. That's what makes her trust me and allows her—in whatever way clients follow therapists—to follow me. I don't think there was any way for us to *not* have that be an issue.

I'm drawn into making those connections. It must be a way of bridging the horror and healing the wounds on both sides—my own as well as my client's. My client is a little younger than I and grew up with some notions about Germans, just as I grew up with some notions about Germans. The reality of what it is to be German probably lies where those two pieces come together. My client talks about going off to a Jewish girls' camp in the summertime and being traumatized as she watched movies about what happened to the Jews in concentration camps.

My mother remarried when I was eight. We moved into military housing in Heidelberg, and I went to the American military school. It was learning by immersion—I didn't speak any English. I ran around with the kids in our building, played with them. They thought I was mute because I didn't speak. They didn't realize I was German. I didn't speak until I knew it would sound perfect. I don't know how long that was. I know I had to speak in school, and I agonized over saying the wrong thing. It was a difficult time. The schools were supportive and the teachers nice, but I felt different—like a fish out of water.

There was a movie theater, and the kids went to the kiddie movies on Saturday mornings. Before the main movie came on, they used to have serials—always about the nasty, ugly, awful *Krauts* and the Americans. There I sat, and I wanted to fit in with my friends; yet, I kept looking for my father's face amongst those nasty *Krauts* on the movie screen. They were always ugly. And they always talked loudly. And they were always mean. And they always died.

And I hated it. I hated going there. But I was never one to say what I wanted, and so I went. Dutifully. To not hurt my mother's feelings, I pretended I had a nice Saturday morning.

I remember being called a Nazi on the playground and wondering what to do with that. A Nazi and a *Kraut*. Weekends I often went back to my grandparents and my German friends. My friends, of course, started seeing me as an Ami— an American. There is no more scathing word than *Ami* uttered in a certain tone by a German. There is nothing more denigrating than *Kraut* said in the same tone by an American.

I don't think I could ever go back and be German again.

I could have during my teens—maybe. But I don't think I can anymore. It's really changed and I've changed. I like my life, and I like my work. It would be nice to think I could have both countries be home. But I don't think that is possible.

I feel often that I don't know exactly where I belong. For a time I felt like a German among Americans, and I certainly now feel like an American among Germans. In some ways it's so familiar, and in other ways I'm really a stranger there. It's sad, that kind of almost schizophrenic existence. Anxiety-provoking. I often feel I can't do it right. For anybody.

I was born in October 1947 in Neckargemünd, a small town outside Heidelberg. My mother's family was very close, and she lived with them until she married my father. A year and a half after I was born, my parents divorced, which at that time, in a nice upper-middle-class family in Germany, was unthinkable. So from the very beginning there was a difference between me and other people. I lived with my grandparents—

they were involved in my life from the beginning. My mother worked for the Americans, which made me different again in a sort of negatively loaded way. She was a very beautiful woman, very stylish. When I think back, she probably was Americanized to some degree and didn't fit in with all my friends' mothers, who were nice *Hausfrauen* with their aprons and little print dresses.

My grandfather really was my father in a lot of ways. Because he'd had a heart attack when he was just forty, they hadn't taken him into the army. Everybody else had gone off to fight. At one point he was probably one of the few men left in town. He was seen as disabled and lived to the ripe old age of eighty-something. He was the first house-husband I ever knew and did all the cooking, all the laundry. My grandmother was the first feminist I knew, although she wouldn't have taken on that label. The first eight years of my life they were more parents to me than my mother, who worked shifts and sometimes slept days. Other times she was gone—I mean, she had to have a life, too. Those years I didn't really feel close to her in a mother-child way.

My father visited, and I visited him in the summers. It was always very pleasant, but the attachment didn't feel paternal. While I have specific memories of my grandfather, my father just sort of floats in and out. At one time he worked as a salesman for a candy factory and drove a panel truck that had a big turtle on the side. He picked me up in this truck. That was a big deal.

In later years my father and I became close, and he told me stories about the war that really had an impact on me. But until I was a teenager we never talked about that. I know he was a pacifist, my father, an opera singer and actor. He avoided serving in uniform until almost the end of the war because he performed instead for the troops. So his life didn't change drastically. I think he also continued to be a performer for the public, doing what he loved best. Music. Hitler valued *Kunst*—art.

One of the most powerful stories I ever heard from my father was that he was sent to an intelligence unit on the border between France and Italy. That unit was supposed to take over a château that had been used as a communications station. My father was in charge. I don't know what rank. The château had been abandoned—not only by its owner, but by the military. My father talks about walking through this beautiful old house. Some damage had been done, and lots of things had been taken, but there was still a music room with a beautiful grand piano. There was sheet music on the piano by some composer who interested my father, and who was banned in Germany because he was Jewish.

My father saw that sheet music, picked it up, and put it in his jacket pocket. And he was appalled with himself. As much as he hated war and despised the violence, he had just participated in his own way, doing what soldiers had always done, taking what they conquered—whether it was sheet music or countries or women—the spoils of war. Thirty years later when my father told me that story, he had tears in his eyes. For him that was the worst moment of the war, even though there certainly were other times when he was in fear of his life. He lost some of his companions—they died in the snow trying to cross the Alps—and he kept walking. Lots of horror stories. But he said the worst horror was knowing there was a seed of that horror in his own heart. That really frightened him.

When he came to visit the States for the first time in the mid-eighties, he asked me: "What's with all the flags?" I tossed it off: "You know, it's the Fourth of July. People are proud of their heritage and proud of their country." He was appalled. "I hate flag-waving—I hate it." I didn't understand where all that came from and thought he was making a big to-do about nothing. He tried to explain to me what was so dangerous about nationalism. He saw our Fourth of July celebration and other nationalistic holidays elsewhere as related to what happened in Germany during the Second World War, to people having some notion of superiority. Now I certainly think about it and don't enjoy fireworks.

A couple of years ago I sat down with my mom, and we went through old photographs. Faces struck her that she hadn't thought about in many years. It was clear to me listening that her whole generation of young men had died. Her boyfriend had lost a leg, and then his hospital had been blown up. All the boys who'd gone to school with her—there hardly were any of them left at the end of the war.

She talked about being conscripted. Young women didn't go into the army, but they had to go to camp for some kind of training and then work in factories or on farms because the men were gone. My mother wound up working in the vineyards, carrying big tanks on her back, spraying the grapes. She was a little bitty thing and didn't last long at that. The farmers decided she would be of better use baby-sitting. While she took care of little kids, the men she would have married died or were crippled.

I just can't imagine. I lived through the Vietnam era, and a lot of my friends were drafted, but it wasn't the wholesale slaughter that happened in Germany. During the Vietnam years, it was terrible to be in Germany as an American. My German friends challenged me big-time: "How can you live in that country?" I tried to tell them: "I'm against the war. I don't believe in that war."

My father's tragic flaw was that he liked women a lot and had affairs. It hurt my mother tremendously. He had all the power in the relationship, being nine years older, more experienced, and so she married his polar opposite, a young man straight off the farm in Mississippi, someone she felt she could control because she was more mature. They were in love. *Ja.* But he saw her as this German *Fräulein,* sweet and little. I don't think he got how powerful she could be.

He was an enlisted man in the army, younger than my mother by eight years. When he first came into our lives, he brought chocolates. He brought all kinds of food. . . . Peanut butter—I'd never eaten peanut butter. Marshmallows—all my friends wanted marshmallows, and we ate marshmallows until we were sick. He would come home from the PX with not one, but three new dresses for me. At that time in Germany you wore the same dress for a week, and then on Sunday you wore something different. He seemed wealthy to us. We'd never been poor, but everything was new and exciting. He not only courted my mother—he wanted me to like him. Americans in Germany at that time were all seen as rolling in dough. They had big Pontiac-type cars, these *Strassenkreuzer,* as they called them.

They got married in May 1956, and they had a very hard time when we first came to the States in 1958. They hadn't thought about what it meant to transfer my mother to the South and to relative poverty. I was ten, and I had figured out that my stepfather was not the knight in shining armor we'd thought he was. We lived on tomato sandwiches for a while and had to borrow money to buy furniture. I remember my mother making my school clothes from curtains. She adapted, but she must have gone through hell, realizing what she'd gotten herself into.

We lived in Georgia, and I remember my mother and me in the kitchen crying to "I'm Dreaming of a White Christmas." It was eighty degrees in the shade, and we were homesick. Ritual was real important, and some of it wasn't transportable or we couldn't afford it. We couldn't buy a traditional Christmas goose in Augusta, and the snow was missing. It was pretty tinselly, and all that Santa Claus stuff did not feel familiar. There was a lot of sadness around Christmas.

And there was the southern accent to deal with. Languages come pretty easily to me, but once again, I was different, and my difference was held up for all to see. My teacher was Southern Baptist—pretty rigid, older—and she made me memorize Bible verses as punishment. She didn't like me—not just because I was the new kid in the class, but because she knew I was German. I can still picture her, and I wonder if she lost somebody in the war, because she made me pay for something I didn't do. The other children felt what was going on. Who wants to be hooked up with the whipping girl? I've been a pleaser all my life, and I wasn't able to please this woman at all. That's the first time I felt I was punished for being German.

I've run into that kind of prejudice since then in minor ways. As an adult, nobody has that kind of power over you—you can walk away—but when you're a kid in school, you have to sit there for nine months of the year and make the best of it. So it was a pretty lonely year for me.

Without the stability of my early years, I might have become really messed up. Since my stepfather was in the military, I changed schools fourteen times before I graduated. I hated the army because it moved us around so much. The human mind is really fascinating, and I never realized until my late twenties that half the moves were not caused by the army but were my mother's choice, her need to be with family. My stepfather would get some sort of undesirable overseas duty like Korea, and my mother and I would go home to Germany, spend a year or two there, and move back to Georgia until my stepfather would get another assignment.

I lived in my childhood home with my grandparents for a year or two at a time. I was going to American schools in Heidelberg and living German. Again, that sort of schizophrenic piece. Where I was living, I was considered German; yet, I had this other life that the German community didn't know anything about. At school I was like everybody—I could talk States and was part of the group, but they didn't know about my other life with my grandmother and grandfather and my mother.

And it never mixed. It was always separate.

It's funny how in your memory you experience life in bits and pieces. I've never really put it all together until now. Well, that's how life was: in bits and pieces. It wasn't a whole. It was parts.

At that time and always, my mother made friends with other German women, and they became very tight. Augusta, Georgia, is a military town, and a lot of German women had gotten there the same way my mother had. Those women sought one another out. It's a bond I've never seen before. They're like second mothers to me. I feel lucky to have experienced that. It's gotten my mother through the hardest years. These women had to create their own family. Part of what makes a family is that you have a history together. There were times when we lived with one of my mother's friends and her daughter while my stepfather went to Korea and Vietnam.

My mom has close American friends, too, but there's always that core of German women: they support each other, and they know where they came from and what the change to the U.S. means; they can say anything to each other about either country and understand how that's meant; they can be critical of Germany and still love it and still pay six dollars a pound for real German *Wurst*.

American women and German women don't share the tragic experience of having a generation of young men crippled or killed . . . their homes devastated . . . their childhoods shattered. The war wasn't fought on this soil. That difference colors how you look at the rest of your life. There's no tragedy that measures up to that tragedy.

I'm not sure how my mother feels the shame of being German—she doesn't talk about it. I know how I feel it a generation later. My mother is pretty spunky, and I think if anything derogatory came up about Germany, she'd get her back up real quick. While I'd question: *What's the grain of truth here? Do I need to explain something to these people that they don't understand about Germans or Germany?* I don't have one feeling about being German. I think for my mother it's clear, and for me it's mixed—plus, minus, plus, minus. . . . Some of the most important, loving, giving relationships of my life are over there, and if I were to hear a negative word about Germany, I'd want to explain, to defend, to share what's wonderful about being German. That's different from my mother, who would be more apt to write somebody off.

Yet, in that explaining is a defensive posture. It's like: *We're not all Nazis. We're not all Jew-haters. We don't all march in goose step. We're not all loud and aggressive and dictatorial.*

There's been a shift inside me. Being German was something I hid for a long time. If people asked, I would say yes and drop it. Most of the time, if you don't give a lot of information, people move on. I didn't spend a lot of time telling my friends about my German heritage until I was well into adulthood, until I got to know my father and listened to him talk about Germany and the war and his experience.

Before that I might have talked about German food. I sometimes fixed German meals and people really enjoyed that. I did let on that I knew something about German wines. I grew up drinking wine. I can remember sitting at the table. My feet wouldn't even reach the floor, but I had my own little wineglass. My grandfather was a red wine drinker—unusual for that part of the country—and he'd pour a couple of tablespoons of his wine into my glass and then fill it up with soda. That was my glass of wine. I preferred red wine because it looked prettier, of course. Well . . . I still prefer red wine. Wine has always been a part of festivities, and I enjoy it every day with a meal.

It seems different the way Europeans and Americans drink

wine. In the past, Americans drank at a party to get loopy, but now more and more Americans are drinking wine the European way where it's just a real enjoyable part of a meal. I like the ritual part of wine drinking, the toasts, and just taking that extra second to look at people before you drink the first sip. It's like a greeting at the table. When my second husband and I got married, the toast during the wedding ceremony was part of the ritual that we wrote for ourselves. We toasted our family and friends. We cited the l'chaim in the Jewish wedding. The Japanese wedding includes drinking wine, and in the Christian tradition the first miracle was at a wedding in Cana.

Every now and then, I have to make *Sauerbraten* and *Rotkohl* and *Schweinebraten* and *Spätzle,* food I grew up with, especially when I'm feeling kind of puny, emotionally or otherwise. It's that nursery-food stuff, I guess. It's comfort. And it's reconnecting to a time in my life when I felt real safe and comforted.

But other parts of being German just were never discussed. There were too many things I might have needed to explain that I couldn't explain to myself yet. What is different now is that I got to know my father and listened to him talk about Germany and the war and his experience. And there it is, you know: somehow what you talk about—even when it's horrible—isn't as bad as what you don't talk about. Now, in the more recent years, I'm up front with where I'm from and talk about it a lot. I find that it's well received. And I make fun of being a sort of rigid German and needing control. I soften that with humor. I make that work for me somehow.

I know exactly where I learned that. There was a lot of humor in our family, and it was used to soften the tough things. I remember my grandfather talking about the radio he had in the basement during the war. He could pick up the BBC. He'd try to find out what was really going on, but then he'd come upstairs and tell my grandmother—who was known as the talker—only what was already in the newspaper, so that she couldn't go out and by accident tell something she wasn't supposed to know. That censorship and secrecy . . . I got a picture of how frightening it was, *Opa*—Grandfather—hiding in the basement and listening to the radio. I could tell there was tension in the story even though it was told in a harmless way. I wasn't told about the fear and about what happened to people who got caught listening to the BBC.

It's not that my mother and her side of the family are silent and inarticulate—they're very cocky people, very extroverted—but there clearly was a limit as to what they talked about regarding the war. I remember an indentation in the floor in my mother's room. It creaked when you stepped on it, and under the linoleum you could feel a hole in the timbers. That's where a bomb went through . . . shrapnel. I was told that bombs came flying and everybody ran off to the woods, but the feelings about that were not conveyed. It's sanitized somehow if you take the feelings out of something. I don't think a kid can know what feelings to put into it. Then as you mature, that story goes with you, but you don't know the feelings that were attached to it.

I can now think about what it must have been like to hear the sirens go off and to run into the woods. And I can attach feeling to that. But for the longest time that was just a story, because that's how it was told, sort of offhand: "Oh *ja,* that's where the shrapnel came through." A lot of war stories were probably told in that sterilized way to protect the people who suffered. Why would you want to recapture that horror?

But then it does leave that gap for the children who grew up listening to those stories.

When my first marriage ended, I was working for the Mayo Clinic in their Department of Psychiatry, and I decided I needed therapy. When you work in the psychiatric community, you know everybody who does therapy. In the phone book were just three names I didn't recognize as colleagues. I remembered seeing one of those individuals at an open house in somebody's office and thinking: *She looks German.* I went to her because there was a piece of my history I didn't have to tell her. She already knew. And that was really useful to me. Sort of a shortcut. I could have spent years explaining all of that to another therapist. She knew.

A lot of my colleagues are Jewish. The field of psychiatry is full of Jews—that's not just the stereotype. One psychiatrist, who is down the hall from me, and I have talked quite a bit about him being a prisoner of war and about me being German. He is an American, who was taken prisoner by the Germans. We've both had tears in our eyes as we've talked about those issues. We both jokingly say, *"Guten Morgen, Herr Doktor"* to one another. We play with it. But we're also real serious about that being part of who we are.

At this stage of my life I'm understanding and tolerating the complexity. I don't have to make it simple. That's true of how I feel about being German. It's a very complex thing, and it's okay that it's that complicated. In fact, it's the complexity that makes it a real gift. I don't wish it away. I don't wish it out of my life.

If you'd asked me at age fourteen, I would have wished it away.

In my thirties I went to the Anne Frank Museum in Amsterdam, and when I came out of there, I could hardly walk. I couldn't talk about it. Prior to that, I don't think I ever did let in what happened to the Jews in Germany. I don't remember when I first understood about the Holocaust, but obviously it must have been before I went to the Anne Frank House. In retrospect, I think I always knew. There were whispered bits and pieces of that horror told at times when I wasn't supposed to listen—it was too terrible for a child. But I heard and knew.

It's fascinating that my grandmother marched with other

women to ban the bomb, told me in gruesome detail about the inhumanity done to the people of Hiroshima, taught me to abhor weapons and war, but never directly talked about the death camps with me. The Holocaust was unspeakable, and the silence—eventually—spoke much louder than the words would have.

We had Jewish friends. It wasn't talked about. They never said. We never said. In my mother's generation, amongst the Germans I know, there's still very little talk about what happened to the Jews.

I was very active in the desegregation of the South. It's the same piece over and over: I don't tolerate bigotry. That's part of my heritage from the war, from the abuse of power, though I wasn't even alive. The political became personal in a very real way for me. Because I lost home and family and country early in life, I have a heart- and gut-level understanding of being disenfranchised and powerless, of being seen as less than and different in a negative way. Outcast. And that's become a life theme for me. I've put myself in positions to champion the underdog—kids who can't read and learn; women who are raped; people who are in pain. In a more global, more political way, I'm trying to make up for what happened to the Jews.

Making those connections is a way of trying to get the whole picture. I can honestly say that it gets richer. The pain is a part of it, but there's so much more. And when the connections happen, when people really talk to each other and understand each other's lives, that enhances and enriches. Some things can happen that avert tragedy when Germans and Jews can talk.

Conclusion

If you listen to someone long enough and very closely, you will find a story. As a writer, I'm always aware of that. Though each of these interviews turned out to be uniquely different, I found major themes that overlapped, most of all the silence that reached into every area of our lives. What Beate recalled about her history lessons in school—"a huge silence about the war years"—did not only affect her, but countless other schoolchildren, including myself. "We happened to get to World War I twice in history class," she disclosed, "and then there was the summer break." Nearly everyone spoke of similar experiences. In Eva's school they "would talk for months about different countries. I knew a lot about America, about Greece. But Germany . . . it was always very brief."

Secrets about the country were often impossible to separate from secrets about the family. Marika's mother believed "children are better off not knowing," but for Marika, not knowing felt worse than the truth. "What you imagine as a child is often a lot worse than reality." We talked about the cost of the secret, the weight of the secret. Katharina confirmed that "what you talk about—even when it's horrible—isn't as bad as what you don't talk about."

Again and again, I noticed that our adult relationships with our parents seem less resolved than the relationships I see Americans of my generation having with their parents. Too much has been left untouched. Unsaid. "Maybe by bringing to light what happened fifty and sixty years ago," Karl hoped, "we can make some sense out of what's happening today."

Our German heritage affects us differently in America than if we had stayed in Germany. During my first year of living here, I found out more about German history than in eighteen years of growing up in Germany. Beate's experience was similar, and she attributed this to living "far enough away to come to grips with my culture and my tradition. People who are out of their familiar surroundings are forced to define it. If you never get out, you don't have to define it."

While some genuinely attempted to understand their cultural heritage, quite a few had stayed within the familiar silence and were afraid or unwilling to look much beyond it. It was not that they didn't speak—it was rather that their silence manifested itself in denial, evasion, repression, justification, defensiveness, and an inability to mourn—not all that different from the response of our parents' generation.

One of the interviewees most deeply locked into that silence was Anneliese, who had traveled six hours to meet me in a city on the East Coast. Since we had already corresponded and spoken on the phone, we moved easily into a personal conversation about our children, menopause, Anneliese's granddaughter. . . . We laughed, identified. But that identification broke off for me soon after I clipped the microphone to Anneliese's collar and began to listen. She flinched when she said she couldn't watch films about concentration camps. "I don't want to know. You couldn't pay me to go into the Holocaust Museum in Washington. . . . Why in the world would I want to go into a pretend cattle car? And I understand they have shoes of the victims." As Anneliese described devastating details to me, it struck me how—by investing such energy in refusing to know—she saw the Holocaust very closely, a private and haunting vision that continues to reach into her sleep with nightmares.

In contrast, those of us who confronted and acknowledged the horrors of our German heritage had arrived at some level of peace with ourselves, coupled with a profound sadness and awareness of our individual responsibility. For Ulrich, a pacifist, this meant staying alert to his heritage. "Even though the individual may not be at fault—I mean, those of us who were born after the war didn't participate in the horrible events and therefore cannot be found guilty by any jury—it's not just the individual. It's the collective. It's the culture that bred individuals who created these problems, and since I'm part of that same culture and my children are to some extent part of that culture, it is at least my responsibility to be aware and to pass that awareness on, because we need to make sure that's not going to happen again. We can't run away."

Sigrid, a lawyer and political activist, cautioned against the notion of a national character. "Some people I've met in Germany are kind of ordinary people. That's the frightening thing—that this can happen in a very ordinary way. It lulls you into complacency to think it takes a certain kind of national character. We seem to have an enormous capacity to be mean and vicious to people whom we define as the other, and then anything is plausible." What Sigrid pointed out was not all that different from what I've heard some of my American friends say in relationship to their own country, that if Americans believe only Nazis *can* commit atrocities like this, they consider themselves immune from ever committing those atrocities. I believe it is important to recognize the capacity to do evil as essentially human and to be alert to what can happen if government legitimizes or rewards evil by providing what historian

Steven E. Aschheim calls an "enabling killing-environment."

While several of the interviewees confronted this capacity to do evil personally as well as globally, others distanced themselves by taking on a defensive posture. "I'm quick to anger when somebody talks about all the horrors perpetrated by the Nazi regime," Jürgen told me, "when there are a lot of examples of other countries. So you can't say that Germans are uniquely predisposed in making it bad for other people." Anneliese, too, pointed out that "other countries are exterminating their unwanted," but Johanna sounded impatient with Germans who "take away from their responsibility by saying others did it, too." She pointed to the "thought-out, planned, organized, rationalized evil that makes it different from all those."

As they spoke of atrocities in other parts of the world, I became increasingly aware of that fine but distinctive line between those who did so to avoid thinking about the Holocaust, and those who looked at it closely in their attempt to understand those other atrocities.

Several disclosed their parents' and other adults' attempts to justify or diminish the Holocaust. Ulrich, who grew up in New York in a large German community, heard comments that "the number of Jews gassed was exaggerated. There weren't that many Jews in the world." When Karl visited Germany as a young man, one of his relatives told him, "There was no crime when Hitler was in power. Hitler cleaned up the streets." Eva, too, heard justifications of the good Hitler had done. As a child, she was told, "The way it started, it was okay. He did so much for the Germans in the beginning. And he did build the *Autobahnen*." Those *Autobahnen* were mentioned in nearly a third of the interviews, but only in quotes of what parents and elders had said.

Several spoke of significant relationships with Jews. Karl was raised by his Jewish uncle, and Sigrid, who married a Jewish man, stayed connected to his family after she divorced him. "Part of his appeal for me was that he came from this large Jewish family, who were very accepting of me. In some ways I married the family as much as I married him." Her son "doesn't see it as a conflict to have a German-born mother and a Jewish father. At this point in his life he's not particularly interested in either politics or history."

Katharina valued her Jewish clients. "My Germanness plays an important role when I work with Jews. It has to be acknowledged. We have to understand that we understand each other through that. Over and around and through that. . . . I want my clients to hear that from me and not discover that in some other way, because that would be a betrayal of trust. They need to have the choice of working with me or not working with me."

Gisela spoke about finding a "healing gift, which is the friendship of Jews. It's as though we're wordlessly creating bridges." She felt certain that "you can't know the truth unless you know both sides," and she pointed out that "research and literature are beginning to discover that German offspring of the war have that same survivor guilt that Jewish offspring have." She told her son "and his Jewish girlfriend that they should feel no burden for what happened before them, that their burden is to always be very conscious in the world, to be aware and sensitive to atrocities of all kinds."

Thoughts about guilt—collective or personal—came up in most interviews. While Beate believed there was a "shadow of a collective guilt" and Katharina defined her deep uneasiness as shame, Karl didn't "feel any sense of collective guilt. . . . Bad Germans did things. Bad Americans have done just the same. I know enough bad people to know who's capable of what."

Heinrich believed strongly that "as a child born during or after the war, you should not be held responsible for what your parents or other Germans did." But Johanna approached the issue of responsibility from a different angle. "I

read somewhere that, being born in 1949, I'm not actually responsible for what happened, but I am responsible *now* every
time the subject comes up . . . in my own reaction."

"What happened in the war, Daddy?" It's a question that
Karl has pondered countless times. "That's something that
has consumed me, preoccupied me . . . trying to sort out who
my mother is and who my father is."

Beate has tried to understand what happened in Germany
by imagining herself into her parents' situation. "I'm glad I
didn't grow up in the Third Reich because I don't know what I
would have done. I'm scared to think about it." She saw definite parallels between her Catholic upbringing and the Nazi
indoctrination. "You obey. You do not question. And the better you obey, the better person you are."

Usually, our parents' focus was on the personal rather
than the political. Sigrid spoke of her family viewing "the war
in a very personal way and not so much on the grander scale."
She said that "they simply were not that political." Most of our
parents only spoke of war incidents that established their own
victimhood. They were more prone to talk about their suffering than about the suffering inflicted on the Jews. As a result,
quite a few of the interviewees' stories about their parents'
war experiences—as well as their personal memories—are
tinged by that defensiveness and denial. There seemed to be a
need to feel victimized as a form of acquittal, an impulse to
say: *You don't understand. We were the victims. We lost so much.*

Katharina's father was unusual in that he exposed to his
daughter how he recognized "a seed of that horror in his own
heart" when he stole sheet music during the war. Although his
theft was minor in comparison to other transgressions, "he
was appalled with himself. . . . He had just participated in his
own way, doing what soldiers had always done, taking what
they conquered—whether it was sheet music or countries or
women—the spoils of war." Unlike Katharina's father, most of

our parents, teachers, and spiritual leaders were not facing this loss of what they once had believed themselves to be.

For Heinrich it was crucial to exonerate his father, a soldier, and his older brother, who'd been in the Hitler *Jugend.* "They really didn't have anything to do with it," he claimed. "They just went through the motions because they basically had no choice." And Anneliese refused to accept that her father—although a member of the SS—could have participated in war crimes. Yet, here, too, she contradicted herself—characteristic for her throughout the interview—already suspecting that "if you were in the SS, you had to have done something."

A tendency to look at some issues openly while evading others came through in many interviews. Although Gisela needed to see her father as a victim—"If he did horrible things in the concentration camps, I consider him just as much a victim of the times as anyone he might have victimized"—she was able to move away from that defensiveness when she spoke of herself carrying "the lessons of the Holocaust: *What is it in a human being that can change that person into a monster?* You do have to ask that question. You can't get away from it without repressing a great deal."

When I asked how much their parents had known, I usually came across a vested interest in repression—even with independent thinkers like Sigrid, who believed that her mother and grandmother "hadn't known about the concentration camps. . . . Once the war came, they were caught up in surviving." Yet, Sigrid was astute in identifying her own defensiveness. "I've never been able to press them past the point of what they were willing to say. . . . Maybe I haven't wanted to think about it. . . . I sound like I'm defending them."

Eva was one of several who figured there must have been people in Germany who had known, yet could not concede that their parents might have been among those. Some reasoned that it had been the strategy to keep people uninformed, and others brought up location as a justification for news not being available, in Eva's case because her family had "lived in a tiny farming community," in Sigrid's because of "an urban environment."

Descriptions of war-torn Germany emerged in nearly every life story, and at times those details were so vivid and immediate that I could picture them. Many Germans fled their homes on foot, in the back of trucks, in cattle trains. Eva's mother had to wait for the birth of her third child before she could escape from the advancing Russians, and Eva never forgot those weeks of walking toward Berlin as a four-year-old. Women were terrified of rape. Eva hid with her mother and aunt beneath a table "when the Russians came. . . . My mother would nurse the baby—she didn't have much milk—just to keep it quiet." Heinrich felt quite certain that his mother was raped by a Russian. "A soldier dragged my mother off, and my aunt was holding me tight, clutching me. Then, a while later, my mother appeared again, and she was crying. . . . She kept saying: 'Abwaschen'—'Wash.'"

Usually, the Russians were described as the bad guys—cruel, barbaric, and eager to inflict death or torture—but Ulrich pointed out that although he'd always heard "that the Germans all wanted to run towards the Americans and away from the Russian soldiers," his uncle told him about American soldiers who "took potshots at anybody who moved when they entered the city." And Gisela's grandfather described to her the "American bombs that would light up the sky like a Christmas tree."

War or postwar memories still affect them today. Several have recurrent nightmares or are frightened of sudden loud noises and low-flying airplanes. Eva "grew up kind of scared, easily intimidated," and Beate remembered "listening to machine-gun fire. I wasn't told what it was, but everyone was very afraid. This probably had a lot to do with that—despite my positive outlook on life—I am fearful of things I don't know."

In every single story I felt a tremendous sense of loss—loss of home, of cultural identity, of dreams, of family, of safety, of parental love. For some, this loss and grief remains unresolved today, making it nearly impossible to form loving and trusting relationships.

Fathers, for the most part, were absent or not very loving. Marika wanted to be close to her father. "Of the people I grew up with and went to school with, I'm the only one who had a father. All other fathers were gone and lost—missing in action, killed in the war, died in prison, died from illness due to the war." Both she and Eva reunited with their fathers in 1946 after long absences, just in time to celebrate their fifth birthdays. Eva smiled as she recalled: "I didn't remember him, you know. He had a little chewing gum and chocolate. He was a prisoner of war in France."

Though several grew up without fathers, they usually had significant adults in their lives, like aunts or grandparents, but most of all their mothers, who became increasingly strong during the war while fleeing with their children and scavenging for food. But all too often their independence was lost to them with the return of their husbands, and they settled back into the traditional family structure where men made the decisions. While Eva's mother "was *auf der Flucht*—on the run—she had to do it herself, but anything after, it was always *Vati*—Daddy. *Vati* made the decisions. . . . She really put him on a pedestal. And she grew a little weaker in this."

Heinrich's loss of a dog may not seem terribly important when compared to the losses that others experienced, but it is significant in that it demonstrates how far the machinery of destruction reached. "That dog was actually drafted into the war. And he was killed. My parents got an official notification that he died with honors. I hate to think what that dog was being used for."

Quite a few spoke of hunger and the fear of hunger. Foraging and stealing meant survival. Heinrich's parents taught him how to gather mushrooms, fruit, and firewood. Still the gatherer, Heinrich brought me plums from his garden when we met for his taping. He told me about bombing raids and how afterwards "huge craters would be left, where rainwater or natural groundwater would collect. We used to play and swim in those wonderful holes. Frogs would be in there, little tadpoles that we caught." Heinrich was the only one who spoke of that childlike ability to find joy in the midst of destruction. "Maybe it's survival," he reflected, "where—given the minimal life support—you didn't expect any more."

Ulrich's uncle butchered "a cow in a pasture to get food for the family, putting his life at risk. . . . Since we were *Flüchtlinge*—refugees, there was very little to eat. Apparently, everybody begged and in some cases stole milk and eggs." Beate described what it was like to be the outsider. "The two main classes there were *Einheimische* and *Flüchtlinge*—natives and refugees. I was the *Flüchtling*, the underdog. So I know exactly how that feels—being different."

This feeling of being different, of being the other, emerged with many as they spoke about their immigration to America. "All through my teenage years," Ulrich told me, "I felt like an outsider." And Hans-Peter, who was eight when he arrived here, the same age as Ulrich, experienced that "when you immigrate, you become somebody else from who you were." Both felt shunned at school. Ulrich "was known as 'the German,' sometimes as 'the Nazi.' . . . I felt that this was a terrible injustice because I was not a Nazi. I was German."

The realization that their cultural heritage was the subject of stereotyping and jokes complicated their adjustment to a new language, new customs, and new surroundings. They usually learned English by immersion, Katharina in an American military school in Germany, Jürgen when his adoptive parents simply stopped speaking to him in German.

Heinrich lived with German-American relatives, who warned him: "Some people don't like Germans over here." They worked very hard at Americanizing him, limiting the times he could speak German, and even modifying his name so it was more American. Heinrich and I laughed when I told him about the first present I'd received here for my nineteenth birthday— a pink electric shaver to Americanize my armpits and legs.

Jürgen, who worked for the government, lowered his voice and glanced around as if worried someone might overhear him whenever he spoke of what he called the "German connection." He said he had to be cautious because "sometimes veiled prejudices are in the air if I talk about my German connection. Somebody might use that negatively, in anger. Then I feel a cultural gulf, a separateness." But the kind of discrimination that Beate reported was the opposite. "People respected me more for being German, and I felt uncomfortable with that. It was the same as feeling badly as a refugee: I had nothing to do then with being discriminated against; and I had nothing to do now with being particularly promoted just for being German. It's ridiculous."

When I asked them if they had any prejudices against others, Anneliese spoke frankly about her racism. "I have a real thing about Indians. India Indians. I don't know why. It's silly. . . . Whenever there are some downtown, I walk far enough away from them." Jürgen seemed to feel justified in his "prejudice toward other cultures." He told me: "There is a lot of concern about illegal immigration. . . . Why should so many people come and change our culture? Europeans don't have preference. Now it's Orientals and Hispanics. It bothers me going to a 7-Eleven and having to work to have English understood." A few interviewees shared that proclivity toward American right-wing views.

But then there were others like Marika, who was visibly ashamed as she disclosed how she was still battling the deep-seated prejudices of her childhood. "I work very hard to overcome this blatant anti-Semitism I was brought up with. It's part of my education in this country, part of the Americanization of me, that I've learned to be more tolerant of other people's beliefs, of other races."

Hans-Peter described the current prejudice in Germany against foreign workers, who do "all the lousy jobs nobody else wanted. . . . Yet you got a lot of factions that would love to throw the foreign workers out, send them home. It's a situation with a lot of violence, and it could be the same theory all over again—that it's only for blond, blue-eyed Germans. I hate to see it." Since Hans-Peter knew what it meant to be a foreigner, he identified strongly. "It's like somebody would throw me out here because I'm from there."

What has immigration done to our sense of identity? There is a definite before and after, a dividing line between Germany and America. While several people I interviewed had thought a lot about what it meant to be German in America, others had to dig deeply as they spoke of their ambivalence. The question of where home is has remained complex and sometimes painful. "I feel often that I don't know exactly where I belong," Katharina admitted. "For a time I felt like a German amongst Americans, and I certainly now feel like an American amongst Germans. . . . It's sad, that kind of almost schizophrenic existence."

Anneliese felt conflicted; she considered herself German although she'd left there as a ten-year-old and had never gone back for a visit. "I have a German passport. Yet, America is my home, and I do feel at home here. But I don't feel like an American." Nearly all of them intended to stay here, except for Johanna, who still wonders about moving back to Germany, and Joachim, who plans to retire in Germany because he has family there.

Our cultural identity seems to shift with time, leading to uncertainty and isolation for some, while others reach a unique state of feeling connected to two countries. Like many of them, I have an accent in both languages now, marking me as an outsider here as well as in Germany. I found it fascinating to listen to their self-revelations as they defined their Germanness or struggled against it. When Karl and Joachim spoke of their uneasiness with so-called positive German character traits, I identified because I know only too well how uncomfortable I feel when others call me responsible or well organized. Joachim, who works as a town manager, is often praised by his community for his German "orderliness and *Gründlichkeit*—thoroughness," and he feels strange because those traits become negative when linked to the German past. Karl "did well in seminary because I'm a German. You do well. You make the trains run on time. I struggle with the fact that I was raised in a way that when you do something, you do it right." To balance things Karl lets them "go to pot sometimes. That's not a very German thing to do."

And Eva described her conscious effort to separate German history from German customs. "It's not that I want to shed everything that's German in me. I cook German meals. Both my children speak German. I kept that because it had nothing to do with the war and Hitler."

Kurt lived in America since he was six years old, but he felt certain that "being from Germany has an awful lot to do with what happened to the rest of my life." Although he was born in 1946, he insisted he is "a product of Germany at a time of war. . . . The only part that ended in 1945 was the hostilities. The Russians and the Americans were still struggling over lines of demarcation. . . . I am literally a survivor of World War II. I didn't have to live through it—but I lived through the aftermath."

Serious was a word that came up only too often for nearly all of us. Johanna was always told she was too serious, but having fun, she reflected, "is not what Germans think is the goal of life." And Marika only learned to make fun of herself when she came to this country. Though she spoke of having freed herself from that seriousness, it is still a very obvious part of her and of others—the shadow of our background.

It has been a learning process for us to enjoy life, to get past that seriousness, and the older we get, the easier we find it to laugh. And we did laugh quite a bit during these interviews, like when Gisela protested our rigid upbringing. "Little German girls are raised to be little good girls. It took a long time to stop being a good girl, and I resent that. One misses a lot in life by being a little good girl. Cinderella was a wimp." With others it was a different kind of laughter, a soft laughter as, together, we tried to fill in the first lines of a song or poem that we half-remembered from childhood, or when we reminisced about traditions that had survived immigration and therefore had become more precious, about German holidays and food, about the German landscape that many of us still loved—for me the Rhine River where I grew up and the Black Forest where my family spent winter vacations. Ulrich and I made fun of the *kitschy* atmosphere in German-American restaurants, the *Biersteine* and the *Lederhosen* and the oompah music. Neither one of us had seen restaurants like that in Germany, and yet that was how most Americans pictured Germany.

What serious children we used to be. . . . Raised within the silence, we lived in communities where the adults were always right, where obedience and loyalty were valued above all. Though it did not surprise me to discover that nearly all of us had experienced abuse during childhood, it was still painful to listen to accounts of severe beatings with fists, with shoes, or—in Marika's case—a riding crop. "I had big welts on the back of my thighs," she recalled. Her mother was "a physically big woman with a man's shoulders, the waist slim, a hunter's daughter. . . . Once she went out in the hall and got her gun from the rack. I thought she was getting ready to really shoot me." Both of Joachim's parents were violent, "pulling at each other's hair, screaming in pain." His mother would hit him "in the head with her shoes, screaming: *Ich schlag dich bis du in keinen Sarg mehr passt*'—'I'll beat you till you can't fit into any coffin.'"

Yet, as Joachim reflected on his mother's threats of mutilation, he wondered if he "had given her cause to do that." This attempt to understand and exonerate parental violence recurred only too frequently. Some felt they must have deserved to be beaten, and they justified brutality at home and in school as being normal, as though they still believed that if only they'd done the right thing, their parents and teachers would have been there for them. Even Marika—so perceptive in her fear of abuse—tried to defend the mother who had threatened to shoot her. "It was her temper. It was her frustration. It was her helplessness. It was her fear."

While Marika promised herself not to mistreat her child, several struggled with the history of abuse in their own parenting. "I inherited a lot from my own father because I was very hard on Tracy," Hans-Peter admitted. "A lot of that was from the old German feeling. I thought she should be a certain way, and that there was no other way." While some regretted that they hadn't been better parents, one man was so afraid of passing on the abuse that he decided never to have children.

Karl told me about an essay he'd read around the time of German reunification by "a Jewish psychiatrist, who had this study done by students, who went to public playgrounds in Copenhagen, Frankfurt, and Italy. They tried to get the same socioeconomic area for each playground. . . . The incidence of physical and verbal abuse in the German playground was much higher. . . . The psychiatrist said he would be a lot happier if he could know what's going on in the German character in terms of why there is all this abuse." From my own childhood I remember only too well that it was socially acceptable for parents and teachers to batter children. There was a word for it—discipline—and it was definitely part of the culture, an aftershock of the Third Reich, sanctioned as a beneficial tool in building character and enforcing obedience.

And if this discipline became excessive—as it often did—there was no public intervention.

Just more silence.

As I listened to all of the people, I was forced to look at myself again and again, and I came to understand fuller how the pervasive silence of our childhood still affects us today, that it is our legacy to be evasive. And that's the hard part to accept, to get beyond, because that legacy has become a tool of preservation. It was only after I'd finished the interviews that I knew I had to return to my own essay to add the passage about my mother's reaction when she found me reading *Das Tagebuch der Anne Frank*. That incident has always been part of my memory, coupled with confusion and shame at my mother's response, and it was a deliberate choice to leave it out. Until now. And yes, it does feel disloyal to the memory of my mother to reveal that she didn't want me to read about Anne Frank. And yes, it does belong there.

My emergence from the habit of silence has taken decades, and it continues. It is a private journey for each of us who comes from Germany. Some choose to travel only a short distance—guarded, defensive, prejudiced—and survive in an atmosphere that's not too different from where we started out. Others fling themselves into relentless self-examination, and as we confront and mourn the past of our birth country and determine our personal commitment of being in the world today, we reach new territory.

The way in which we balance those worlds defines much of our present.